PRESENT TENSE

Present Tense

A Radiohead Compendium

Edited by Barney Hoskyns

CONSTABLE

CONSTABLE

First published in Great Britain in 2019 by Constable

1 3 5 7 9 10 8 6 4 2

A CIP catalogue record for this book is available from the British Library.

ISBN: 978-1-47212-944-4 (hardback)
ISBN: 978-1-47212-943-7 (trade paperback)

Typeset in Minion Pro by SX Composing DTP, Rayleigh, Essex SS6 7EF

Printed and bound in Great Britain by Clays Ltd, Elcograf S.p.A.

Papers used by Constable are from well-managed forests and other responsible sources.

Constable
An imprint of
Little, Brown Book Group
Carmelite House
50 Victoria Embankment
London EC4Y 0DZ

An Hachette UK Company
www.hachette.co.uk

www.littlebrown.co.uk

Contents

Introduction

In the fine essay included here on Radiohead's 2000 album *Kid A*, Simon Reynolds asks why we shouldn't consider its predecessor – 1997's *OK Computer* – to be the best British rock album ever made.

It's a more than legitimate question. I've regularly listened to *OK Computer* for over twenty years and can't see too many rivals to such a crown: not *Revolver*, not even *Exile on Main St.*; certainly not *Sgt. Pepper* or *London Calling* or *The Stone Roses*. Yet in the *Observer*'s 'One Hundred Greatest British Albums' listicle of June 2004, *OK Computer* polled no higher than 24 – a reflection, one might suggest, of the residual suspicion towards Radiohead's seriousness, their emotional grandeur, their willingness to risk pretension and complexity in their playing. The UK's rock-critic consensus never quite abandons its dim view of the 'progressive' tendency in pop music.

To get from the neo-Nirvana abjection of 1993's breakthrough hit 'Creep' to the anguished six-and-a-half-minute prog epic that was *OK Computer*'s 'Paranoid Android' in the space of just three albums remains astounding. Few listeners who bought the group's debut album *Pablo Honey* (1993) would have given Radiohead much chance of evolving beyond what John Harris called the 'angst-ridden paroxysms' of their early sub-grunge emoting.

Second album *The Bends* was, of course, a key transitional work. Within minutes of the opening 'Planet Telex' it was clear they'd taken a giant stride forward from 'Creep' and the sour 'Anyone Can Play Guitar'. Yet the suspicion around them remained and even grew, rooted in an inverse snobbery towards middle-class boys from Oxford in the era of Britpop. For what were Radiohead if not, inadvertently, the anti-Oasis – a band with scant interest in being big for the sake of it, public schoolboys bored of the hoary trappings of rock stardom. They wanted to take rock beyond the stale conventions of the mid-'90s and had a number of attributes to help them: principally the musical gifts of Thom Yorke's singing and Jonny Greenwood's brilliance as a guitar player and all-round sonic architect – but also the considerable contributions of their colleagues Colin Greenwood (bass and older brother of Jonny), Phil Selway (drums), Ed O'Brien (guitar) and, not least, exemplary engineer-turned-producer Nigel Godrich.

Radiohead were also willing to stare humanity's dystopian hi-tech future in the face and question where we were all heading. In time, this convinced the group to leave traditional rock elements behind them – at least temporarily – and embrace the textures and signifiers of electronica as they moved into the new millennium. Yet they never entirely abandoned the beauty of their melodies, and even when Yorke's lyrics were at their most elliptically irritating he could move you to tears with the seraphic yearning of his vocal lines.

INTRODUCTION

While *OK Computer* remains a musical Matterhorn that neither they nor anyone else are likely to top, Radiohead have consistently delivered music which confirms their stature as the most daring of major rock bands. Are there any more intoxicating bursts of popular music than '2+2=5' or 'Burn the Witch', any Smiths-inflected anthems more drivingly potent than 'Knives Out' or 'There There', any ballads or downtempo lamentations more beautiful than 'Nude' or 'Pyramid Song' or 'Sail to the Moon' or 'Give up the Ghost'? Other contemporary acts may have had their great phases (PJ Harvey, Joanna Newsom, Feist, Arcade Fire, Interpol, Grizzly Bear, Queens of the Stone Age), but few have amazed and surprised us for so long.

It's been a genuine pleasure assembling the reviews and interviews for *Present Tense*: to travel from Ronan Munro's prescient early reports about On A Friday (what a relief they dropped *that* name) to the exceptional reportage, portraiture and commentary of writers such as Reynolds and Will Self, Ann Powers and Adam Thorpe, John Harris and Pat Blashill, Will Hermes and R. J. Smith – and of Mark Greif, whose towering essay in *n+1*, 'Radiohead, or the Philosophy of Pop' may be the most extraordinary thing ever written about the group.

Do Radiohead, by virtue of their radical intelligence and engagement with our terrifying times, elicit more intelligent critical writing than Oasis? And is it rock snobbery to suggest as much? Judge for yourself as you read *Present Tense* and follow the band's twenty-eight-year journey to the tense present day of 2019.

Barney Hoskyns, Rock's Backpages, April 2018

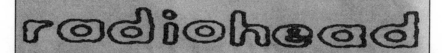

PLEASE NOTE

ON A FRIDAY
HAVE CHANGED THEIR NAME
TO

radiohead

FIRST E.P. OUT IN APRIL

One: Friday On My Mind

1

Review of On A Friday at the Jericho Tavern, Oxford

Ronan Munro, *Curfew*[1], September 1991

I spend the entire set tonight desperately trying to think what exactly On A Friday remind me of. Not so much the music as the vocals. The next day it hits me: Kirk Brandon! Yes, he of Spear of Destiny and silly haircut fame.

Now, On A Friday's singer Thom hasn't got a silly haircut (in fact, he's hardly got enough hair to have any kind of a cut), but he does possess a voice very reminiscent of Brandon – the way he elongates every syllable and almost howls rather than sings – and it's the way it's so at odds with the rest of the band that's so intriguing.

I'm sceptical after the first couple of numbers, which come a little too close to that Manchester sound for comfort, but delve a little deeper into On A Friday and a whole new angle on them opens up. While the drums and bass (with a little help from the keyboard player) do evoke an indie-dance groove thang, there's

1 Local Oxford music magazine, since retitled *Nightshift*.

an almost country and western feel to the band at times, more R.E.M. than Kenny Rogers though, fortunately.

Confusing? Not if you see them live for yourselves (which you all will when they inevitably become extremely famous and you swear you were here at the beginning). In my book it's a good thing when you can't easily place what you're hearing, and when you can dance to it as well then even better.

There's an impressive turnout tonight, justifying the early buzz surrounding the band (they've already been recommended by the Candyskins); certainly their sound is well tuned to what's going on at the moment and it shouldn't be long before they're attracting major label attention.

Just a couple of questions, though: doesn't the bass player, Colin, look like Christopher Walken from *The Deer Hunter*? And what's with the subliminal backing vocals? They make the inside of your head go all funny, like.

2

The First Demo Review

Ronan Munro, *Curfew*, November 1991

Currently my favourite local band, On A Friday here prove just why they are with a highly impressive – albeit old – two-track demo. 'What Is That You Say?' is what good commercial indie guitar music should be about and shows you don't have to sell out to break out.

On A Friday are a well-polished band with highly imaginative songwriting ideas and are possessed of an unusually talented lead singer who would appear to have a pitch-bend lever inserted in his throat. How he manages to retain control as he switches from the low to high notes in the way he does, I don't know. The band also manage to make proper use of a backing vocalist, which is something that too many bands never get the hang of.

'Stop Whispering' sees another storming vocal performance while the guitars hover dangerously in the background. Halfway through, the song begins to deliberately break down before a scream brings it all rushing back with a weird organ sound fighting with a very Velvet-Underground-sounding guitar for supremacy. Lovely.

PRESENT TENSE

On A Friday are due in the studio this month to record with Slowdive's producer and the result should be with us in November. Until such time try and see them live if you can – you'd be a fool not to.

3

On A Friday:
an Interview

Ronan Munro, *Curfew*, November 1991

At the end of October, Oxford's thinnest band (the Wild Poppies split up ages ago), On A Friday, played the Jericho Tavern to a good-sized crowd and there was a man from EMI there.

A mere two weeks later they are playing the Tavern again and the place is heaving. There are twenty-five record-company A&R men there and, what's more, they have all paid to get in. To put it bluntly, On A Friday are happening.

It's a good job, then, that we've chosen this month to put them on the front cover. If we'd waited any longer, they'd be splashed all over the nationals and we'd be left with egg all over our faces.

The first time I saw On A Friday, I was so drunk I couldn't remember a single thing about them. The second time I saw them I thought they were really rather good, if a little weird. Ironically, I finally realised what a great pop group they were at a pathetically-attended gig at the Poly, with crap sound and a ludicrously curtailed set.

While On A Friday's music is lively, catchy, intense and easily good enough to stand up on its own, what makes them just that much better is singer Thom's voice. He is possessed of that rare and special thing: a naturally musical singing voice. How many bands have you seen ruined by a bad or boring singer? I lost count many years ago. Thom doesn't just deliver his lyrics; he uses his voice to interact with the other instruments, almost as if it were one itself. This often makes the words hard to comprehend. What are the songs about?

Thom: 'Erm . . . well, "Nothing Touches Me" is based on an artist who was imprisoned for abusing children and spent the rest of his life in a cell, painting, but the song is about isolating yourself so much that one day you realise you haven't got any friends anymore and no one talks to you.'

Sounds pretty miserable – but your music is quite happy, isn't it?

'Yeah, I'm just aggressive and sick.'

Twenty minutes later, Thom reveals that he doesn't really know what the songs are about.

On a Friday, far from being a singer and his backing band, are a collective of five individuals, each with a strong input into the band's music. All stamp their individual influences and tastes on the music, and this means that the end product doesn't really sound like anyone else. Thom, Phil (drums), Colin (bass), Ed (guitar) and John (guitar and organ) find common ground in bands like the Buzzcocks, R.E.M., the Fall and (ahem) Peter Paul and Mary (this could be a wind-up), but beyond this they go for anything from Curve to Bootsy Collins to techno. They also seem to argue lots.

They've just been into Courtyard Studios with Chris Hufford, producer of Slowdive's album.

Colin: 'He heard about us through a mutual friend and came to see us at the Jericho. Afterwards he was almost shaking. He said we were the best group he'd seen in three years and invited us to record with him at the Courtyard. We see it as an investment.'

And the investment seems to be about to pay off sooner than they expected. The five songs they recorded show a massive leap in depth and professionalism from their last demo, impressive though it was. The new tape should be available from Manic Hedgehog by the time you read this and it's well worth forking out three pounds for. In short, it's a stormer.

All five members of the band are Oxford-born and bred and all have returned to their home town after time away at college. How much influence has Oxford had on their songs?

Thom: 'Loads. "Jerusalem" is all about Oxford. So is "Everybody Lies Through Their Teeth". It's such a weird place and it's very important to my writing.'

It's the subject of Oxford – in particular, music in Oxford – which provokes the arguments. Wildly differing views are thrown out as to why Oxford has, or hasn't, got a decent music scene . . .

' . . . if the Tavern closed, there wouldn't be any scene at all.'

'No? What about the Dolly and the Venue?'

'And the Old Fire Station? I know it's crap, but there are a lot of towns the size of Oxford haven't got a venue like that. Oxford has got a lot more soul than, say, Cambridge, but it comes from places like Cowley rather than the university. Students come here for three years and leave without contributing anything.'

'I don't think it's all the students' fault. It's the people who run the university who are the problem. They control everything in Oxford from their corridors of power. They have a say in all the licensing of clubs. That's why we get terrible places like the Park

End Club. Oxford is crying out for a couple of decent nightclubs. And it's the dons who say that bands can't play in the colleges, not the students . . . '

The argument continues with no real agreement or fixed conclusions. Everyone agrees that things could be better, but they could be a lot worse.

'There are a hell of a lot of bands in Oxford for its size, and the Dolly and the Venue and especially the Tavern are good venues. The Old Fire Station looks like it was designed by the people who build Little Chefs. The stage is almost an afterthought, you feel like you're playing on a salad bar.'

On A Friday also say some very complimentary things about *Curfew*, which makes me feel like my life isn't totally wasted. And indeed, if this humble and overworked editor's gushing opinions can help On A Friday towards the mega-success they are due for, then *Curfew* will have achieved at least one useful thing in its time. And successful On A Friday will be. No ifs and buts with this lot. This time next year they will have outgrown all the venues they talk about, and for once I think I may just have got it right. Are they ready to be stars?

Thom: 'People sometimes say we take things too seriously, but it's the only way you'll get anywhere. We're not going to sit around and wait and just be happy if something turns up. We are ambitious. You have to be.'

4

Review of On A Friday at the Venue, Oxford

John Harris, *Melody Maker*, 22 February 1992

Terrible name. Apt for beer-gutted pub rockers, perhaps, but ill-suited to the astonishing intensity of this bunch.

On A Friday swing between uneasy calm and crazed desperation, hinting at extremes that belie the just-got-paid/let's-get-pissed overtones of their moniker. Like Kingmaker, they've opted for the rock-as-catharsis principle, exorcising demons at a rate of knots and steering well clear of anything approaching frivolity.

Their angst-ridden paroxysms frequently depend on their sheer volume – without warning, piercing screams will fly from the stage while the band pound their instruments. Within seconds, they'll revert to a disciplined, razor-edged mode, revealing a schizophrenia that gives songs like 'Stop Whispering' a frighten-ing volatility, furthered by the frantic movements of their singer: a diminutive, close-cropped young man whose jerky demeanour sums up On A Friday's screwed-up appeal.

PRESENT TENSE

They leave us with a speeding hymn to megalomania entitled 'Nothing Touches Me' – a perfect example of their manic-but-melodic charms, and an indication of credible self-confidence. 'Promising' seems something of an understatement.

Two: Pop Is Dead

1

Review of Radiohead at the Richmond, Brighton

Paul Moody, *New Musical Express*,
27 February 1993

We couldn't have waited much longer, really, could we? What with Suede so colossal, and the likes of the Auteurs and Kinky Machine still rubbing their eyes and blinking in the spotlight, *somebody* had to come along and remind us what greatness looks like.

So, thank God it's Radiohead. In the depths of the Richmond (sold out and cluttered with gawky, grinning boys and swaying, dreamy-eyed girls) they manage to take pop music – forget 'indie', *please* – and coat it in a glitter-dust not seen since Suede at Central London Poly and T. Rex, oh, anywhere. You can tell they're going to be dazzling from the moment Thom – even more scrawny and whey-faced than usual – bawls 'I wish something would happen!' during 'You' and mop-haired lead guitarist Johnny answers with these skyrocket, glam-chord progressions that sidle up to you and then scream in your ear.

It's their vulnerability that makes Radiohead so compelling. Thom may belt his guitar and glare stone-faced at us from deep behind his fringe, but look a little closer and cracks open up a mile wide and the whole thing suddenly crumbles into sand. 'Creep' is the obvious example. The song Pulp's Jarvis Cocker could never give up playing Twister long enough to write, it sets the controls on slow burn and then bursts into flames the moment he screams '*I wish I was special – You're so special!*', like the furious little brother of Ian Brown circa 'I Wanna Be Adored'.

'Lurgee', too, is more medicine for the soul – a chilling, chiming thing that could give 'Back to the Old House' a bear hug if it saw it in the street. It marks the moment at which the girls at the front fall in love with Thom and the entire Richmond gulps audibly in recognition.

There are lesser moments, sure, when you gather your senses and realise that third guitarist Ed has got his shirt wide open and is busying himself with the Bernard-from-Suede Guide to Rock Posture, and that anybody with three guitars must by law have something in common with the Family Cat, but that's about it.

Besides, next single 'Pop Is Dead', with its crashing death-rattle snare and '*It's no great loss*' refrain lets you know that Radiohead are fully aware of how ridiculous the notion of being in a pop group really is; that young males should have something better to do than stare glassy-eyed at motorway junctions through transit van windows and eat overpriced meals in late-night service stations.

The whole thing finally implodes with the appropriately named 'Blow Out', which applies the basic principles of foot-on-monitor theory (find riff and attack savagely), finds all the newly lovestruck girls dancing wildly and Thom grinning beatifically

– until, that is, his final 'See you again!' when the soundman applies a ridiculous stadium-rock reverb which leaves his words hanging in the air.

It's so un-Radiohead it's unbelievable, and when Thom pulls a spastic face and skulks off as a result, he becomes the most misunderstood and put-upon peroxide singer in a rock'n'roll group ever.

For this week, at least.

2

Review of *Pablo Honey*

Simon Price, *Melody Maker*,
20 February 1993

They say we're repressed, us Brits, don't they? So the cliché goes – brilliantly personified by the encounter between Basil and Mme Peignoir in the 'Wedding' episode of *Fawlty Towers*. We bottle up all our passions behind a reserved exterior, until one day we get arrested for marching stark naked down the high street.

You want another cliché? Boys Don't Cry. In this respect, Radiohead's promisingly imperfect *Pablo Honey* is as British and Boyish as they come. Thom Yorke spends most of the time expressing himself in the most hackneyed – and therefore meaningless – language possible, the language of the emotionally mute ('*You are the sun and the moon and the stars are you*', is the album's first line) and then he'll suddenly crack, take a fall (as in Albert Camus' *La Chute*, or Thom's own line '*You're free until you drop . . . without a ripcord*'), strip himself stark naked and emote in the most extreme terms: '*I wish I was special, you're so fucking special/But I'm a creep, I'm a weirdo/What the hell am I doing here?*', or '*I'm better off dead*'.

Radiohead aren't the new Suede (despite guitarist Jon's frantic glam poses), but if Suede are the New Smiths and if we must play these games (this *is* the music press, so I suppose we must), I'd hesitantly put Radiohead down as the New Jam.

Much of *Pablo Honey* is very *Setting Sons.* (Historical note: The Jam, a classic Boys' Band, sang about the UK's decay and The Unbearable Shiteness Of Being with mixed emotions of fury and fondness. Every kid at school thought they were gods. The atmosphere when 'Going Underground' went straight in at No. 1 was a million times more intense than anything surrounding 'Teen Spirit'. They were fucking MASSIVE.)

Sometimes Radiohead err too far on the side of Boy-Rock. 'Ripcord', with its muscular, slashed chord progression, recalls Steve Jones on the Pistols' 'Stepping Stone', while 'How Do You?' is all 'Into the Valley' heroics, Thom's voice occasionally breaking into the strained, declarative holler that Bono left behind when he finally realised the absurdity of it all. And, strangest of all, 'Blow Out' starts exactly like Dire Straits' 'Sultans Of Swing'.

'Anyone Can Play Guitar' is either a hilarious parody of Carter USM's 'Do Re Mi So Far So Good' or it's a case of simple melodic plagiarism. A lyric like *'And if London burns, I'll be standing on the beach with my guitar/I wanna be in a band when I get to Heaven/Wanna grow my hair, wanna be Jim Morrison'*, suggests the former. So does the song that precedes it, 'Thinking About You' (*'Your records are here, your eyes are on my wall/Your teeth are over there, but I'm still no one and you're now a star/I still see you in bed, but I'm playing with myself'*). Coupled together, the songs form a believer's/cynic's dialogue on Pop Stardom. Then again, what if Radiohead really do just wanna be Mega City Four? It's a close thing sometimes.

The thing that tips the balance in their favour is Jon Greenwood's guitar. When he makes that grotesque crunchy noise in 'Creep', just after the words *so fucking special*, it sounds like the prison door being slammed and locked on a man's entire hopes and aspirations. Why do I keep coming back to this song? Not just because it was one of *the* songs of 1992 (inexplicably absent from our critics' chart – you had, by law, to be American or Suede) but because it seems to have touched a nerve among you (witness the extraordinary devotion on the faces of the kids who recited every fucking word of every song when Radiohead played my club at ULU last month). And it will, let's face it, be the main reason you'll buy *Pablo Honey*.

So fucking special . . .

3

'Creep' Stumbles Onto Fame

Jim Sullivan, *Boston Globe*,
8 October 1993

It's barely noon, but Radiohead's Thom Yorke has been awake
for a very un-rock'n'roll-like four hours. This certainly can't be
one of the perks of nascent stardom. He's been in his hotel room
staring at the TV, getting rudely acquainted with US televange-
lists' custom of begging for dollars. He's feeling sorry for all those
people dialling in to pledge.

But why did the young Englishman rise with the roosters in
Norfolk, Virginia, anyway? Yorke, on the phone, mutters something about being tossed off the tour bus at an ungodly hour but
adds, with a laugh, 'I don't quite know why. I don't have complete
control of my fate at the moment.'

Success will do that and, at the moment, the young band is in
a very enviable position: the group's debut album, *Pablo Honey*,
just turned gold, signifying sales of 500,000 copies. 'Creep', the
first single, has become a from-out-of-left-field hit.

Sings a fragile, envious Yorke: *'I wish I was special/You're so*
[expletive] *special/But I'm a creep/I'm a weirdo/What the hell am*

I doing here?/I don't belong here.' Jonny Greenwood's scraping, stuttering guitar licks explode into a full-throttle frenzy as Ed O'Brien and Yorke join him. It's an anthem for anyone who has ever felt left out of the mix or cast aside. Hurt, but verging on hostile.

'Creep' first found a home on alternative radio, but it has crossed over to the pop charts (up to No. 29) and album-oriented rock stations. When played on the latter format, its delicate chords, nervous arrangement and self-loathing viewpoint provide a rather sharp contrast to the strutting, testosterone-prone fist-waving bands that dominate.

'Actually,' says Yorke with a laugh, 'live, there are elements of that strutting stuff in us. But still, at the same time, [we're] fully aware of it. I have a real problem being a man in the '90s, anyway. Any man with any sensitivity or conscience toward the opposite sex would have a problem. To actually assert yourself in a masculine way without looking like you're in a [hard-]rock band is a very difficult thing to do . . . It comes back to the music we write, which is not effeminate, but it's not brutal in its arrogance. It's one of the things I'm always trying: to assert a sexual persona and on the other hand trying desperately to negate it.'

'Creep' is a most inadvertent hit. Bostonians Paul Q. Kolderie and Sean Slade were in England, producing *Pablo Honey* with Radiohead. The band ran through the song in the studio to allow the engineers to set the proper levels. It was an old song, explains Yorke. There was no plan to even record it until Kolderie and Slade said they thought Radiohead had something there. And they had the tape rolling.

'It was just a song we were doing that hadn't worked very well in rehearsals,' says Yorke. 'We didn't really have an angle on it.

And then we discovered we didn't need an angle on it, except maybe Jonny's guitar . . . "Creep" just grabbed people by the throat. It wasn't intentional.'

The inspiration, Yorke suggests, came from the fact that Radiohead was an untested entry in this vast 'alternative' rock field. Did the five belong? 'It was at a crossing point in my songwriting,' Yorke says, 'because I'd gone from writing songs in my bedroom to being somebody who had huge [record company] figures over my shoulders listening to me.' In other words, he was a potential commodity.

Fans of 'Creep' are no doubt pleased that it's not the only worthy song on *Pablo Honey*. And fans of *Pablo Honey* may be pleased to hear that, in concert, Radiohead has improved over its early recording days: more fury, more clamour, more hypnotic guitar bliss. 'That's simply a question of [the fact that] since we started we must have done 400 gigs and you learn quite fast what works and doesn't work,' says Yorke.

Radiohead's 'Stop Whispering' is moving up the alternative charts. All this success – the band co-headlines with pals Belly – has forced the band members to reconsider their relationship to the music industry.

'There's very much the British feeling of "I'm not worthy, why am I here?"' says Yorke. 'Certainly, there's an implicit neurosis about how the press is going to treat you . . . And when we signed with our record company there were a lot of weird political things going on. It's learning to actually isolate yourself from relying on people around you. I'm kind of a kid about things like that. It stresses me out. I'd like to go back and play with my building blocks and just let my parents worry about the record.'

4

From the Bedroom
to the Universe

Paul Lester, *Melody Maker*,
23 October 1993

I've heard screaming before, but nothing quite like that. At once exhilarated and anguished, it is the scream of a girl on the verge of a nervous breakdown.

'I love you, Thom!'

The scream is four syllables long, very sharp and extraordinarily loud, somehow managing to pierce the commotion of the Providence, Rhode Island, crowd and the noise blasting out of Radiohead's enormous PA.

'I love you, Thom!'

There it goes again, sharper and louder now, a terrifying mix of frightened child, ecstatic weenie, and wailing banshee. Of course, I have no trouble hearing the scream – everyone in club Lupo's (Jesus, everyone in Providence) can hear the yell-from-hell; it's just that I don't seem to be able to work out where the fuck it's coming from.

'I love you Thom!'

That does it, I've got to find out who on earth is responsible for this orgiastic-moan-cum-death-rattle. So, as Radiohead build towards the climax of their finale 'Pop Is Dead', I wade into the fray, a claustrophobic crush of pretty preppies, frat-house freaks, cropped jocks, sweaty crowd-surfers and all-round psychos. And there she is again, squashed between the 'Beavis-and-Buttheads', the tiny kid with the giant voice.

'Hey! Look at this!' the drenched (new) waif calls out, instantly recognising me from the hotel where Radiohead and the *Maker* have been staying and on whose doorstep she has been camping out over the last few days in the vain hope of catching a glimpse of her heroes. The girl – Sharon, twenty-one, from Massachusetts – is shivering, not from cold, but like she's just seen a ghost or Christ or the ghost of Christ.

'Oh my God,' she sighs, 'that was the best thing I've ever seen. They are just awesome.' Suddenly, Sharon starts pulling up her sweatshirt to reveal her midriff. It is purple. So determined was she to get close to Thom E. Yorke – Radiohead's singer, guitarist and reluctant messiah – that she braves the mêlée, risking, in the process, such irrelevancies as life and limb.

I guess that's the kind of thing you do when you're in love.

'He is sooo gorgeous,' swoons Sharon, prodding at her equally bruised thighs and grinning, oblivious to the gawping hordes, oblivious to the *pain*. Clearly, she can't feel a thing. Obviously, she would do it all again.

''Course I would!' she beams. 'Anyway, it doesn't hurt a bit.'

Brett who?

———

I've seen bigger bands. I've seen better bands. I've seen U2 in Germany, New Order at Reading, Public Enemy at Wembley and Barry White in Manchester. So, no, you can't possibly blame me for assuming I'd seen everything. And I have, in a sense. But I've never seen five undernourished ex-college boys from the home counties inspire such reckless enthusiasm, such devotion, such *love*. I've never seen a fan letter for an 'indie' band from a man in death row before. I've never seen a bunch, tagged 'ugly losers' by hacks in their home country, make so many luscious teenies (male and female) on the other side of the Atlantic quiver and shake. And I've never seen a group of hicks from the sticks make some poor bastard stuck in a wheelchair at the back of a concert hall smile so hard he could cry.

I see all of this and more in America with Radiohead.

Yeah, *that* Radiohead. The Radiohead we all used to studiously ignore when they were called On A Friday. The Radiohead we sort of began to notice when their monument of misery, 'Creep', crawled out of Parlophone last September. The Radiohead we begrudgingly gave press space to when their next slabs of caustic plastic, 'Anyone Can Play Guitar' and 'Pop Is Dead', scraped the charts (respectively Nos. 32 and 42) and their debut album, *Pablo Honey*, reached the Top 30. The very same Radiohead we pushed aside in our rush to sanctify Suede and who we're now being forced to (re-)assess in the light of the 'Creep' re-issue (No. 7 with loads of bullets) and the band's impressive Stateside success – the LP has shifted upwards of half a million units, while estimates suggest it will have sold a cool million by the end of the year.

Yes, indeed. *That* Radiohead.

Embarrassed? *Nous*?

No. Not us. Never. We know no shame and have even less

pride. Besides, Radiohead, we now realise, are worth every cringing second of the shameless *volte-face* it takes to be granted an audience with them. Certainly Thom E. Yorke – a man who seems to have taken Elvis Costello's early 'revenge and guilt' persona and multiplied it several-fold – is becoming a fascinating figure at the centre of British pop. If the sensitivity, irritability, suspicion, rage and anxiety displayed in Yorke's words are anything to go by, he should be a chap with a chip the size of a small banana republic on his shoulder. And if the savage riffing and thrillingly conventional ('Music for lapsed rock fans' is how I describe Radiohead later, to the band's assent) attack of the players is any measure, then Jonny Greenwood (lead guitar), Ed O'Brien (rhythm guitar), Colin Greenwood (bass) and Phil Selway (drums) will be bullish and brash, defensive and aggressive, in the mould of the young Joe Strummer and Paul Weller.

Wrong! Radiohead are disarmingly charming, articulate on every subject from representative democracy to *fin de siècle* Muggletonian asceticism, erudite from morning till night and educated to the max. Their received pronunciation has more in common with royalty than rockers. And they could probably knock out the odd authoritative political column for the *Guardian* in their spare time. I can't help wondering, as I watch Thom leave the Providence gig, head towards the tour bus and reduce a startled female to a trembling wreck (Sharon!) and the Greenwood brothers get swamped by autograph hunters, whether these strange (banal?) pop rituals are beneath them. And I can't help wondering just who are these pale young men whose songs and sounds, eyes and skin are exciting thousands of music lovers thousands of miles from home.

'He's great, but what is his problem?' asked Steve Mack of That Petrol Emotion when he first saw Thom E. Yorke at a Radiohead gig last year. The crusty kitten-hunk had a point. Yorke may well be as much of a gentleman as the others in the band; it's just that he's rather more prone to bouts of moodiness. And don't forget that the enigmatic singer is the man responsible for this little litany of lacerating self-loathing: *I'm better off dead* ('Prove Yourself'); *I failed in life* ('Stupid Car'); *What do you care when all the other men are far, far better?* ('Thinking About You'); *All my friends said bye-bye* ('Faithless The Wonder Boy') and, of course, *I wish I was special* ('Creep').

Back in the Providence hotel bar and bearing in mind his reputation for sporadic fits of pique, even black periods of nihilistic despair, I approach Thom cautiously and repeat that Petrol enquiry: what *is* his problem? Nursing a bottle of Beck's in the corner, he reasons that 'I'm a lot of different people when I write.'

I hear you've been in a steady, happy relationship for three years. How come you sound so haunted and hurt, fierce and fucked-off/up in your songs? 'You can feel those things in any relationship,' he explains, eyeing me from beneath his Cobain-ish blonde fringe, apparently unaware of the fact that Sharon (again!) is spying on him, à la *Fatal Attraction*, from a nearby table.

'Am I for real?' he repeats. 'Good question. I am sincere about what I do.'

How about that line from 'Faithless': *I can't put the needle in* – have you ever been tempted, in one of your more downer moments, to try hard drugs? Or were you just flirting with heroin imagery?

'I wouldn't be that pretentious to play the Kurt Cobain,' he winces. 'That phrase is more about trying to get back at people, get nasty.'

Tonight, you introduced 'Yes I Am' (the B-side of 'Creep') by saying, 'This is for all the people who shat on us.' What made you say that?

'That was just . . . I wrote that song about the sensation of being the underdog for so long and how suddenly everyone's nice to you. And it's like, "Fuck you",' he snarls, offering a glimpse of the human behind the hysteria.

More glimpses: Thom was born in Scotland twenty-five years ago (it's his birthday on the day of this bar confessional. Ed and Colin present him with a book by leading dissident intellectual Noah Chomsky), moving to Oxford when he was seven. His childhood was all right, but he hated his public school ('It was purgatory,' he says. 'It nurtured all the worst aspects of the British middle-class: snobbery, lack of tolerance and right-wing stupidity.').

After a tortuous failed romance ('Have you ever seen *Who's Afraid of Virginia Woolf?* It was like that for a year and a half, lots of fighting in public'), Thom went to Exeter University, where he studied English and fine art, shaved his head, started DJing and discovered he had a dangerous taste for drink ('I almost died from alcohol poisoning once,' he shudders at the memory. 'I lost it for a bit.').

Thom doesn't say whether or not things got so bad he ever thought about ending it all ('Might have done, might not have done,' he half-laughs), but he does agree with my theory that 'Creep' is the exact inverse of the Stone Roses' 'I Wanna Be Adored': the former is fuelled by self-pity, the latter by arrogance – both by egocentricity bordering on narcissism.

'Creep' is saying 'I Wanna Be Abhorred', isn't it?

'Yeah, definitely.' Thom is quick to agree but slow to disclose any more. 'It's about [pause] . . . it's about sympathy [longer pause] This is all very hard. If, erm . . . Yeah, I s'pose. Mmmm [very long pause]. As soon as I say this, everyone will take the piss. It's just, I think [pause for several centuries] . . . part of me is always looking for someone to turn around, buy me a drink, give me a hug and say it's all right,' he says at last, breaking the painful silence. 'Because I just go off on one. For days I can't talk to people. And it shocks me because I'm still doing it. I want to be alone and I want people to notice me – both at the same time. I can't help it. There's this book, *The Famished Road*, where the main character has these forces following him around and pulling him about – I feel like that.'

Thom continues to bare his soul and disprove the idea that commercial reward + public acclaim = emotional stability. 'It sounds really tossy, this. If I was a painter, it would be like, "Wow! That's wonderful!" But this is pop and in pop you're not meant to say things like this.'

———

You are if you're Radiohead. You are if you're Thom E. Yorke. And you are if you're one of the dandy Greenwood duo.

Jonny is twenty-one, Colin is twenty-five. Their father died when they were young, leaving their mother to worry about her two wayward sons. 'She thought Jonny was being dragged away by the forces of evil,' confides Colin the day after the Rhode Island gig, chain-smoking Camel cigarettes inside the tour bus now parked outside the Avalon – the venue for tonight's Boston show. 'She got a bit better when she saw us on *Top of the Pops*.

Mind you, she thinks everyone on that programme's a drug-taking lunatic. Actually, she's not happy unless she's worrying. Very Radiohead, that. We're all worriers, you know. Even when there's nothing left to worry about.'

Jonny, who left Oxford Polytechnic after one term to concentrate on the band, is Radiohead's resident musical genius, the Bernard Butler to Thom's Brett Anderson. Something of a prodigy at school, he played viola for the Thames Valley orchestra, then began hanging around with Colin and co. as soon as the group started. Pretty soon, all five members were sharing a house in Oxford, just like the Monkees.

'No, *Banana Splits*,' corrects Jonny, joining me in the scorching Indian summer heat on the pavement – sorry, sidewalk – outside the Avalon.

'Which of us was the father figure? No patriarchs! We were all mothers.'

I ask Jonny whether he thinks Radiohead have achieved success in the States rather quicker than Suede because the latter are more of a tease and Americans mistrust any ambiguity of any kind.

'Are we more boyish? Ooh, no,' he grimaces, genuinely peeved at my proposal. Jonny later admits to being more than slightly repulsed by a nipple ring given to him by a female fan who appeared stark naked at his hotel door a few nights ago and asks me, at the end of our chat, not to mention the gender of his partner back home. Meanwhile, Jonny's staring at the sun, telling me this: 'We get fans of both sexes. Groupies? That's a terrible word. How seventies. No, we don't get offers. We're not the Manic Street Preachers. We're a testosterone-free band. We didn't form this group to unleash our libidos on the general public.'

Colin, who has a degree in English from Cambridge University, spent his formative years in the kitchen at parties with Thom, wearing black body-stockings and garish mauve and green shirts and generally, as you do, trying to halt the hegemony of goth. Another one of Colin's favourite pastimes was outraging the boys at school (Radiohead attended the same school, although – apart from Colin and Thom – they were all in different years) by getting off with their male friends. Then he went to college and really let his hair down.

'We all pretty much shot our load at college in terms of drinking and drugs,' admits the most candid member of the band, squinting at the sun coming through the bus window and closing the blinds as scores of Radiohead's new American fans mill about on the street below, waiting for their bass-playing idol to emerge. 'It was nothing extreme,' he adds, sounding for all the world like an Oxbridge don with an epicurean bent. 'Nothing more than speed or dope. Smack? No! People can't afford that indulgence in terms of time and money these days.

'I remember at college,' he goes on, furiously inhaling and exhaling, 'there was this chemist on the corner – it was the local methadone-dispensing clinic. I used to walk past and see all these junkies queuing up. Then I'd walk round the corner and they'd be shooting up, which wasn't very nice . . .'

Colin has already informed me that Brett Anderson's celebrated remark – 'I'm a bisexual who's yet to have a homosexual experience' – was lifted from the notorious slacker manual *Generation X*. What about those early gay encounters of yours, Colin?

'Yeah, well. Yeah, well. Yeah!' he laughs, momentarily embarrassed before divulging: 'Well, yeah, I had a couple of flings at college with some guys. But my girlfriend knows about them, so it's all right. She doesn't like me hanging out with her gay friends in London too much, just in case I get tempted! I'll show you a photo of her if you want. She's a biker. She's more rock'n'roll than me. She's a biker woman. She got three bikes on our holiday in Greece. You know, I was the only guy in Greece on the back of a bike with a woman on the front!' he chuckles, leaping up to dig a photograph of Madeleine, his crazy biker-chick girlfriend, out of his travel bag.

Ed is the only member of Radiohead who doesn't have a partner back home. There are advantages to this. For one, he has more money than the others. (A homesick, love-struck Colin has spent about £600 ringing Madeleine every night. Drummer Phil doesn't disclose a precise amount for his nocturnal calls to girlfriend Kate, but he does tell me that he wishes he'd bought shares in British Telecom.) For another, he gets to flirt with women on the road. Like Tanya Donnelly of Belly, for example, who – take note, True Stories fans – has just broken off her engagement with her US rocker boyfriend. Even as we speak, Radiohead's playmate Tanya is jumping down the steps of Belly's astrodome of a tour bus and interrupting my chat with Ed as we sit in the shade outside the Avalon.

'Sorry!' Tanya squeals in my general direction after bounding towards Ed to plant a big kiss on his cheek, that legendary 'shark-with-lipstick' smile forming on her face. 'I thought you were just some college geek doing an interview.' (Memo to 4AD: you can forget about any more Belly front covers.)

Ed's parents split up when he was ten, although he moved back in with his father in Oxford five years ago – he's twenty-six now, but his dad, a Happy Mondays fan, is pretty cool. After a regular adolescence ('I used to think girls hated me,' he says. 'I couldn't speak to girls till I was seventeen'), Ed went to Manchester University, then 'did his Jack Kerouac bit', taking a Greyhound bus around America, exorcising most of his Bacchanalian tendencies.

'Someone held a party for us the other night and none of us went,' laughs the handsome, blue-eyed, six-foot five-inch guitarist. 'Drinking just depresses me nowadays. Until recently I was drinking very heavily and I loved it. But then it started to act as a depressant. I like to smoke dope a lot, but that's about it. Crack and coke? We've been offered it. I *am* intrigued, but . . . the same goes for girls – there's a hidden rule that no one goes with groupies. I hate that side of things, it's so dirty and seedy. It might be all right in a Guns N' Roses video, but it's not for us. We're quite a moral band, you know.'

––––––

I don't speak to Phil Selway – who only last night was stopped outside the band's tour bus by a girl and asked whether he was 'the roadie or just a hanger-on? Oh, and can you get me Thom's autograph?' – until after Radiohead's storming appearance in front of three thousand devotees at New York's Roseland Ballroom. I know it was storming because Thom's skinny-rib black jumper is hanging over a heater pipe in the band's dressing-room after the gig and it is dripping with sweat. Really. Drip, drip, drip.

I also know it was storming because all sorts of record company and MTV types are schmoozing and salivating and generally declaring Radiohead to be the best new band since whoever, the cure to all known diseases, etc. etc. You wouldn't know it was storming to look at Ed, who, after a puff or twenty-seven of, well, puff, has got what he calls 'the fear'. And you definitely wouldn't know it to look at Thom E. Yorke. Evidently, schmoozing with record-company and MTV types comes just below verruca removal on his list of likes.

Fearing the onset of one of Thom's 'moods', I drag Phil into a corridor and ask him why he thinks Radiohead have Made It Big in the United States, as opposed to – just to pick a name at random – Suede. (Interesting fact: Suede immediately faxed their congratulations on hearing that *Pablo Honey* had gone gold.)

'Americans like our Englishness,' says the drummer, Liverpool Poly graduate and former Nightline counsellor (true!), leaning against a drab grey wall. 'It's a far more abrupt kind of Englishness than Suede's – more energetic, more frenetic and direct.'

Just as Phil is starting to get into his stride, a rude American strides over to where we're standing and starts listening to our conversation. Surreally enough, it turns out to be Michael O'Neil, production assistant on MTV, better known as the voice behind America's latest lobotomised cartoon cult Beavis,[1] of *Beavis and Butthead* infamy.

'Radiohead rock, man!,' O'Neil/Beavis announces unprompted, as Phil and I exchange looks of the 'An Uzi, an Uzi, my kingdom for an Uzi' variety. 'Are they gonna be big? Let's quote-unquote: "Bigger than U2!" Definitely. They know how to write songs, they know how to sing and they know how to play. They're cred. They've got attitude. They're alternative crossover! They're like

---

1 Editor's note: the man who *actually* did the Beavis voice – and Butthead's too – was, of course, their creator Mike Judge. Exactly why Michael O'Neil claimed he voiced the snickering, sexually frustrated thoughts of Beavis must remain a mystery.

Jim-Morrison-meets-Jimi-Hendrix. MTV love them. They're rockin' the country!'

Huh-huh, huh-huh. Only this time, the joker's not joking. Radiohead's acid anthems and simply twisted pop are just what Europe, America, the world ordered.

One million people can't be wrong. Can they?

Three: Round *The Bends*

1

Review of *The Bends*

Ted Drozdowski, *Rolling Stone*,
18 May 1995

Luck and lyrics that capped the zeitgeist's ass made Radiohead's 'Creep' the summer radio hit of 1993.

The song initially stiffed in the band's native England, where the pained introspection of its *'I'm a creep/I'm a weirdo'* refrain collided with the glib irony of [the London] Suede and other codifiers of pop taste. Even Radiohead guitarist Jonny Greenwood hated the tune, and his sputtering guitar – a neural misfire signalling the final explosion of singer Thom E. Yorke's constipated synapses – was attempted murder. Nonetheless, 'Creep', which buoyed the otherwise unspectacular debut *Pablo Honey*, bullseyed our national inferiority complex and left Radiohead and James the last great UK hopes for America's brass ring.

Radiohead's reach may fall short with *The Bends*, a sonically ambitious album that offers no easy hits. It's a guitar field day, blending acoustic strumming with twitches of fuzzy tremolo and eruptions of amplified paranoia. Only Catherine Wheel's riptide of swollen six strings approximates the crosscurrents of chittering noise that slither through these dozen numbers. And as with Catherine Wheel, Greenwood and co-guitarist Ed O'Brien's devout allegiance to pop steers them clear of the wall of bombast that Sonic Youth perfected and that countless bands have flogged into cliché.

Yet pop allure also trips up *The Bends*. Yorke is so enamoured of singing honeyed melodies that he dilutes the sting of his acid tongue. In 'High and Dry', whose title is spun into one of the album's best hooks, Yorke gently sashays through the lines *'Drying up in conversation/You will be the one who cannot talk/All your insides fall to pieces/You just sit there wishing you could still make love'*. There's no hint in his presentation of the poison such abject isolation secretes. Elsewhere, oblique lyrics – an English inclination – erode the power of Yorke's decayed emotions, especially in a song like 'Bones', whose big riffs and swaying bass otherwise bellow for airplay.

'Creep' whacked Americans because its message was unfiltered. That's what we've come to expect of our contemporary rock heroes, from Kurt and Courtney to Tori Amos. Which doesn't mean *The Bends* won't grab that brass ring. But it'll be a difficult stretch.

2

World Class: How Radiohead Gave Us *The Bends*

Wyndham Wallace, *The Quietus*,
3 March 2015

You see that figure over there with the fuzzy ponytail poking out from under a Greek fisherman's cap, his jeans torn at the knees, his ankle-length grey raincoat rescued from a charity shop's neglected racks? That's me, the music editor of Exeter University's *The Third Degree* magazine, an expensively educated former private schoolboy desperately looking for a way in life that won't lead him to join the army, like his father, or to work in the city, like many of the people around him plan to.

See that guy, seated with me at the same wobbly coffee table, scanning the Student Guild coffee shop, from beneath a wild mop of bleached hair, for an excuse to stand up and leave? That's Thom Yorke, who's too well brought up simply to walk away. He's already living my dream, I'm sure, but he's not especially happy. It isn't my fault: his band's first record has been delayed by a couple of weeks. His label has forgotten to 'sell it in', the name given to the process of persuading shops to take stock of forthcoming releases. His gripes seem wholly justifiable.

It's May 1992 – just under three years before Radiohead will release *The Bends*. The *Drill* EP, which is currently languishing in EMI's warehouses, is the group's debut release, though they've been knocking around since 1985, when they formed – under the unpromising name of On A Friday – within the centuries-old grounds of Abingdon school, outside Oxford, where Yorke and his bandmates were boarders. I studied three and a half miles down the road at an even grander establishment – or at least that's how many of its staff and pupils haughtily thought of it – but this isn't something we've discussed. We've not discussed much, in fact: I barely know the man.

By now, Yorke has left Exeter University and returned to live in Oxford. I, meanwhile, still have over a year left to go. Nonetheless, we share a couple of friends. There's Paul, whose hair showers down his back to his beltline and who books shows for the students, generously ensuring I'm on the guest list any time I want. In later life he'll teach special needs kids and any of his wilder tendencies will be indulged instead on a vintage motorbike. Then there's Shack, the dreadlocked individual behind technology-loving duo Flicker Noise. He'll go on to enjoy a career as a musician and DJ – under various names, including Lunatic Calm and Elite Force – but he and Yorke used to play in Headless Chickens, an indie punk act featuring Thom on guitar and backing vocals. You can hear Thom on their only recorded track, 'I Don't Want to Go to Woodstock', part of a showcase seven-inch for local label Hometown Atrocities. It features two other woefully-named acts, Jackson Penis and Beaver Patrol, alongside the rather more prosaic Mad At The Sun. If you really care enough, copies are available these days for about £75.

I try to placate Yorke's concerns about their debut, informing him I've given it a great review, like I expect him to care what I think. I've described it as 'a storming opener to their career, a noisy guitar affair reminiscent of the Catherine Wheel', but I don't tell him I've given Kitchens Of Distinction's 'Breathing Fear' and Suede's 'The Drowners' joint Single Of The Month status. Nonetheless, I'm excited to see the band perform and I'm particularly keen to see if he can replicate that fifteen-second wail at the end of 'Prove Yourself', the lead track, though I don't articulate that last thought out loud. I'm actually far too nervous: Yorke's the first person I've ever met whose band has signed a deal.

As a student music critic I've met other musicians, of course, but they were already with a label by the time our paths met. Yorke, on the other hand, was a DJ at the university venue, the Lemon Grove, up till the end of last summer, and Paul reckons he's probably the best they've ever worked with. Yorke would entertain my friends and me on Friday nights as we sank Snakebites and Black until our limbs were loose enough to dance. Sometimes I'd make requests – the Stone Roses, the KLF, maybe Happy Mondays – and I far preferred Yorke's indie playlists to the club-fixated Saturday nights, which were hosted by Felix Buxton, later of Basement Jaxx. Back then, Exeter's Oxbridge rejects were far more privileged than they could ever have guessed, for many more reasons than they ever realised.

This encounter is the first time Yorke and I have talked for more than a moment or two over the record decks. Despite not really knowing him, I've still got this nagging feeling. He seems focused and self-aware, his bearing suggestive of a man confident that his choices will prove worthwhile. The music I've heard has helped: the *Drill* EP isn't an exactly stellar start to their career, but it's a convincing debut. It sounds like it was recorded in a budget-priced, provincial studio by a band excited at the possibilities newly available to them: the vocals distorted and artfully buried in the mix, the guitars raw and fluid, the bass lines imaginative, the snare drums tightly tuned. In the flesh, too, Yorke is just like a budding rock star should be and, though his mildly aloof demeanour makes me feel a little uncomfortable, it's something I can't resent, the existence of our mutual acquaintances making me feel quietly loyal to him. In years to come, I like to think, I'll be able to tell people I used to have coffee with Radiohead's Thom E. Yorke.

Six months or so later, I'm behaving like the worst kind of student, shitfaced, most likely stoned and, more worryingly, high on a sense of my own importance. A white label of 'Creep' landed on my doormat only a few weeks earlier, and it's the most exciting thing I've heard in a while. This time I honour Radiohead with a Single Of The Month – 'This has to be one of the best pieces of rock since Everest,' I write, oblivious to how this will make me wince in my future – and now they're playing at the university. I get to hang in the dressing room for a little while with a couple of friends, enjoying what I like to think of as Thom's victorious homecoming. These companions include one of my more glamorous associates, who, with admirable premonition, swiftly displays a fondness for Jonny Greenwood's prominent cheekbones. He, inevitably, behaves like a gentleman.

His brother, Colin, is similarly polite, and there's no sense coming from any of the band that this represents the fulfilment of a long-held rock'n'roll fantasy: there's no hurried necking of beers, no backstage shenanigans, no foolish conduct of any sort. Life spent on the road with Radiohead is no Valhalla.

I talk to them eagerly about the brilliance of 'Creep' and they seem neither uninterested nor unusually responsive. Naturally, no one's rude, so I stay there a while, albeit driven by my enthusiasm for their music and my solidarity with their cause rather than any sense of intimacy. But while no one would notice if I weren't there, I never once feel as though they wished I were someone or somewhere else. I'm simply a face to whom there's no need to be impolite, and they're really only concerned with the job they've come here to do. Still, I have this feeling that I, alone with the few, have recognised untapped potential, that I'm – though the phrase has yet to be coined – an early adopter. I'm convinced that 'Creep' is such an unmistakable anthem that there's no way it can be overlooked. I'm just one of the lucky ones who knows this because I've got one of the first copies. It's obvious others will soon agree.

Fifteen sheets to the wind, however, isn't a good place to be when you're in the mood to show off. Soon after the band start playing their new single, I edge my way to the front of a sparse crowd and, as Jonny Greenwood crushes out those iconic chords, I throw my arms into a crucifix and bellow along with the lyrics, directly beneath Thom's microphone stand. Worse still, I do so with my back to Thom, taking on the responsibility of cheerleading with an uninhibited passion. My hands rise and fall as I exhort others to sing along with me. They stumble back, embarrassed, leaving me isolated in front of the singer. I carry on regardless: I am Radiohead's champion. I am a complete disaster as well, but soon enough everyone else will look stupid for not having been down there with me.

Another few months pass and I drive three-plus hours from Exeter to north London on a rainy Sunday afternoon in March 1993. Belly are headlining the Town and Country Club in Kentish Town, and the Cranberries – currently seducing the British music media on the back of their debut single 'Linger' – are on first. Former Throwing Muse Tanya Donnelly's stab at mainstream stardom is all the rage and I know I should be excited to see both bands, but really it's the middle act, Radiohead, that are the main reason for my trip. By now, 'Creep' is a hit Stateside and it's infiltrating the UK too, having been recognised as a Single Of The Year by a number of publications. Their debut album, *Pablo Honey*, meanwhile, has been on the shelves for two weeks, stirring up what I describe in *The Third Degree* as a buzz as big as Suede's the previous year. 'That was quite some buzz,' I add, not as droll as I think I am.

I remember little of the show, sadly, aside from being excited at the chance to say 'Hello' to their tour manager and consequently ingratiate myself backstage. I find my way to their dressing room, but they've already got their fair share of hangers-on, so – having briefly said 'Hello' to the four of them I can find – I ask where I might find their frontman. There's a nonplussed reaction, a collective shrug of the shoulders. Sandwiches wilt under mirrored lights. Stepping outside into a concrete corridor, I can hear laughter coming from Belly's dressing room, out of which people are spilling into the passageway to my left. To my right, some dozen feet away, steps lead down towards the stage, and I hear a shuffling sound, or maybe a cough, emanating from a hunched, gnomish figure lurking at the top. It's Thom and he's alone. I hesitate, then shamble over. We exchange pleasantries but conversation stalls and Thom begins to look increasingly gloomy. It's time to get me coat.

Fast-forward another twelve months to 27 May 1994. It's almost two years since Thom and I shared that awkward coffee on the eve of Radiohead's debut. That's me again, clinging to the balcony railing of London's Astoria club. What's happening in front, from the moment Radiohead tear into 'You', is an almighty revelation. Whatever I may have thought of them in the past, there's an unprecedented urgency to their performance that nonetheless refuses to diminish the fluency of their playing, the ragged sketches they'd drawn on *Pablo Honey* delivered as sculpted, muscular beasts, elegantly wild yet mature. In a sign of their growing confidence, they drop the unfamiliar 'Bones' second song in and 'Black Star' follows after a furious 'Ripcord', Yorke introducing it with a pre-emptive, self-deprecatory apology for performing another new track.

It's far from the last, too: soon we get 'The Bends', 'Fake Plastic Trees' and 'Just', Yorke, in his Hawaii '81 T-shirt, bug-eyed and snarling, jerking his head convulsively to one side like Ewen Bremner in Mike Leigh's *Naked*. To his left, Greenwood Jr, his own shirt several sizes too small for him, handles his guitar like he's trying to tame it, while his brother lurks in the shadows, calmly bobbing his bobtailed head as he uncurls ingenious basslines. At the other end of the stage, Ed O'Brien – dressed like he's auditioning for Mandy Patinkin's role as Inigo Montoya in *The Princess Bride* – wrangles unforeseen chords from his instrument, slapping meat back onto the bones of their songs as though he'd previously underestimated his capabilities. Behind them, calm and unobtrusive, Phil Selway holds things together. I'm slack-jawed, wide-eyed and bowled over.

They return for an encore, playing 'Street Spirit (Fade Out)' for possibly the first time in public, revealing a sensitivity that 'Creep' only hinted at, its understated beauty seductive and spellbinding. Afterwards, I'm unusually speechless and, when the band appear in the Keith Moon bar later on, while I'm sinking dirty pints at an adrenalin-fuelled pace, I'm far too over-excited to even consider saying 'Hello'. I'd realised during 'My Iron Lung', unveiled almost half an hour into the show, that I'd never talk to them again. The way that barrage of explosions from Jonny Greenwood's guitar blew apart Yorke's artless melody, tearing it violently from the cotton wool of the song's coiling guitar lines and consciously dragging bassline, ripped a hole in the world around me. This faultless exhibition of sustained tension and release confirmed that Radiohead had become what I'd always hoped they'd be. Within little more than a year, the world would at last agree.

———

So what does *The Bends* mean, two decades on from its March 1995 release? Personally, it represents the end of a rite of passage: in the three years since Yorke and I had shared a coffee, I'd graduated from university, worked briefly in a record store and then moved to London, where I worked as a publicist for a variety of American acts. I took my job seriously: however late I stayed out partying, I was always behind my desk by 10 a.m. in an office above a piss-stinking alleyway a few metres off central London's Oxford Street. I'd left behind my comfortable upbringing to live in a shabby Soho flat – built for two, if shared by four – which provided a base for adventures I'd never expected to enjoy: I'd got drunk with Guided By Voices, barred Liam Gallagher from the Afghan Whigs' dressing room and smoked Snoop Dogg's weed at *The Word*.

It wasn't always easy being posh in the world of indie rock: I was gullible and over-sensitive, unsure of my place in – and unfamiliar with the customs of – London's thriving music industry. But I felt like I'd come of age and, when I first heard *The Bends*, it seemed to me that both Radiohead and I had reached the end of a crucial portion of an ongoing, thrilling journey. We'd shared similar backgrounds, had pursued comparable trails and had even crossed paths along the way. In my mind, their triumph was emblematic of what I too had achieved: the fulfilment of my long-held dream of an alternative existence in the music business.

To empathise with this far-fetched sentiment, there's something you need to understand: despite all the opportunities fee-paying schools might offer, they're not designed to propel people along such a path. (They weren't back then, anyway.) A 1980s middle-class upbringing hardly groomed one for success outside the traditional professional establishments, and though there were rebels – the smokers, the tokers, the drinkers, the thinkers – for most of them it was a stance, an opportunity to enjoy freedom before they settled down in the home counties with a well-spoken partner, a couple of precocious kids, a favourite seat on the London train and an inflated nostalgia for their misspent youth. 'Just like your dad, you'll never change . . . '

Having left university, I knew that my parents wished the time I was spending writing uncommissioned reviews for *Melody Maker* and *NME* was instead being spent preparing applications for jobs in more respectable fields. They weren't unsupportive, but this wasn't what they'd had in mind when they'd put my name down at birth for a fiercely competitive place at a prestigious educational establishment. Still, if private schools insisted on one thing back then, it was instilling in their pupils a sense of responsibility. My own headmaster called this one of 'the right habits for life', as important as keeping your fingernails clean and your hands out of your pockets when talking to staff. Whatever route was undertaken, you learned, you were to apply yourself fully to the task in hand. It's one of the few things I grasped during those ten bleak years away from home that has ever proved useful at all.

It's not too far-fetched to suppose that, like me, Yorke and his colleagues were reasonably cautious before they decided that music was a valuable pursuit. When families spend tens of thousands of pounds educating their children, only a few of their offspring dare reject the expectations that have built up around them. Even Jonny Greenwood, one imagines, spent a few sleepless nights at Oxford Brookes University before he walked out three weeks into his music and psychology degree to sign the band's deal with EMI's Parlophone imprint.

Not that such a background makes things harder than it is for those from state schools. Far from it, obviously: the familial financial cushion that most privately educated school-leavers have is unquestionably a significant reassurance for the ones willing to take a risk. But you can hear in Radiohead's *Drill* EP a need to be taken seriously; to – as the song said – 'prove' themselves. Its songs are lean and considered, balanced by a rough-and-ready sound that suggests they're scrupulously self-aware, uncommonly determined and attentive to where they want to sit in the grander scheme of things. You can bet that their teachers soon claimed a part in the band's global success.

But what does *The Bends* mean beyond my own narrow existence? It emerged on the back of an era in which music's tectonic plates had been shifting violently. Shoegaze had roared, then whimpered; the baggy movement had collapsed in a comatose haze of its making; Britpop had gorged itself upon its own noxious legend and, by the time *The Bends* was finally released, even grunge's poster boy Kurt Cobain had been dead for a year.

Judging from Thom Yorke's DJ sets at Exeter University, the band would have been familiar with all of these movements, shifting from the predominant domestic British sounds of their school days to explore noisier sounds coming in from the US, their common thread a sense of independence and a distaste for the status quo. This kaleidoscopic amalgam of potential inspiration informed everything Radiohead did in those early days, even if it was yet to be distilled to its essence.

The *Drill* EP is, inevitably, stamped with the indie production tropes of its time. Truth be told, it doesn't sit entirely uncomfortably alongside the likes of Kingmaker and Cud. But, by the time *The Bends* hit stores, Jonny Greenwood would be seen on Sunset Strip billboards wearing a T-shirt he'd bought at a show by Cell, a New York band championed by Sonic Youth. One member still recalls with pleasure how Thom Yorke once told him – after a show headlined by Radiohead – that Radiohead should have opened for them.

The quintet embraced influences that felt disorientating, smudging familiar genre boundaries and pursuing avenues that dismayed as many as they excited, albeit on a smaller scale than the band would later attempt. But it wasn't just critics that were confused about where they fitted in. Despite their efforts, Radiohead barely knew where they stood either. Everyone was scrambling for a new Seattle, a new Britpop, and times were becoming so desperate that, within months of *The Bends'* delivery, the media would be championing 'Romo'. Wherever you tried to place them, Radiohead failed to conform. This wasn't what was expected of them.

If *The Bends* came from anywhere, it was from a desire to comprehend this confusion of influences. After all, the members of Radiohead, one senses, didn't become a band because they wanted to make a noise, but because they wanted to make music and, crucially, knew how to make it. Some groups form because of a need for camaraderie or rebellion or escape, but none of these reasons seem relevant to Radiohead. Working together was simply the smartest option available to them: collectively, they could carry one another to their goal. They became a band, just as they've since become what they now are, because they embraced the duty of being Radiohead.

Becoming Radiohead took time, too: there was much to digest, so much to learn, before they could understand just what this responsibility meant. *The Bends* is consequently the sound of five men fighting their way out of a tangled web of conflicting convictions and prejudices with an uncommon earnestness, reconciling their tastes and their ambitions, sifting through the Pixies and the Smiths and Dinosaur Jr and the Beatles and Talking Heads and Happy Mondays and Elvis Costello and Tim Buckley. It's the sound of five men taking an exploratory dive into deep waters, finding themselves lost, and still somehow redrawing the map of where it is they should resurface. It wasn't called *The Bends* for nothing.

Before that, though, there was 'Creep'. Love it or loathe it, it represents a critical juncture for Radiohead in their development, just as it embodies for me the night before the morning I realised in what an undignified way alcohol could make me behave. It's common knowledge that the band has leaned towards a negative sentiment for this song for years: even Greenwood's first, extraordinary interjection of noise apparently stemmed from his attempt to mess up a song that he thought was far too fey. (One might say he had a point.) But, in drawing upon what was happening on both sides of the Atlantic, 'Creep' combined a grumbling Englishman's indie sensitivity with the sometimes nihilist, always principled spirit of the US guitar underground. Predictably, with Cool Britannia approaching its zenith, it was left to America to be first to 'get' it: in the UK, the track peaked upon its first release at No. 78 in the charts. But after it became a hit Stateside, the band conceded to a UK reissue that made it into the Top 10. They'd just adopted their albatross.

Listening to 'Creep' now, it's understandable that they were unenthusiastic about its British re-release and why they soon found it so unbearable that it failed to make it onto their set lists for most of the 2000s. The appeal of such lyrical transparency soon dwindles when you're forced to stand in front of crowds repeatedly denouncing your significance. What once appeared honest is rendered almost ridiculous by virtue of its repetition – for both the singer and the audience. No wonder Yorke looked so genuinely nonplussed in 1997 as he sang the song at Glastonbury: '*What the hell am I doing here? I don't belong here . . .* '

Feasibly, there may be yet another dimension to their uncomfortable relationship with the song. By virtue of their upbringings, these well-bred boys were most likely indoctrinated with the conviction that such declarations of self-pity were hardly becoming when uttered from beneath a stiff upper lip. To sit about whining and whingeing is decidedly non-U – *infra dignitatem*, you might say – if you came from the kind of establishment they did (though God help anyone who tried). These may not have been conscious beliefs, but they probably coloured their growing distaste for a track that had been very good to them. Still, whether or not this is correct, the truth is that 'Creep' contains none of the complexity of the music they were soon writing and, even amid other songs they were already playing, it seemed a little . . . trite. To some, their subsequent decision to bench it may seem precious or at least disrespectful to fans, but honestly: imagine yourself, night after night, in front of increasingly huge audiences, having to pretend, in a tremulous voice, that you're still the same jerk you were on that lonely night you first wrote the song. You'd soon start feeling sorry for yourself too.

In the year between 'Creep''s two deliveries, Radiohead released two other singles. 'Anyone Can Play Guitar' was the first and coincided with the release of their patchwork debut album, *Pablo Honey*, in February 1993. It ridiculed the idea of pop stardom with unusually acerbic bitterness, something that perhaps contributed to its commercial failure: '*Anyone can play guitar/And they won't be a nothing anymore*', Yorke growled, adding wickedly, '*Grow my hair, grow my hair/ I am Jim Morrison* . . . ' 'Anyone Can Play Guitar' appeared to be a reaction to the spotlight that 'Creep' had attracted and, a year later, 'Pop Is Dead' – which, tellingly, never made it onto an album – was even more alienating for the media, as well as the general public and, presumably, the band's record label too. '*Oh no, pop is dead, long live pop/It died an ugly death by back-catalogue*', Yorke sang, echoing Morrissey's line from 'Paint A Vulgar Picture' – 'Reissue, repackage, repackage! Re-evaluate the songs' – in an ill-advised video that found him carried in a glass coffin, heavily made up like a dead fop.

Furthermore, Yorke wasn't finished. 'We raised the dead but *they won't stand up*,' he went on, 'And radio has salmonella/And *now you know you're gonna die*,' before he concluded, ahead of a whirring squawl of guitars, that '*pop is dead, long live pop/One final line of coke to jack him off/He left this message for us*.' If the song's meaning wasn't clear enough, though, Yorke would elaborate on it at the band's London Astoria show in 1994 with the words, 'Dedicated to members of the press, as it always has been,' altering the lyrics to '*one final cap of speed to jack him off*', then muttering, 'fucking bunch of losers'. 'Pop Is Dead' appeared so contemptuous that it was hard even for Radiohead's biggest fans to like.

Fortunately, *Pablo Honey* itself contained enough notable moments to maintain belief in their explorations. Admittedly, almost half of its songs were already available – the whole of the *Drill* EP was included, for one thing – but, if one accepted that the best songs were indeed the ones that were most fresh, it indicated that the band were developing at a pace. Sure, they still struggled to stand far above many of the other acts that were scoring 7/10 reviews in the music press: 'Vegetable' was merely lovable if one really wanted to love it, for instance, and 'How Do You?' could only just summon up enough bile to satisfy a sweaty teenage audience too young for the Sex Pistols. But in its two closing tracks it provided a signpost towards where they were moving. 'Lurgee''s quiet compassion and 'Blow Out''s lysergic drama displayed a mature aplomb that would prosper on *The Bends*, their willingness to let the music define them an overdue replacement for the record-company styling to which they seemed to have fallen victim: the red-and-white striped trousers, the dubious haircuts, the 'received wisdom' that seemed to inform many of their visual decisions. *'You do it to yourself, you do, and that's what really hurts . . .'*

These intriguing fumblings, with moments of generous inspiration scattered amid them, were a tentative reconnaissance, a preliminary warm-up, a necessary step in Radiohead's evolution. In fact, *Pablo Honey* was an application letter, one might say. *The Bends*, of course, would be the interview.

First, though, in October 1994, there was a stopgap EP, *My Iron Lung*, its opener in fact lifted directly from the tapes of the band's monumental Astoria show, with only Yorke's vocals newly tracked. *'This is our new song,'* he wailed, *'Just like the last one/A total waste of time/ My iron lung'* and, every time I heard this, I'd remember that disconsolate Yorke at the top of the steps at the Town and Country Club in '93. They still loved making music, while playing live could be satisfying and they probably enjoyed each other's company too, but already Radiohead were learning that they didn't like being in a band: all the rigmarole that came with it seemed only to inspire revulsion. Maybe this was less true for the rest of them, but Yorke in particular seemed to be struggling to come to terms with the games that they'd been led to believe needed to be played.

The Bends was made as Radiohead first stepped on the treadmill, and already they wanted off. It was, one suspects, a record upon which they knew they'd stand or fall, informed by everything that preceded it. In many ways, it feels more like a debut album than *Pablo Honey* – with its mixed bag of strengths – ever did, as though it were the culmination of a lifetime's work. Second albums are notoriously difficult to make and, by all accounts, *The Bends* suffered a more than troubled gestation, yet it still comes out sounding fully formed, defining them in a way that *Pablo Honey* by and large failed to do. The privileges and the prejudices, the accolades and the rebukes, their pasts and their presents: all of these and more converged as one, crashing and grinding into each other until they found their place, only to soar off on a new, graceful trajectory. It was the end of a rite of passage.

The songs themselves only need to be recollected here because *The Bends* became so omnipresent and inescapable, so much a part of the sound of summer and winter 1995 that its over-familiarity bred a certain degree of fatigue. At the time of its release, however – in the wake of *Definitely Maybe* and *Parklife* the previous year – it appeared unusually literate and accomplished, and, in some people's minds, towered above everything championed by an over-excitable press for years.

If they'd been little more than the sum of their influences on *Pablo Honey*, now Radiohead were like no one else at all – like no one apart from Radiohead, that is. Even this was a concept that would soon be demolished: each new record from the band would swerve passionately away from where they'd last paused. They'd reinvent themselves repeatedly, first reshaping alternative rock, then dragging intelligent techno and electronica into the mainstream, before exploiting their well-earned, hard-won independence by at least attempting to disrupt conditions precipitated by the arrival of the internet.

That was to come, though: in March 1995, they staked their first real claim to greatness with a forty-nine-minute collection of accessibly timeless, visionary songs that may have gathered a little dust since but which stand up remarkably well. Admittedly, *The Bends* was only quietly revolutionary: there were no heroics, no ill-suited bursts of attention-grabbing histrionics, merely layer upon layer of intriguing arrangements that demanded repeated plays to unravel. But that mysterious sound of empty space being filled by shimmering guitars at the start of opening track 'Planet Telex' now seems prescient: Radiohead were taking up camp in territory few people seemed interested in investigating. This worked because *The Bends'* lyrics were more elliptical and the songs more intelligent, than anything they'd previously tried. Indeed, they were smarter than almost anyone in mainstream 'alternative' music was trying to be, a far cry from the wilful idiocy and tabloid realms in which direction every other band seemed to be drunkenly heading.

The sonics of the album, too, were polished, yet rarely drew attention to themselves. Yorke's voice, meanwhile, still seemed to slur from note to note in his quieter moments – though he continued to rage bitterly at other times – but he seemed to be inhabiting the songs rather than testing out a role, whether amid the crunching guitars of the title track or the tender acoustic strums of the heartbreakingly puzzling 'Fake Plastic Trees'. On 'Just', the band might have given in to their American influences, but they still packed the song with colourful fireworks and 'Bullet Proof . . . I Wish I Was' boasted a haunting, peculiarly English desolation. Then there was the lilting grace of 'Nice Dream''s strings and Yorke's impressively feminine falsetto, which gave way to an impressively dramatic flurry of squealing guitars while, in 'High and Dry' and 'Street Spirit (Fade Out)', they mapped out a terrain towards which a pack of other songwriters would soon rush: anthemic, gutsy, mid-paced songs of unapologetic but never over-egged sentiment. Few would ever do it as well.

Radiohead, of course, would soon leave these copycats trailing and many of us would travel with them, leaving *The Bends* behind. In fact, in a sense – especially in the light of what came after – *The Bends* nowadays sounds a little gauche, as if it's tied to a period of Radiohead's lives, and indeed our own, whose ideals have long since withered. Since then, we have grown wiser with experience, and the cultivated excesses of *OK Computer* and the stubborn experimentalism of *Kid A* and *Amnesiac* have underlined the band's insistence that great musicians have a responsibility never to stand still, a reminder of an older generation who challenged themselves to constantly refine their talent and explore new domains with each and every release.

The Bends, therefore, is attached to the 'old' Radiohead, a band who, for a while, were compromised by major label practices but who, in overcoming their distaste and disenchantment with the institutions into whose beds they'd unwittingly climbed, surpassed the promise others saw in them. It may exude an awkward, sometimes unwelcome nostalgia, but remember that it once offered far, far more than that. Without *The Bends*, one imagines, Radiohead might never have become what they are.

So – you see that man up on stage, his arms twitching spasmodically, his voice like an angel's, his colleagues filling up arenas with ever-restless inventiveness? That's Thom E. Yorke, lead singer of Radiohead, one of the greatest groups to have emerged in our tiny little lifetimes, and it all started with *The Bends*. Now, you see that fellow buried deep in the crowd, his balding pate lit up beneath the moon, still struggling with ghosts from his entitled youth but determined to leave them behind? Yeah, you guessed it: that's me, once again.

Did I tell you I knew them when I was younger? They couldn't give a damn, of course, but I'll be proud till the day I die.

3

Don't Call 'Em Britpop

Clare Kleinedler, *Addicted To Noise*,
May 1996

Britpop. It's all over the place all of a sudden. There's Oasis, the Beatles rip-offs trying to emulate the Rolling Stones' drug-taking, groupie-filled past. Then there's Blur, the self-described 'middle-class' darlings of the UK music scene who just can't seem to make a dent in America. Don't forget Elastica, Pulp, Supergrass and Echobelly. But whatever you do, please, please do not include Radiohead in the list of Britpop bands.

The only thing Radiohead have in common with the above-mentioned bands is that, yes, they are from England. What makes them different from their fellow UK musician brothers and sisters is that Radiohead do not limit themselves to playing recycled '60s music and they do not engage in public spats with other bands. Nor do they spend their free time bragging about how 'fookin' great' they are. They don't have to talk the talk. Radiohead's songs and live performances speak loud enough for themselves.

Radiohead's current album, *The Bends*, alone made 1995 a year of great music. Every single song on the record is amazing;

from the breathtakingly beautiful melody of 'Street Spirit' to the ear-piercing, guitar-wailing 'Just'. And after over fifty weeks on the charts, people are finally beginning to take notice. The album is currently bobbing in and out of the Top 10 in Britain and is enjoying its first break into the Top 100 here in the states. MTV can't get enough of the band's video for the single 'High and Dry', and virtually every other music critic in the US and the UK voted the album as one of their Top 10 for last year.

Not too shabby for a band that used to play to a crowd of about, um, two people at parties ten years ago when they first started out. Having met at an all-boys private school in Abingdon, England, singer/guitarist Thom Yorke, guitarists Jonny Greenwood and Ed O'Brien, bassist Colin Greenwood and drummer Phil Selway formed the band out of sheer boredom. The group put the band on hold to attend college (except for youngest member Jonny, who stayed behind at school) but rehearsed during breaks and holidays. By the summer of 1991, the lads re-grouped and decided to take this whole music thing seriously.

They called themselves On A Friday and started gigging around their home town of Oxford. Though in retrospect Yorke says that 'we were pretty crap', their appearance at Oxford's Jericho Tavern in October of 1991 attracted about 25–30 A&R guys and inspired a journalist from a local zine to write: 'And successful On A Friday will be. No ifs and buts with this lot. This time next year they will have outgrown all the venues they talk about and for once I think I may just have got it right.'

The journalist was right. The band changed their name from On A Friday, a name that proved confusing on flyers if they played a gig, for example, on a Thursday, to Radiohead and scored themselves a record deal with Parlophone. The band recorded their debut album *Pablo Honey* in three weeks and released it to minimum hype and enthusiasm. In 1993, the band's single 'Creep' was re-released and the rest is history.

'Creep' was probably the best and worst thing that has ever happened to Radiohead. While the single propelled *Pablo Honey* into gold album status in the states, the song became somewhat of an anthem for the band, especially singer Yorke. Much to the band's dismay, Radiohead became 'that "Creep" band' and Yorke became the weirdo of all weirdoes, the misunderstood, reluctant poster boy for a generation that identified with the agonising lyrics '*I wish I was special/You're so fucking special/ But I'm a creep!*'

MTV picked up a heavy rotation of the video and even invited the band to play to a crowd of bikini babes and frat boys at the channel's Beach House. Seeing the video of that performance proves how undiscriminating the whole 'Creep' obsession was; frat boys banging their heads to Radiohead? Creepy.

Although many bands dream of having a hit single early on, the men of Radiohead loathed the idea. The band was immediately pressured to come out with another 'Creep' and the recording of their follow-up album became a nightmare. Yorke and co. 'crawled' around the studio with producer John Leckie (Stone Roses, Ride) for three months, driving Leckie and each other crazy. According to the group, it was a major low point for the band, a time that saw each member go through bouts of self-doubt and depression. Finally, Leckie ordered everyone to go home, with the exception of Yorke, and made him go to work. The band went back out on the road for a bit, came back and in two weeks *The Bends* was finished.

Since the release of the album in March of 1995, Radiohead has been a non-stop touring machine. The band has done several headlining club tours around the globe and supported R.E.M. last year in America, giving them the opportunity to play arena-size venues. While touring is very much a part of the rock'n'roll lifestyle, off time is spent in a very un-rock'n'roll manner. The members of Radiohead prefer books over parties and each keeps a fairly low profile in the public, choosing to stay in Oxford rather than join the Britpop masses in London or Manchester. Often referred to as 'the most polite band in music', the guys are pleasant, with the exception of an occasional stress-induced outburst from Yorke.

I've personally experienced both aspects of the band. The first interview I'd ever done was on the phone with bassist Colin Greenwood. As fate would have it, during the interview my computer crashed, as did my tape recorder. Of course, I didn't realise until after I'd hung up with Greenwood that my tape was blank. In fear of losing my job, I frantically called Greenwood back, explaining through tears what had happened.

'No problem,' he replied calmly. 'Call me back in two hours and we'll do it on my lunch break.' A gesture I will never forget.

On a heavier note, I had a run-in with Yorke on a bad day last year during the KOME Almost Acoustic Christmas Show in San Jose, California. 'I just got here! Leave me alone!' he shouted as I approached him for an interview. Completely shattered and feeling like a worm, I crawled into the corner, and wondered if I had chosen the right career path.

So it is that dreadful memory that's weighing heavily on my mind as I arrive at the Phoenix hotel in San Francisco for my interview with Yorke and guitarist Jonny Greenwood. My heart pounds and my palms begin to sweat as tour manager Tim walks me over to meet Yorke.

'Hi. Have we met before? You look familiar,' says Yorke, pleasant as can be.

'Um, yeah,' I stammer. 'We definitely have.' I wait until later to let him know the when, where and how. Yorke and I have a seat on some plastic lawn furniture next to the pool. His hair is a blinding orange today, contrasting sharply with the oversized black-black sunglasses on his face. Seems he is nursing quite a hangover but is in good spirits nonetheless. Jonny bounds over, shakes my hand and slides into a chair. The reluctant girl-magnet of the group, he's got 'cheekbones that could start a war' (according to my friend Cat) and a bob of shiny black hair that hangs carelessly into his eyes. Noticing a painful-looking shaving cut on his chin, I inform him that he is bleeding.

'Oh, I know . . . I enjoy it, though,' he says, pressing his hand against the cut. Staring at the splotch of blood on his hand, he looks surprised. 'Cool! Should I go and mop?'

'No. Bleed on the table,' says Thom, sarcastically.

The two of them could be brothers. They don't look anything alike, but they do weird things like finish each other's sentences and repeat every other word the other is saying. Jonny's real-life brother is Colin but, after hanging out with these two, I'm beginning to wonder if they were related in a previous life. They even play-fight over who will answer what question, constantly cutting each other off, competing to see who can be cleverer. But it is all in fun. No Liam/Noel-esque punch-outs here in Camp Radiohead.

Addicted to Noise: How is the tour going so far?
Thom Yorke: Pretty good. It's quite exciting, but I've got to stop
        drinking.

ATN: Better than the last tour?

Thom: Yeah, it's sort of . . . yeah. I think so. And they've all sold out, which is pretty amazing.

ATN: **Did you ever retrieve any of the stolen equipment from the Soul Asylum tour? (The band awoke one morning in Denver to find their entire truck, filled with all of their gear, had been stolen right out of their hotel parking lot.)**

Jonny Greenwood: Nothing at all. Not a musical sausage.

Thom: Not a bleeding sausage.

ATN: **Let's start from the beginning. You all met at school . . .**

Jonny: It was a dark, moonlit night . . .

Thom: A dark, moonlit night . . .

Jonny: We should make it more romantic than it was. It was a boring afternoon at school, probably.

Thom: I'm still fond of Jonny coming in and playing every instrument that he could possibly think of to get into the band . . .

Jonny: Yeah, turning up with gel horns.

Thom: Yeah. He started with the harmonica and we weren't into that.

ATN: **Is it true that none of you knew how to play your instruments when you first started the band?**

Thom: It's all relative, but I would say it was true . . .

Jonny: [To Thom] Really?

Thom: Well, you were quite good.

Jonny: Well, we just didn't play in public. I don't think we were as bad as most bands . . . we just sort of . . . we didn't think we were very good.

73

Thom: It was more a low opinion of oneself, you know, but justified low opinion, I think.

ATN: You all seem to have different musical influences: jazz, Scott Walker, XTC, Magazine, various trip-hop groups . . . How do you all write music together?

Thom: Well, it's not like you go to a recording studio or rehearsal going, 'Well, we're gonna make it sound like this.' It's pretty bad if we do anything like that, because there would be no point. I think, like, if you were a painter, you wouldn't, like, argue about who to copy, you know. You presume you get over that. It's not really an issue. If we were all into the Pixies and nothing else, then it would be pretty obvious what the band would sound like. I think it's the same with any band, really. I mean, if you talk to R.E.M., their influences are pretty disparate . . . about as disparate as you can get, really. Anyway [looks at Jonny], he's got me into jazz now. Bastard.

ATN: So finally *The Bends* is getting some recognition. Why do you think it took so long?

Thom: Well, the nicest thing is that *Billboard* thing. They have three journalists with their faces going [makes a fake grin] and we were No. 1 in two of them and three in the third, I think.

Jonny: It's weird. It's been kind of a reversal from *Pablo Honey*. We had an album that sold a lot but wasn't taken much notice of and now we've become that horrible thing of a bands' band or a critics' band.

Thom: Frightening.

Jonny: Which is kind of a big reversal for us . . .

Thom: Because they're even more fickle than the public.

Jonny: It's a nice change from the first album.

ATN: **Is this kind of what you wanted from the beginning, to slowly climb up the charts?**

Jonny: Yeah. At least now, when journalists miss the point and reviewers miss the point, then we can sort of disagree with them. But when reviewers are saying bad things about the first album, we just sort of half-agree with them. [Thom lets out an enormous laugh.] There's some truth to what they're saying. If they say [*The Bends*] is rubbish and no one has said that, so it makes sense, really.

Thom: It makes us a little nervous.

ATN: **What are your inspirations for your songs?**

Thom: [They] change all the time. Mostly books about politics at the moment.

ATN: **Speaking of politics, do you plan on pursuing a career in it, since you're involved in the Rock the Vote UK and you have a new song called 'Electioneering'?**

Thom: Oh yeah. I think I wanna become a politician. Well, I wanna actually get into the arms trade first and make my money there. Pop stardom, arms trade, have it all.

ATN: **What has been the highlight of your career thus far?**

Jonny: Career? You sound like my mother . . . she says that. 'When are you going to get a career?'

Thom: Yeah. 'Why have you chosen this career?' A career is going in the army.

Jonny: Career suggests long . . .

Thom: Longevity . . .

Jonny: . . . and planning. There's something quite depressing when you hear a band say, 'We want to make music together for another 20–30 years'.

ATN: (jokingly) **You don't want to do that?**

Jonny: I don't know what I want to do, really. Music. That would be good, but you know, I don't plan on anything, really.

Thom: Peter Buck, he said . . . we were at this bar, and these two girls came up and tried to pick a fight with us. They started on me by saying something like . . . Oh . . . there was a Vancouver show where I walked onstage and said, 'We've been all over the world and you're the rudest fucking audience we've ever met' [laughs] and a fight ensued [laughs harder] and she sort of tried to pick a fight with me about that and that didn't work. Then she turns to Peter Buck and says, 'R.E.M. guy' and started pushing him and stuff. It was really fucking weird! We both just stood there, and he said, 'Well, you gotta sort of cultivate a healthy sense of the absurd,' which I thought was pretty cool. Then I said, 'Yeah, it's all gonna mean shit diddly when you're dead.' And he said, 'No, no, it will mean nothing well before that.' So, that resounded in my head.

ATN: **So what have been the highlights in being in Radiohead?**

Jonny: I heard one of our songs used by the BBC for a trailer for *Match of the Day*.

ATN: **What's that?**

Jonny: Oh, you know, sort of [announcement] on BBC1 tonight. [Mimicking the announcer] 'We'll be showing the Everton match.' And they'll play a Radiohead song to it. It's usually something like Tears for Fears or something . . . [Thom making drum noises in the background.] It's surreal, yes.

ATN: **How about lowlights?**

Thom and Jonny: Lowlights?

Thom: Is that code?

ATN: **Highlights, lowlights . . .**

Thom: Oh, lowlights. Oh sorry. I thought it was a type of milk or something. Lowpoints. Soul Asylum was pretty fucking low, I think.

Jonny: Yeah, that was pretty bad.

Thom: That was pretty low [laughs]. Just having one's gear stolen, then having to carry on with the tour. It wasn't much fun. Especially since we just came off R.E.M., so you couldn't really go down further. Couldn't really get much more let down. Handy link to a song. [One of Radiohead's new songs is called 'Let Down']

ATN: **You all seem to stay away from the Britpop party scene. Why is that?**

Thom: There is one at the moment, apparently. We don't really like cocaine that much.

Jonny: We're from the wrong city, as well . . . Oxford.

Thom: Yeah, deliberately. They don't let us out.

ATN: **So much of what is written about you in the press tends to focus on your volatile personality. Why do you think the papers are so obsessed with that aspect of Thom Yorke?**

Thom: Because most people in my position have learnt to behave and I haven't and I'm just not very good at behaving . . .

Jonny: I think people like their pop stars easy.

Thom: Like film stars, really. You can't be temperamental; you're basically a distraction.

Jonny: I think they want 'Pop Star Lite', really. L-I-T-E.

Thom: Someone from R.E.M. was saying to me the other night, 'Get nervous when you realise you can do it. When you can go through a whole evening having talked to fifty people and not remember a fucking word of any of it. Then you really are in trouble.'

ATN: **I've read somewhere that you've been writing down happy thoughts for the next album. Have you written anything down so far?**

Thom: Nearest I got was writing about the colour of the sky in LA.

ATN: **That's happy?**

Thom: Yeah, because that particular day it had rained the night before and you could actually see the sky. That's as happy as it's got, so far.

ATN: **That's all?**

Thom: Yeah, that's it. [Both laugh]

ATN: **What can we expect from the next album? Do you plan to put some of your current B-sides on it?**

Thom: There's been talk of doing a B-sides album at some point.

Jonny: Yeah, they are rather good and do get lost . . .

Thom: But then that's sort of cool. Otherwise we'd be getting into Prince territory and release three albums a year and there would be no quality control and people would see through it, wouldn't they, really, frankly?

Oh . . . Um . . . [to Jonny] what can we expect from this next album? Jon? It'll be analogue.

Jonny: Um, it will be, yes, sort of western.

Thom: Analogue.

ATN: **Western?**

Thom: Western analogue. Communist.

Jonny: Post-techno-gothic.

ATN: **Will it be somewhat experimental like the B-side remix of 'Planet Telex'?**

Jonny: I think we'll do more stuff that will be experimental, but again, it will be as unlike 'Planet Telex' as . . . [it will be] weirder than anything else.

Thom: The best indication of what we're going to do is that we're building our own studio, we're producing it ourselves and it's going to be a fucking mess.

ATN: **Why are you going to produce it yourself this time?**

Jonny: Because we sort of always wanted to and we were used to it when we were recording in bedrooms and it's not really that much different . . .

Thom: Yeah, we just really want to get that bedroom mentality of not giving a fuck and not worrying about it being a record.

ATN: **Where are you building your studio?**

Jonny: That's a secret.

ATN: **I don't mean the address! Where, like [the] city, [the] place . .**

Jonny: [laughing] 17 Turnpike . . . No, it's a sort of old apple storage place or banana storage place . . .

Thom: Lots and lots of upside-down trees.

ATN: **Do you think that is going to be good for you to be out in the middle of nowhere?**

Thom: Oh, very good. There's no toilet . . .

Jonny: Chi . . . good for the vibes.

Thom: [To Jonny] The chi? Is that as in tai chi?

Jonny: It flows up through the ground. Farms nearby. I mean, we've always been the kind of band . . .

Thom: [cuts him off] Is that what chi is?

Jonny: Yeah [trying to finish his sentence] That's recorded . . .

Thom: Does that come up through the ground?

Jonny: Yeah [continuing the story]. That's why . . .

Thom: [again, cuts Jonny off] I thought that was sewage.

Jonny: No. That's why [it's good to] be barefoot and not wear shoes.

Thom: Really?

Jonny: Yeah. So anyhow . . .

Thom: [Cuts Jonny off again] Fucking hell, I didn't know that!

Jonny: So, yes. We're recording there. We've always been the kind of band who records in picturesque village holes rather than in city youth centres, so yeah, that's probably a good thing. I don't know.

ATN: **Can you talk about some of the songs that you've already written for the album?**

Thom: OK, what can we say about the . . . I don't know if they're any good, really.

ATN: **I heard 'Electioneering' is excellent.**

Thom: Yeah, it's all right. I don't know. I don't like any of it, really. Some days I like all of it, some days I don't like any of it. What do you think, Jonny?

Jonny: Yeeess. Sometimes all of our songs don't sound good, sometimes they all sound great.

ATN: **How are they sounding like today?**

Jonny: People keep telling us we sort of sound like Queen, uh . . . Pink Floyd. Someone said we sounded like a skiffle band last night . . .

ATN: **A skittle band?**

Thom: You know, skiffle. Rockabilly . . .

Jonny: So it's anybody's guess. Sort of skiffle-Pink Floyd that sounds like Queen. Yeah, that's us. Easy to categorise, as you can tell. That cliché, that old pigeonhole that we fit into so well.

ATN: **A lot of bands like Garbage, R.E.M. and even k.d. lang refer to Radiohead as their favourite band. How does it feel to be admired by fellow musicians?**

Thom: I don't get it. Well, we're not that good. You know . . .

Jonny: I don't know. I feel their band is better than ours.

Thom: A lot better than ours.

Jonny: We always have a feeling that we can do better. There's always acres and acres of room for improvement. Just about everything we do, from every interview to every song we record, every concert. But maybe that's what keeps us going. Imagine being satisfied with something.

Thom: Satisfied is when you get fat and, like, go home.

Jonny: And have so much confidence in yourself that you don't worry . . .

Thom: Try to find more satisfaction by eating more . . . that's what I do. So that's why I come on the road.

ATN: **If you weren't in Radiohead, what would you all be doing?**

Jonny: We'd be asking k.d. lang, or Garbage, or R.E.M. for jobs. I don't know, what would we do?

Thom: I would be um . . . I'd be a politician!

ATN: **No, really.**

Thom: I would!

Jonny: I'd stick with college, really. And I'd be graduating this

year and have an honorary doctorate degree in
something . . .

ATN: **Where did you all go to school? Thom, you went to
Exeter, right?**

Thom: Yes, I went to Exeter and I did English literature and
fine art.

ATN: **[to Jonny] And you were in college when the band got
signed?**

Jonny: Yes. I did four weeks or something like that.

Thom: Then your tutor said, 'Leave!'

Jonny: [laughing] Then they turned up in a white van and
dragged me up to some concert somewhere.

ATN: **What about the others?**

Jonny: Colin went to Cambridge.

Thom: [in royal-esque accent] Cambridge! English literature!

Jonny: [also doing accent] Philip probably went to Liverpool . . .

Thom: [accent] We can't remember what he did!

Jonny: Edward did politics in Manchester [laughing].

Thom: [accent] Politics and economics . . . mostly politics!
Northern Irish politics!

ATN: **Then he can be your campaign manager.**

Thom: Oh yes!

ATN: **Tell me about your songwriting process. How does it
all come together?**

Jonny: It's quite defecatory.

Thom: Yes, it's very defecatory and it's a friggin' mess and, um,
often you'll have a song for a year, which you won't
know what to do with, and then Jonny will change one
note and it'll all fall into place. And some songs are
completely automatic, like 'Lucky', where there was

absolutely no thought process or anything involved. We just played it one day and that was it. I played the chords once around and everyone joined in and that was the song [laughs]. It was just frightening, frankly.

ATN: **Tell me some interesting fan encounters.**

Thom: Mostly people trying to convert me to God.

Jonny: There's some people who follow him around and say, 'You should use that power you have to spread the word of our lord Jesus Christ!'

Thom: And I say, 'I'll spread something else instead.' I had someone come knocking at my door in Oxford. And I was forced to slam it in her face. Because that was the line that was drawn and she went across it . . . [laughing . . . trying to have a sense of humour about it]

Jonny: Someone grabbed me when I was onstage at a Canadian show and said, 'Quick, write your name on my arm.' Which wasn't a first, but they showed up at the next show, which was like three hundred miles away, which was quite strange. But stranger still was that my name was sort of, very roughly . . . didn't even look like my name . . . they had it tattooed on . . . permanently.

Thom: There's a lesson there. Always write neatly.

Jonny: Yes, that's a good lesson.

ATN: **Did that freak you out?**

Jonny: Nooo . . . I just wish they would've asked Thom to draw something. It's better than an anchor or a lion's head.

ATN: **So you just signed 'Jonny'?**

Jonny: Well, it was more like Jeremy, actually . . . [laughing]

ATN: **Do any of you have tattoos?**

Thom: No. I get a transfer occasionally. I find [tattoos] very sexy. Hmmmm.

ATN: **But you don't want to get one?**

Thom: Well, not on me.

Jonny: Yeah, standing in the mirror admiring your own tattoo . . .

Thom: And getting off on it. Anyway, ohh . . . that could get really messy.

ATN: **OK . . . I have some questions that have been emailed to me by the members of the Radiohead emailing list. Some of them are very strange.**

Thom: Yes, let's answer those.

ATN: **First question. Thom, why are there so many car references in your songs like 'Killer Cars', 'An Airbag Saved My Life', 'Stupid Car' . . .**

Thom: First of all, where did you get the title 'An Airbag Saved My Life'?

ATN: **Everyone on the Radiohead emailing list is talking about it.**

Thom: Oh fuck! Never mind.

Jonny: That was quick!

Thom: Yeah . . .

Jonny: It hasn't been recorded or filmed live yet . . .

Thom: Or done anything at all . . .

ATN: **Someone already has it on tape.**

Thom: Ah fuck! London!

Jonny: How? When did we do it?

Thom: We did it in London for XFM.

Jonny: Oh yeah. We did it well, though, so that's all right.

Thom: No, we did it dreadfully.

Jonny: No, it wasn't.

Thom: Really?

Jonny: No, it was good.

Thom: Oh, OK. Why are there so many references to cars? Well, I'll tell you why. It's because when I was younger my parents moved to this house, which was a long, long way from Oxford and I was just at the age where I wanted to go out the whole time. I used to have this one car, and I very nearly killed myself in it one morning, and I gave my girlfriend at the time really bad whiplash in an accident. I was seventeen. Hadn't slept the night before. Anyway, eventually, my dad bought me another car, a Morris Minor, you know, and when you drove around corners in it, the driver door used to fly open. And I'd only do fifty miles an hour and on the road that went from my house to Oxford, there were fucking maniacs all the time, people who would drive a hundred miles an hour to work and I was in the Morris Minor and it was like standing in the middle of the road with no protection at all. So I just gradually became emotionally tied up in this whole thing.

ATN: **What are your feelings on vegetarianism?**

Thom: I think we were right and the rest of the world's wrong [referring to mad cow disease]. Yeah . . . we were right . . . nah, nah, nah . . . so there.

Jonny: I find it increasingly hard to do, because you discover with horror that your favourite chocolate sweets have gelatine in them . . .

Thom: And cheese, when they put the rennet in . . . that's the most disgusting thing imaginable! I think, basically, that it's the responsibility of the supermarkets to fucking get themselves sorted out, you know. Because basically people rely on supermarket chains and they're really the ones that should be endorsing vegetarianism. 'Cos if they don't, then it'll never happen, you know.

ATN: What do you want fans to see in your work?

Thom: The word of God!

Jonny: Yes.

Thom: [Notices my silence, waiting for him to finish] That was pretty good, I thought! [laughs] Um, if people get it, they wouldn't think it's depressing. When people sort of say, um . . . all that fucking annoying thing about, 'Oh your work's so depressing, na, na, na . . .' Well, it's not because those are just the words. The point is I put the words to music which I think is incredibly uplifting, otherwise, there would be no point to doing it at all.

ATN: Several people on the list want to know this: Jonny, do you have a girlfriend?

Jonny: I have hundreds, yeah. A different one every day. No, no, I'm not interested in women or sex or anything . . .

Thom: No. Messy, smelly . . .

ATN: How do you feel about the whole promotion aspect of the US?

Thom: I sort of envision myself in a sort of a Billy Graham role, you know . . . shake hands and spread the word of God and fuck off and take the money and run . . .

Jonny: We have money?

Thom: Apparently. Apparently, it comes later. We haven't seen any money yet.

ATN: What do you do in your off time?

Thom: Off time? Don't have any. Try and sit still. Can't do it.

Jonny: We usually sit around and think about what we're going to do with our on-time, sadly.

Thom: Yeah. It's really, really, really pathetic. In fact, we all need to get hobbies.

ATN: **You told me last time we talked that you were going to travel to Japan for vacation. Did you go?**

Thom: No, I was going to. The reason I didn't was because it's so fucking expensive and we haven't seen any money yet.

Jonny: The Japanese are the most . . . I think the most stylish nation on the earth.

Thom: Yeah . . . it's embarrassing. Makes the rest of us look like ill-dressed spazzes.

ATN: **So I take it you like touring Japan?**

Thom: Yeah. Any opportunity to go back will be gladly received [laughs]. We keep trying but they say they don't want us.

ATN: **That's not true. My sister just called from Tokyo this morning and asked when you're coming.**

Jonny: The official line, allegedly, is that we're going to go back when we can sort of . . .

Thom: . . . sell something new.

Jonny: No, when there are clubs that have room for about a thousand people. And after that it's like 15–20,000 people . . .

Thom: Oh, right. So we don't go back 'til then? [sarcastic]. Oh, yeah. That really makes sense. I think someone's lost the plot [reaches up in the air as if trying to grasp Jonny's meaning].

Jonny: We hope we can play Budokan and we'll go back when we can sort of . . .

Thom: What is the Budokan?

Jonny: It's a horribly big, scary place.

ATN: **Didn't the Beatles play there?**

Jonny: Blur played there too.

ATN: **Well, if Blur can sell it out, you should be able to . . .**

Jonny: Well, this is what we're vaguely trying to hope, yes.

Thom: How big is it?

Jonny: It's like Wembley Arena.

Thom: Oh, fuck that. I'm sorry, but people are losing the plot here, thank you very much. That's not my idea of a good night out. At all.

Jonny: Hmmm. We'll see.

Thom: [Back to the previous question] Um, as I said, trying to sit still, which was something I tried to do over Christmas. Sit in front of the television for more than twenty minutes without just shouting at it and getting up and moving out again. And I find it very, very, very, very difficult indeed. Other than that, I play with my Macintosh. All day long. Very sadly.

ATN: **Games?**

Thom: No, I don't play games. I do sort of art work, but it's actually usually related to the band. I always find that I'll do this image and put Radiohead above [it] and I'll go, 'Fuck, I'm doing it again! Shit!' Yeah . . . so I think we all need to get hobbies.

Jonny: Macramé. It was very big in the '70s. It's like crochet, I believe. It's made of crochet material.

ATN: **Do you weave them?**

Jonny: I think so. I'll let you know next time I see you. I'll take it up.

ATN: **Are you going to make me a pot-holder?**

Jonny: I'll make you a tea cosy.

Thom: How about shoelaces? And decorate my house.

ATN: **In pot-holders and tea cosies.**

Jonny: Do you want to get married?

ATN: **Excuse me?**

Thom: [waving his hand in front of Jonny's face] No, that was my gag!

Jonny: Because I can legally marry you now.

ATN: **What?**

Thom: Well, I could actually . . . [trying to cut in]

Jonny: [cutting Thom off] No, we're reverends . . .

Thom: [cutting Jonny off] Oh, yeah, we're reverends . . . we're all reverends.

Jonny: We started our own church.

Thom: The Holy Church of Waste.

Jonny: Well, we can legally marry people and bury people in thirteen American states, including California.

Thom: So if anybody needs, you know, to get married, we can do it for them now. [To Jonny] How much did it cost us? Twenty dollars?

Jonny: Ten dollars or something. So we are going to conduct a mass community-style wedding at our LA show, that's tomorrow.

Thom: Waste packaging is going to be the next thing.

ATN: **Your fan club and newsletter are called W.A.S.T.E. . . . what's the obsession with waste?**

Thom: Waste? Well, um, just waste, really. You know,

everything about it. Waste, waste, you know . . . it really fucking does my head in, man! It does, honestly. I sound like a real idiot, but it's true. Think about it, when you go to the supermarket and you come home and you have your vegetables and they're in cling-film . . . and what do you do with it? You put it in the bin, and where's it go?

ATN: **Recycle.**

Thom: Well, not in our country it doesn't.

ATN: **You guys don't have a recycling programme?**

Thom: They do not have anything like that in Britain. Britain is so backward, it's frightening.

Jonny: They put a little curly thing [on packaging] where they sort of have a little recycle sign, and you think 'great' then you look at it a little closer and it says 'recyclable'. Instead of 'recycle'.

ATN: **But there's nowhere to recycle?**

Thom/Jonny: Yeah.

Thom: I think the most important thing for anyone to do at the moment is that, really. That's why I'm becoming a politician, so I can find a way to get rid of my rubbish.

Jonny: I think if you drive far enough, you can get your paper recycled. That's about it, you know.

Thom: [But] you cannot recycle plastic in Oxford or London. So where the fuck does it go? And it's not like it even costs that much to do it! Anyway, that's far more important than Radiohead. That's why we formed a company called Waste.

ATN: **Can't you just bring your own bags and put produce in that?**

Thom: Can't do that in Britain. You can do this thing where there's this farm and you get a big hamper of food every weekend and they come deliver it, and that's your food for the week. And that's what we're going to be doing when we get back. But I mean, if you need to dash out and stuff, you come back with bananas in cling-film . . . and you put them in a bin, and it's like . . . and that's why we formed the Holy Church of Waste.

ATN: **To start the recycling programme going on in Britain?**

Thom: Yeah.

Jonny: And marry people.

Thom: And marry people.

Jonny: And bury people.

Thom: We can christen people . . .

Jonny: . . . into the Church of Waste. I mean, there's nothing derogatory about the idea. There are a lot of people in the public in England, like the Reverend Ian Paisley, who actually have no qualification . . .

Thom: Yeah. He woke up one morning and decided that he wanted to be a reverend.

Jonny: And people tend to use titles like that to get people to throw their money. It's quite easy to get master's degrees and doctorates . . .

ATN: **It is?**

Thom: Oh yeah. It's a piece of piss! I actually got one for being mad from Oxford!

ATN: **Oh, like the honorary ones?**

Jonny: No, no, actual ones. Where they send you booklets, and you have to answer . . .

ATN: **Oh, mail order ones.**

Jonny: Yeah, but they're all legal. You can get mail order anything. You can be a rabbi if you wanted to. It's very, very disrespectful.

Thom: Never leave your house. It'll all turn up in big packaging and bits of foam and cardboard, which you'll then put in the attic . . .

Jonny: [yells over to a roadie] Cline!! Clare, can Cline be in our photo shoot?

Thom: No! He doesn't go with any of our clothes . . .

[Jonny and Thom are both distracted for a minute]

Thom: Sorry, we're not behaving. I'm sorry about the KOME thing . . . I'm really sorry about the KOME . . .

ATN: **It's OK, don't worry about it. Any last thoughts?**

Jonny: Yes, lots. Why do Americans express the word 'say' with the word 'like'? Like, he's, like, let's do this and he's, like, let's do that . . .

ATN: **[Tries to explain] I don't know where it started . . . maybe with the whole Valley Girl thing in the '80s . . .**

Thom: Valley Girl? Valley Girl? That's an interesting phrase.

ATN: **I can't get out of it either and English isn't even my first language . . .**

Jonny: What is your first language?

ATN: **Japanese.**

Jonny: All right!

ATN: **But I've forgotten it all . . .**

Jonny: Nooo! I know pidgin Japanese . . . *Phil-san wa, doco desu ka.*

ATN: **You're better at speaking Japanese than I am.**

Jonny: Nooo! *Jonny no* Radiohead *desu*. Can you remember how to count? [Jonny and I count in Japanese together]

Thom: [waving disc player] All the new songs are on this. It's a mini-disc-Walkman-recording-thing.

ATN: **You can record onto a disk?**

Thom: Yeah. And you can name them as well, which is the cool bit. So when every track comes up, it's got a different name on it . . . Three hundred pounds it cost me, but it's amazing. You can make records on that. It's like a DAT, you know . . . but it's easier to use. You can use it as a data input-and-output thing using the optical line in . . . so it can be like a hard disk if you want it. It's got, like, instant access to each track as well . . . just go [pushes the button] and it's there . . . it's not like rewinding a tape or anything . . . So, I'm giving it the hard sell.

ATN: **Well, that's all for now.**

Jonny: *Domo arigato.* (Thank you very much)

ATN: *Doitashimashite.* **(You're welcome)**

Jonny: *Hai. Dewa mata.* (See you again)

Four: Neurotics Anonymous

1

Party On!

Tom Doyle, Q,
June 1997

Brightly early most weekday mornings before 9 a.m., when other rock stars still have at least a good six hours of kip ahead of them – or have yet in fact to go to bed following another night of drunken or chemically-induced shenanigans – Radiohead's curiously angular guitarist Jonny Greenwood can usually be found in the middle of a field in the quiet Oxfordshire countryside, flying his kite.

If the widescreen possibilities of this undeniably evocative scene have a touch of Pink Floyd-like imagery about it, then that perhaps is no coincidence, since the soundtrack on the rake-thin twenty-five-year-old man's personal stereo is *Meddle*, an album released in 1971, the year he was born. This evidence alone may not be enough to suggest that Radiohead are slowly, surely mutating into the New Pink Floyd. But then there are other factors which have to be taken into consideration. Not least the fact that singer Thom Yorke warmly recalls recording parts of their self-produced third album, *OK Computer*, at their recently acquired studio farmhouse while, outside the window, herds of Jersey cattle lumbered lazily through sunny fields. In the background, an industrial chimney belched acrid smoke into the sky. 'It was the Floyd,' he enthuses before – perhaps typically – feigning vomiting in self-disgust at having been forced to draw this seemingly unthinkable parallel himself.

Bassist Colin Greenwood has his own thoughts about his brother's kite-flying plot to turn Radiohead into a progressive rock ensemble. 'Jonny made us all watch *Pink Floyd Live in Pompeii* and said, "Now this is how we should do videos",' he offers, grinning, his already frighteningly voluminous eyes widening in mock disbelief. 'I just remember seeing Dave Gilmour sitting on his arse playing guitar, and Roger Waters – with long greasy hair, sandals and dusty flares – staggers over and picks up this big beater and whacks this gong. Ridiculous.'

Nevertheless, there is no getting away from it: Radiohead's keenly-awaited third album is a sprawling, hugely experimental affair that cannot be described without using the words 'out' and 'there'. The return single, 'Paranoid Android', by way of indication, is a six-and-a-half-minute epic in three movements. Jonny Greenwood admits that, during the making of the record, he had found himself becoming involved in a brave but perhaps futile pursuit: trying to unearth half-decent prog rock albums.

'It's been very disappointing because most of it is *awful*,' he softly admits in his engagingly posh way. 'I've got it into my head that prog rock albums must be good because they attracted a lot of fans. So far, I've just trawled through fairly tedious Genesis albums.'

Aside from all of this, there has also been the suggestion that Radiohead have been gradually morphing into R.E.M. since the Oxford quintet's extended supporting sojourn on the Monster tour in the summer of 1995. Certainly Thom Yorke's friendship with Michael Stipe – who made the onstage pronouncement that 'Radiohead are so good, they scare me' – has been well-documented. In fact, Yorke and Jonny Greenwood have just returned to Oxford from London, where they were collaborating with Stipe on tracks for *Velvet Goldmine,* the glam-rock-scrutinising film that Stipe is currently producing. Notably, on *OK Computer,* there is evidence that Yorke's approach to lyric-writing has taken on a distinctly more oblique, Stipe-like bent.

Whatever comparisons are being made, it's clear that Radiohead have gone through something of a transitional period. It seems reasonable to declare that toying around with groundbreaking studio techniques and constructing wildly ambitious musical atmospheres now figure heavily in their collective imaginations. Queen for the '90s, anyone?

'I've been building up my chest just now so that it looks good in a white vest,' warns the small and slight-framed Yorke, with his characteristic level of sarcasm. 'Christ, you should've seen the 'tache I had last week.'

———

After coming down from such a high as Radiohead experienced when R.E.M. took them under their wing and nursed them through the crucial period when they learned how to get their music across to stadium-proportioned crowds (Yorke claims that his most deep-rooted nightmare is to become Jim Kerr at his worthiest), the band were given carte blanche to record and self-produce their next album. As a consequence, *OK Computer* unarguably finds them breaking into new territory, from the looped-up, all-fronts assault of 'Airbag' through the searingly anthemic 'Electioneering' to the soothingly effective 'Exit Music (For a Film)', ostensibly 'She's Leaving Home' retold with a panicky edge.

Preliminary sessions began – in a stroke of magnificent indulgence, at actress Jane Seymour's mansion near Bath – in the spring of last year, the very same place where the Cure initially developed the commercially disastrous *Wild Mood Swings*. The previous summer, Johnny Cash had rented the house before an appearance at Glastonbury. The flowing-locked English rose could be reassured that Radiohead were rather less of a rock'n'roll proposition. Although they did rearrange the furniture.

'We recorded in her library,' Jonny Greenwood explains. 'It was wonderful going somewhere that wasn't designed for recording. Recording studios now tend to be quite scientific and clinical. You can't really impose yourself without getting over the fact that there are fag burns in the carpet and gold discs all around. It's good to go and decide that we'll turn this beautifully furnished sitting-room into whatever.'

While they are a five-strong band of self-confessed 'neurotics anonymous', the fact that Radiohead are so keen to guard the rural location of their studio farm headquarters, where the album was completed, is indicative of their growing status as the archetypal art-school-grounded English rock band afforded the Imperial-Leather-like luxury of creative freedom. This, it would seem, is a direct result of the fact that, throughout their five-year existence – while everyone's heads were turned in the directions of (initially) Blur, then Suede and now Oasis – Radiohead have quietly grown into a formidably successful act. Their second album, *The Bends*, has now achieved platinum status in Britain, a trend more or less followed in most record-buying nations.

When, at the beginning of 1996, Parlophone Records released 'Street Spirit (Fade Out)', the fourth, campaign-closing single from *The Bends*, its hypnotically languid tone rendered it too dark and sombre to be playlisted on Radio 1. It still debuted with a one-fingered salute at No. 5. On the release of War Child's *Help* album the previous September, Radiohead's magnificently moody contribution, 'Lucky' (oddly included on *OK Computer*), proved to be the stand-out – although the band had been forced to complete the track in an intensive five-hour period to meet the required deadline, after a day spent posing for a War Child camera crew dispatched to film them *pretending* to record. 'They were waiting for us to record the song and we were waiting for them to go,' smiles the unnaturally lofty Ed O'Brien, credited on the group's sleeves for supplying 'polite guitar', as opposed to Jonny Greenwood's 'abusive guitar'. Of the video footage depicting casualties of the Bosnian conflict that was subsequently set to the track, Yorke – never one to understate his emotional reactions – simply says, 'It had me in tears.'

Today the five members of Radiohead, fresh from tramping through the fields of rape for their *Q* photo session, mill around the management offices close to their recording studio, seemingly a relaxed and quietly polite bunch who enjoy a laugh of wry and knowing variety. O'Brien, lightly stoned this afternoon, since this is effectively a day off for the band – although pockets of them will frequently disappear into the adjoining recording room to continue work on B-sides – is charming and affable and has earned a reputation as the band member renowned for his on-stage acts of over-exuberance. The band gleefully recall the guitarist once disappearing over the lip of the stage at a theatre gig in North Carolina, tumbling into the orchestra pit and then struggling for ages to clamber back out.

Groomed drummer and, impressively, ex-Samaritan Phil Selway proves suitably genial for someone who has had a Japanese fan club – Phil Is Great – set up in his honour. Another of the Phil Is Great club's meetings is planned for the following week, when Radiohead make a promotional trip to the Pacific Rim.

The Greenwood brothers, who share no distinctive physical resemblance, are polar opposites. Jonny rarely touches alcohol; Colin can regularly be located in a pub after frenzied searches five minutes before the band are due on stage. Jonny is silent unless coaxed; Colin is effusive when engaged in the topics of books, records and other bands. Jonny was likely described as 'a dreamer' by his teachers, his head seemingly operating at some cloud-high altitude; Colin is sharp and wary and likely the cornerstone of Radiohead. When together, both share an inscrutable look if questioned on any subject. Colin admits to feeling guilty of acting a touch cruelly to his colour-blind younger brother when they were growing up: he would mix up the crayons, which the guitarist claims 'retarded me'.

'We share the same gene pool,' states the elder, directing another meaningful look towards his sibling.

'But I got the shallow end,' adds his toothily blessed younger brother, without any detectable hesitation.

Meanwhile, the boyishly-proportioned Thom Yorke pads around barefoot in blue canvas jeans, Radiohead fan club T-shirt and Gaultier shades, his short, spiky hair dyed black after extended periods as peroxide blond and retina-damaging orange. Quietly intense, he is a man possessed of a bitingly sharp sense of humour, although an air of brow-beaten cynicism can be detected in his every utterance. The others simply describe Yorke as 'a bit of a worrier', but it would seem that his enduring reputation as a troubled and overly angsty individual is reasonably well-deserved, despite his claims to having recently 'learned to relax a little'. He talks with his head bowed and eyes closed, covering his face with his hands and peering through his fingers, sometimes curling his limbs up into a tight ball, as if he is under physical attack. The prospect of Radiohead performing this summer to forty thousand people in Ireland as well as headlining a major festival (interestingly, on the same weekend as the strategically unannounced Glastonbury bill) seems to fill him with dread.

'I can't see why we're doing these big gigs,' he shrugs. 'Thing is, whoever it is up there, it's not the person sitting here. It's a completely different state of mind that you have to spend a long time getting into. I can't switch it on and off. When even the logistics of these big gigs are discussed, I just fucking freeze up. It's not something I'm emotionally capable of dealing with yet. Hopefully I'll get back into a different frame of mind where it won't worry me.'

While there is a certain fragile quality to Yorke, the two sides to Radiohead's chief songwriter are exemplified in those moments when his distinctive singing voice swoops down from a choirboy falsetto to a low, anguished snarl. Similarly, in conversation he can suddenly cop an attitude, turning shirty and argumentative. O'Brien remembers his first impression of the young Yorke when the two were involved in a play – the former acting, the latter providing musical accompaniment – at the Oxford school where Radiohead first met as teenagers.

'There was this tense dress rehearsal,' O'Brien remembers, 'and Thom and this other fella were jamming freeform cod-jazz throughout it. The director stopped the play and shouted up to this scaffold tower thing they were playing on, trying to find out what the hell was going on. Thom shouted down, "I don't know what the fuck we're supposed to be playing." And this was to a teacher.'

———

Born with one eye closed on 7 October 1968, the infant Thom Yorke had already endured five major operations on his paralysed eyelid by the time he was six. Made to wear an eye-patch during his early school years, he was cruelly mocked by his schoolmates. He half-bitterly brushes off suggestions that this may have caused him to have a slight chip on his shoulder.

'Oh no,' he states, sharply. 'I was sweet and lovely and nothing ever happened to me. [Cagily] When I was younger I was in the music room most of the time, anyway. It was great. No one came down there and there were these tiny rooms with sound-proofed cubicles. I suppose I'm quite an aggressive person. I was a fighter at school, but I never won. I was into the idea of fighting [laughs hysterically]. I've had to calm down a bit, otherwise I'd go nuts.' Yorke recalls the moment in his younger life when he realised that he was not perhaps quite as handy with his fists as he'd imagined. 'In first year at college, I went through this phase where I was into this granddad hat and coat I had,' he quietly explains. 'They were immaculate and I was into dressing like an old man. But I went out one night and there were these blokes, townie guys, waiting to beat someone up and they found me. They said something, I turned around, blew them a kiss and that was it. They beat the living shit out of me. One was kicking me, one had a stick and the other was smashing me in the face. That put me off fighting a bit.'

Back in mid-'80s Oxford, where Radiohead first bonded and began rehearsing, essentially as the school band, they called themselves On A Friday. Selway was in the sixth form, O'Brien in the fifth year, Yorke and Colin Greenwood in the fourth and Jonny Greenwood – the last to join – in the third. 'We're still in our same classes and years, really,' the elder Greenwood grimly decides. 'The thing about having been together for such a long period is that there are some heinously embarrassing group shots from ten years ago when we were in adolescence with varying styles of haircut and demeanour which would now be openly laughed at in the street.'

During this era, of course, the quiff was king ('You'd literally take a photograph of Morrissey to the barber and say, "I want it like that"') and if On A Friday resembled the Smiths visually, they had yet to find a foothold musically. The four others remember tapes of Thom Yorke's early compositions as being 'schizophrenic'. 'One track, "Rattlesnake", just had a drum loop that Thom did himself at home on a tape recorder with bad scratching over the top and kind of Prince vocals,' Jonny Greenwood remembers. '"The Chains" had viola and was meant to sound like the Waterboys. "What is That You See" was a feedback frenzy. After hearing it, I knew Thom was writing great songs and I knew what I wanted to do.' Nevertheless, the younger Greenwood's ambitions were thwarted by the group's reluctance to let him join. Described to them as 'a precocious talent' who would whip through an assortment of instruments in an attempt to impress his potential bandmates, Jonny sat onstage, in Phil Selway's words, 'with a harmonica, waiting for his big moment' at On A Friday's first gig at Oxford's Jericho Tavern in 1987.

As each member wandered off to college or university, rehearsals would take place only during their lengthy summer breaks as students. But On A Friday were improving by leagues and, by the summer of 1991, when their first real demo went into circulation (released as the *Drill* EP in 1992), there were suddenly legions of A&R men cramming into the Jericho Tavern. Within weeks, On A Friday signed to Parlophone and, out of 'sheer embarrassment', changed their name to Radiohead.

———

As imageless as a police identity parade and embodying such extremes of stature and build that Ed O'Brien probably towers a whole foot above Thom Yorke, Radiohead initially found it difficult to attract attention during the lifespan of their debut album *Pablo Honey* when other, more fashion-conscious outfits were hogging the limelight. On its initial release in the UK, the second, self-hating single, the possibly classic 'Creep', stiffed. As with the Fixx before them and Bush afterwards, Radiohead suffered the indignity of being rejected by their motherland and embraced by America when 'Creep' became a slacker anthem after an extended period of over-exposure on college radio. By the time Radiohead arrived in America for their first tour, 'Creep' was already in the *Billboard* Top 40 and for the summer of 1993 its mutant guitar crunch and soaring melody spilled out from car radios and apartment windows all over America. Its follow-up, the bracing 'Stop Whispering', failed to maintain the momentum and the band found themselves performing to capacity audiences interested in hearing one song. For a time, Yorke re-christened the song 'Crap'.

'At that time the whole so-called alternative rock thing happened there,' remembers Yorke, 'populated by sad programmers from the '80s who didn't have a clue what they were putting on and "Creep" suffered from that. It was a good song, but afterwards it was, "Well, let's have more like that please because the pro-grammers understand it," and it's like "No, sorry.""

'We didn't know what was normal in America,' Jonny Green-wood muses. 'We went over there and we'd turn on MTV and "Creep" would be on again. We thought, Oh, that's good.'

'People were being very nice to us over there because "Creep" was doing so well,' adds Selway. '"Stop Whispering" didn't do quite so well, so that opened us up to the more cynical side of it.'

'We were hysterical,' decides O'Brien. 'One moment we'd be giggling, the next we'd be really down. Our reactions were extreme.' Regretfully, it was around this time that Radiohead, under pressure to visually reinvent themselves, became the tightly-trousered, big-haired rock band they felt America expected of them. Jonny Greenwood and Yorke even accepted modelling assignments for American fashion magazines, the latter sporting a hellish tangle of hair extensions atop his cranium.

'I *was* rock,' winces the frontman with an embarrassed laugh. 'There were so many elements to that period, but the hair was the worst. It was such a weird trip anyway, because suddenly we were seen as this big investment and there was money being thrown at us. It didn't last long enough to mess us up, but then I suppose, for a while, it probably did.'

The most positive knock-on effect of 'Creep"s US success was that on its re-release in the UK, it reached No. 7. On the negative side, Radiohead were in danger of looking like a one-trick pony. Immediately they set to work on *The Bends*, titled after the dramatic side-effects of emerging from the depths too rapidly. Cutting between *Zooropa*-fashioned loop collages ('Planet Telex'), folk rock ('Fake Plastic Trees') and hushed atmospherics ('Bulletproof'), the record managed to distract the listener for long enough to forget that 'Creep' existed. Of course, America couldn't get its head round it.

'There's this assumption, especially over here, that Radiohead are big in America,' O'Brien offers. 'Radiohead are not big in America. We had "Fake Plastic Trees" as a single and it was played on a radio station. They did a survey of their listeners – 18-to-25-year-old males who drive four-wheel-drive jeeps – and it came bottom of the list. The thing with Radiohead and America is that we had one pop hit there.'

'And they don't remember it anyway because they've got the attention span of insects,' Yorke mutters darkly. 'Our so-called success in America was that it allowed us to do lots of things, but it also meant that somehow we owed somebody something. But I couldn't work out who and I couldn't work out how much.'

––––––

Flying in the face of the drug-hoovering, groupie-rogering rock band image, Radiohead present themselves as Evian-sipping abstainers, content to play a hand of bridge on their tour bus, thank you very much. Nevertheless, the punishing eighteen-month touring schedule that followed was not without casualties.

There is an undercurrent of obsessiveness within the group, a matter most evident when they play live. Jonny Greenwood plays his guitar with such teeth-grindingly frantic force that he unknowingly lacerates his fingers. Recently, he has taken to strapping on an arm brace, which could be seen as a unique guitar-hero affectation. However, Greenwood insists he's been ordered to wear it since it was diagnosed that his playing style was causing repetitive strain injury. Similarly, he is keen to point out that the bulky headphones he sported throughout the latter half of the Bends tour are industrial ear shields he was advised to wear after suffering from a dangerously leaky lughole.

'My ear was ringing and bleeding for two weeks on the American tour,' he reveals, with strangely calm detachment. 'There was this terrifying gig in Cleveland, where I was nearly fainting. I was taken to hospital at three in the morning and the doctor said the situation was really grim. I'd love to do without both of them, but the arm brace I'm still going to need. It's conceited to deny there's any affectation but, having said that, I enjoy putting on the arm brace before I play. It's like taping up your fingers before a boxing match. It's a ritual.'

The most memorably grim incident of the tour, however, occurred in Munich, when Yorke blacked out and collapsed on stage. 'That had been building up,' he mumbles while wriggling uncomfortably in his seat, head in his hands. 'There'd been an incident in America where I'd really been as sick as fuck. This cold had got to my throat and whacked me out. It turned into laryngitis. The promoter takes you to the doctor, that's the normal standard thing, and the doctor says, "Oh, no, you're fine to play." You argue with them. They say, "No, take these drugs and you'll be fine." Then you realise the promoter is paying the doctor. It got bad again in Germany because we were sleeping on a cold damp tour bus in the middle of winter. This doctor turns up – usual thing, paid by the promoter – with this huge bag of drugs. All sorts of shit, man. He offered to inject me with steroids, which I refused. I didn't take anything because I thought I could get through it. We did the soundcheck, and I was like, "Oh shit, this is really bad." My voice was not there at all. By that point, it's too late, you can't cancel. I go on and third song in, I lost it. I remember hitting the floor and then I wasn't there.' He pauses and his face contorts into a perverse smile. 'It was great, actually.'

Most things about Thom Yorke's burgeoning rock-star status seem to trouble him deeply. The word he uses most frequently is 'doomed'. While he claims not to suffer from an acute fear of fame ('it's just that I have no respect for it'), he admits that his growing friendship with Michael Stipe has involved the R.E.M. singer offering guidance on how Yorke should deal with his concerns, although the Radiohead frontman is protective of their relationship. 'If you don't have any semblance of a normal life, then you won't be able to write,' he muses, 'and if you can't write, then you won't be there. He's helped me deal with most things I couldn't deal with. The rest is not anyone else's business and that's what's great about it. Anyway. Whatever. It sounds like I've been touched by an evangelist or something.'

Why still bother making music, then?

'Because I can be very drunk in a club in Oxford on a Monday night and some guy comes up to you and buys you a drink and says that the last record you made changed his life. That means something. It makes you chill about it.'

As a result of the anguished nature of your lyrics, are Radiohead fans obsessive individuals as a whole?

'They were. In the letters they can be, yeah. But when you meet people it's a different thing. People put pen to paper for different reasons, some of them quite weird. It was set up like that from the first record because of "Creep" and all the hyperbole around that, but actually we lost most of that debris when we brought out *The Bends*. Murderers have stopped writing to me to say how much they relate to "Creep", so that's cool. Now it's just people who're into what we're doing and there's respect on both sides.'

So your motivation is purely and simply the music you make and the reaction you'll get from it?

'[Sarcastically] I know it sounds awful, but, yes. [Changes mood] But y'know, that's probably lies as well . . .'

You do seem to eat yourself up about everything.

'I'm not eating myself up,' he continues defensively. 'It's just that if I read that last statement, I would think, "Wanker". Because whoever's said it isn't being honest.'

There was a certain point at which Nirvana had to pull back because they felt they were getting too big and they couldn't handle it. Can you see yourself doing the same if you get *really* famous?

'Yeah, I've got the pull-back button ready. You have to have. That hotline back to the President.'

How would you do that? Release a few seventeen-minute singles?

'No . . . no, there's other ways to do it. There's other shadows you can find. You can still be there. That was the thing I've had to learn recently. But it still gets to me.'

Do you ever fear for the ill-effects of increased success on your mental health?

'Oh, yes,' he exclaims, his mood strangely and suddenly lifting. 'Thank you, yes.'

Later that afternoon, as the light begins to fail, Thom Yorke appears to have returned to a more balanced state and almost rhetorically enquires, 'I don't think that this has been about moaning, do you?' Pulling an 'urgh' face when his band mates invite him down to the beer garden of a local pub for some light tea-time refreshment, he wanders off instead in the direction of the studio to continue work on the B-sides for 'Paranoid Android'.

As the others wend their way through the winding country lanes on the way to the hostelry, the talk turns to the fact that their frontman seems to be bearing so much intolerable weight on his shoulders.

'It's weird to see the public representation of Thom,' ventures Jonny Greenwood after a time, 'because it's quite different. I find Thom to be very affectionate and child-like.'

'Yeah,' his brother adds, 'but we don't draw the curtains of our bedrooms at night when we're going to sleep and see all these people staring up at the window. We don't have to deal with that. It's different graduations of stress, I suppose. What's important to him is that if he can have two different personas it's a way of protecting himself.'

'Well, I shared a room with him for four years,' Selway laughs, before tellingly adding, 'and that's not the man in the interviews.'

Deeply weird bunch, Radiohead. Insular, posh, irrationally paranoid, yet capable of creating achingly beautiful songs resplendent with mind-warping sonic tricks. They might just have the potential to re-chisel the granite face of rock music if their new-found prog-rock edge doesn't devour them or they don't disintegrate in the process. God help them if they ever get into proper drugs.

'Us on hard drugs? That would be horrible,' Thom Yorke had stated earlier, in a lighter mood. 'We'd probably end up sounding like Bryan Adams.'

2

Review of *OK Computer*

Nick Kent, *MOJO*,

July 1997

———

Because it's so damnably hard to pigeonhole effectively, you'll probably be seeing the new Radiohead album described in all manner of half-hearted ways over the next few weeks.

Some will glance at titles like 'Paranoid Android', hear what sounds a bit like a Mellotron (but probably isn't) swelling up on two or three tracks, note the strange song structures throughout and lazily conclude that the Oxford quintet have decided to come over all prog rock, like some late '90s manifestation of early King Crimson. Others will hear the spacey mix and all those freaky guitars buzzing around and immediately think, This must be their 'psychedelic' record. But I can only imagine someone listening to it on hallucinogenic drugs having a pretty grim time. It's not punk rock, lad rock, Britpop or grunge, either, and you can forget about 'easy listening' right now. There's little that's 'easy' about this record, little sugar-coating on the pill this time, no temporary oasis of perfect pop escapism and calm to bury yourself in while you try to come to terms with the trickier stuff.

Thom Yorke may be big mates with the lofty likes of Michael Stipe these days and he may accept the odd prestigious music-industry award standing alongside Brian Eno but, on this record, fame and success haven't removed the considerable chip still weighing on his shoulders.

From the very outset of their career, Yorke and Radiohead have always taken a pride in their perceived status as rock's rank outsiders. They've never belonged within any cosy community-minded groups, while their best-known song – 'Creep' – is as close to a definitive anthem for outsiders as has been written in the last twenty years. Now they've been allowed to produce themselves – and it can't be over-emphasised: the fact is, they've done a great job – Yorke and co. have finally created their own little sonic galaxy, part enchanted planet, part outsiders' club, with Yorke the ultimate anti-glamour rock star, sneering and seething – often with tongue not altogether out of cheek – while his co-workers content themselves by performing some of the most ingeniously arranged guitar-bass-drums-with-a-bit-of-synth-based music ever made.

'Airbag' has a stately but slightly tortured 'lost-in-space' feel, a bit like early Pink Floyd but more melancholy. The mix is alive with flanged guitars weaving among each other like snakes; '*I am born again*,' sings Yorke, but the abjectly mournful tone his voice elicits would lead one to feel this could be a curse and not a blessing. Next up, 'Paranoid Android' is the frankly audacious choice for first single, so you've doubtless already been confronted with its deeply eccentric, plaintive-acoustic-ditty to paranoid-screaming-electric-noise-and-back navigations, topped off with a sequence that sounds not unlike a bunch of pissed monks chanting in an abbey somewhere in the depths of Czechoslovakia.

'Subterranean Homesick Alien' counters 'Android's giddy changes by being a slow, beautifully languid piece led by a jazzy electric piano that features one of Yorke's most beguiling vocals to date, as he sends out a touching message of comfort and sympathy to alien life-forms trapped discontentedly on this planet. It helps to know that 'Exit Music' was written for the close of Hollywood's recent grunge re-styling of *Romeo and Juliet*. Lyrically, *all hell* is about to break loose, the song's heroine is having trouble with her breathing and yet the music moves at such an eerily calm pace it feels as if everyone – singer and musicians – are on the verge of losing consciousness.

'Let Down' is the album's one potential anthem-rocker, full of luscious chiming guitars and a haunting melody that could easily charm its way into the higher regions of the international singles chart. Then things swiftly turn weird and ugly again with the arrival of the vindictive 'Karma Police'. '*That's what you get/When you mess with us*,' Yorke snarls/sings by way of a chorus, but the slightly turgid rhythm makes you wonder whether he's being malicious or just ironic. Echoes of *White Album* John Lennon are well evident here, specifically the somnambulist lurch of 'I'm So Tired' and certain of the chord changes of 'Sexy Sadie'.

'Electioneering' is the full-tilt anarchic rock bash-up and sounds a bit like a splendidly warped deconstruction of dear old Alice Cooper's 'School's Out'. On the edgy 'Climbing Up the Walls', Yorke takes a detour onto Tricky's turf with a claustrophobic trip-hop vibe and distorted vocals before bringing in the rest of the group to return the sonic thrust closer to the guitar-based heart of Radioheadland. 'No Surprises' is the other potential hit here: an enchanting guitar ballad – somewhat in the vein of the

Velvets' 'Sunday Morning' – this could ultimately turn out to be Radiohead's very own 'Losing My Religion'. 'Lucky' you probably heard on the *H.E.L.P.* benefit album a couple of years ago. As haunting as ever, it fits in here perfectly as an extended melancholy farewell alongside 'The Tourist', the remarkable last track. Deep, slow, deeply soulful – just beautiful.

What does it all add up to? Certainly a record to which the adjectives 'dour' and 'dense' seem particularly appropriate when hearing it the first few times. Because there's so much going on here it can get a bit hairy at the beginning. It opens up quickly enough, though, and once you've been hooked, it never stops growing on you. Better than *The Bends?* Probably. Record of the year? Conceivably. Others may end up selling more, but in twenty years' time I'm betting *OK Computer* will be seen as the key record of 1997, the one to take rock forward instead of artfully revamping images and song-structures from an earlier era.

3

Radioheadline

Adam Sweeting, *Esquire*,
September 1997

A couple of hours earlier, Radiohead's Thom Yorke had looked like a bedraggled refugee who'd hitchhiked all the way to California from Sarajevo, slouching about in floppy striped trousers and a black leather jacket so worn out it was beginning to disintegrate. Even with four-inch-thick soles on his scruffy trainers, he seemed shrunken and stunted. You'd never imagine he was a rock star. You'd be more inclined to buy him a bowl of soup.

Yet now, here he was on stage at the Troubadour on Santa Monica Boulevard, looking like he was about to murder somebody by sheer willpower. Radiohead were in the midst of playing 'Talk Show Host'. As they stoked the song to a climax, Yorke became Robovocalist, strutting across the stage like a starship trooper ruthlessly subjugating some unsuspecting new planet, thrashing manically at his guitar. As the tension seethed upwards and began to verge on the unbearable, with Yorke and guitarist Ed O'Brien combining in a cyclone of whiplashed chords and ear-popping reverb, Yorke's eyes narrowed to a squint and his lower lip began to jut out obscenely.

He advanced to the edge of the stage, and his gaze fixed on a hapless onlooker in the front row. For what felt like hours, with the band raging around him, he glared pitilessly down at his target with an expression of concentrated hatred. It seemed that, at any moment, steam would come out of his victim's ears, his eyeballs would melt and his head must surely explode. Then suddenly the song was over. Yorke spun contemptuously on his heel, and the spell was broken. I made a mental note never to stand in the front row at a Radiohead show.

Yorke is the grand enigma of Radiohead, the central mystery of a band that a few sceptics still claim are merely English pomp-rock revisited, perhaps because their background recalls the arty educatedness of veteran progressive groups such as Genesis and Pink Floyd. It's as if they were created to be the polar opposite of the professional yobbishness of Oasis's Gallagher brothers. The quintet are articulate and cerebral and all live in Oxford, determined to steer clear of the backstabbing ferment of London. Where Oasis play primitive meat-and-potatoes rock with stubble and underarm hair, Radiohead's new album – their third, OK Computer – is fifty-three minutes of complex, allusive music, often unbearably emotional and as intricate as classical music or jazz. The band's growing confidence in their own abilities and judgement was written all over the disc's first single, 'Paranoid Android'. As if to cock a snook at frothy trivia such as the Spice Girls or Hanson, it was a six-minute micro-symphony in four movements, complete with a 'destabilising' passage in 7/8 time.

'There was this popular conception that we were all set up to do the big third crossover album,' reflects lead guitarist Jonny Greenwood. 'I think people who know *The Bends* [their second] will like it, but I'm not sure it's going to cross over into middle-American kids.'

'I don't think it's quite as people imagined it would be,' adds Yorke, with a twisted smile. 'A lot of people have experienced a nasty shock.'

It's possible that, without Yorke, Radiohead would be too technical for their own good. With him, they've grown into a formidable combination of expertise and musical ambition, given focus by Yorke's eerily affecting voice and the howls of rage, anguish and disgust that teem through his lyrics. 'At the end of the day, the vocal is the most important thing,' says O'Brien. 'It's more important than any guitar textures or rhythms or anything. The vocal is the thing that pulls you into the song.'

At the soundcheck before the Troubadour show, Yorke put the group briskly through their paces, trying out most of the songs they would play during the set later on. There was an absolute minimum of time wasting, though during pauses to fiddle about with drum mics or O'Brien's amplifier, Jonny Greenwood squatted down on stage to speed-read the last few pages of a Paul Theroux book.

'Let's do "The Bends",' said Yorke sharply, so they did. He cut them off after a couple of choruses. 'Let's do "Planet Telex".' Thirty seconds in, Yorke waved his arms impatiently to signal a halt. He had a problem with his guitar. The others didn't notice and kept playing, so Yorke scrubbed grumpily at his Telecaster to shut them up. Everybody jumped smartly to attention.

But Radiohead are intelligent and adult enough to accommodate everybody's personality foibles, small or large. The quintet have known each other, and played music together, since they all attended Abingdon boys' school. All of them read music to some extent and four of them have degrees. Jonny Greenwood is the exception, although you'd hardly call him the thick one. With his long, gangling frame, thick flop of black hair and dramatically angular bone structure, Jonny could have stepped out from an early Pink Floyd album sleeve, especially when he wears bell-bottom jeans and skinny T-shirts. Being the youngest, Jonny had to quit his psychology and music course to stick with his graduate fellow-musicians as they sought to turn the band into a serious professional enterprise.

Bassist Colin Greenwood, Jonny's smaller but less shy elder brother, has an English degree from Peterhouse College, Cambridge, and is usually reluctantly cited as Radiohead's leading intellectual. Top of his hit-list are modern American poetry and English Renaissance literature. If he wasn't in a band, he murmurs, he wouldn't have minded having a go at writing. Between them, the Greenwood brothers bring an aura of dreaming-spired bohemianism to Radiohead. It's the sort of thing that makes some music critics spiteful about the band's intellectual middle-classness. Radiohead try not to take any notice.

'We've never hidden it,' shrugs O'Brien, rolling himself some Golden Virginia while slouched beside the swimming pool at the pseudo-Camelot of Hollywood's Chateau Marmont hotel. An inflatable shark and a baby dinosaur bob in the blue water, perhaps subliminal reminders of the prevailing Los Angeles business ethos and the monstrous success of Steven Spielberg's *The Lost World: Jurassic Park*, at that moment devouring the nation's box offices. O'Brien is as personable and gregarious as you could wish, and makes such a marked contrast to the furtive, twitchy Yorke that they could be a comedy writer's idea of the perfectly mismatched couple.

'I was amazed to hear that Joe Strummer went to public school,' O'Brien reflects languidly. 'Well, we're not very good actors. We haven't paid our dues. We went to college and stuff like that and that's all part of the make-up of the band. It's very important for us. We carried the band on during college, but we were able to go off and do different things. Thankfully, we didn't get a recording contract when we were eighteen [although they did have a demo tape rejected by Island Records] and the fact that we signed when we were twenty-two or twenty-three meant we didn't need to seek out the rock'n'roll lifestyle. Our student days were fairly wild and we got it out of our system to a certain extent.'

Yorke's view is angrier and more melodramatic. 'The middle-class thing has never been relevant. We live in Oxford and in Oxford we're fucking lower-class. The place is full of the most obnoxious, self-indulgent, self-righteous oiks on the fucking planet, and for us to be called middle-class . . . Well, no, actually. Be around on May Day when they all reel out of the pubs at five in the morning puking up in the streets and going "Haw haw haw" and trying to hassle your girlfriend. It's all relative.' And that's not all. 'The thing that winds me up about the middle-class question is the presumption that a middle-class upbringing is a balanced environment when, in fact, domestic situations are not relevant to class,' he hisses. 'A bad domestic situation is a bad domestic situation. It's just such a fucking warped perspective on things.'

Calm is restored by drummer Phil Selway, the oldest member at thirty. He briefly held down a 'real' job as a desk editor with a medical publishing firm in Oxford. O'Brien remembers how the others recruited Selway when they were still at school and he'd already left, lending the sticksman an aura of experienced adulthood. A summit meeting was arranged in a local pub and they all pussyfooted gingerly round the subject of his recruitment so nobody should lose face. It's rare, I suggest to Selway, for a band to have stuck together as long as Radiohead without a single personnel change. Not even a Spinal Tap-style exploding drummer.

'It's odd in some ways, because on some levels you feel you're still stuck at that stage of your life and you've never actually left school,' says Selway drily. 'I think the original feeling about the band and the loyalty to each other and the friendships are still very much intact. You have to allow each other a lot of scope for development, especially when you're working so closely together, and I think we've managed that.' Selway is aghast that the press has discovered he used to be a Samaritan. 'God knows how this ever got out in the first place,' he winces. 'It's hideously embarrassing, because it's supposed to be confidential and you're supposed to remain anonymous. I'm sure any other Samaritans who read that are thinking: "jumped-up little tosser, putting himself across as some kind of saint".'

On the other hand, it could be very useful to have a practised sympathetic ear inside the pressure-cooker of a hard-working rock band. The stresses of touring have driven apparently well-balanced musicians round the twist, let alone a character as volatile as Thom Yorke. Some of his morbid, isolated lyrics on their last album *The Bends*, as well as the band's self-hating 1993 hit 'Creep', have drawn assorted freaks, emotional cripples and even convicted murderers to the band. R.E.M.'s Michael Stipe, a Radiohead admirer who is accustomed to having meanings he never intended foisted on his own lyrics, suggested that Yorke could do himself a favour by masking the bleeding edge of his emotions. *OK Computer* thus finds our small but feisty hero making a conscious effort to look outside himself.

For all its bleak, psycho-medical imagery, Yorke reckons *The Bends* did him a power of good. 'I realised afterwards there were a lot of things that had been sorted out in my head. I've always used music to sort myself out, because that's what it's there for. At the end of *The Bends*, I felt charged by external things and I wasn't internalising everything. Everything became much less of a personal trauma, which is why it was a bit of a strain to read that that is still the way people see us.'

But transforming the public perception of Radiohead will take time, particularly when *OK Computer*, for all its subtleties and melodic grace, is frequently as jocular as a midnight coach ride through Transylvania. While to some extent the band only have themselves to blame for starting the 'miserablism' bandwagon rolling, episodes such as the notorious *Melody Maker* article which lined up Yorke as the man most likely to follow Kurt Cobain into DIY oblivion still rankle. 'It was awful for the rest of us, seeing a friend go through that,' says O'Brien. 'I wanted to go down to the *Melody Maker* offices and say, "Do you know what you're doing? The impact your writing has on someone's character?" It's really irresponsible.'

The extent to which listeners' responses can be brainlessly pre-programmed is astonishing. One American journalist automatically assumed that 'Exit Music (For A Film)', despite its painstakingly literal title, must be about suicide. In fact, it was written to play over the end credits of Baz Luhrmann's movie of *William Shakespeare's Romeo + Juliet*.

'I think it's got to the stage of, fuck it, you can't be responsible for people being screwed up and unstable,' reckons O'Brien. 'When you have people writing in from Death Row, it's quite a heavy burden on young shoulders, to put it mildly. Patti Smith said something about a song capturing a time, and that's it, you can't be responsible six months later if people take it differently. I think people have seen over the last year that Thom is not the tortured artist, and he's really enjoying being able to look outside himself.'

'I've always seen our songs as being quite positive, really,' Selway argues. 'They confront very painful topics but at some time there's always a sense that there's a struggle with them and an attempt to overcome them, so I don't think there's anything in there that would intentionally incite people to do anything. You can't censor yourself overly, can you? You would just get a very half-baked second-guessing album. I think we are quite direct, both musically and lyrically, and long may that continue.'

Radiohead have a perverse streak which makes them kick against expectations, and they're deeply suspicious of doing the obvious. *The Bends*, from 1995, was a majestically brooding piece of work whose gleaming production and string of powerfully melodic songs made it feel suspiciously like a mainstream American rock album. The new disc, by contrast, is exactly what your average FM radio programmer would not have ordered. You have to figure that Thom Yorke is the ringmaster, the *éminence grise*. The group seem to need Yorke's edginess and unpredictability to keep goading them forwards. One moment he'll be sunny, charming and glad to talk. Then he'll be withdrawn and tetchy and will growl at you if you ask him a question. It's as if he lacks a protective layer between his emotions and the outside world. He's like a sheet of emotional blotting paper. If he feels angry, he'll bleed hot, red anger. If he feels frustrated, his pinched face and clenched body-language scream 'frustration'.

'It all comes from Thom, really, and they all sort of gather round and support him,' according to John Leckie, who produced *The Bends*. (The band didn't use him on *OK Computer* because they say they no longer needed a 'father figure' in the studio.) 'It's a good chemistry because Jonny's pretty wild, you never really know what he's going to do. When they're in the studio, they jump around the same way they do on stage and knock things over, and Thom rolls on the floor just doing a guide track. It's pretty exciting.'

Anything else? 'They're drug-free, as you probably know. The occasional little puff or something with me . . . it's not so much that it's frowned upon, it's just something they don't connect with. And they do the *Guardian* crossword every day. That's the most important thing, I'd say. Things like that, which set them apart from the usual lads' kind of thing.' Leckie also recalls that debates about such topics as which song should be the next single would go on for weeks, with nobody able to take a final decision, but Yorke thinks the band have become more outspoken in their dealings with each other.

'I think we're much more used to shouting at each other now, which is good. There used to be a lot of serious in-fighting under the guise of reasonable discussion and now it's lots of shouting and eventually we'll decide, so that's kind of cool. It's sort of like a marriage, when you learn to shout at somebody and that it's a good thing. I could very easily walk in and say we're going to do this, this and this, but it won't work because it's going to sound flat. I think the most exciting thing is when everyone in the band feels they can try things out, but there's a point where you have to say, "No, we've got it." I think it's a case of recognising when you've got it; that's the difficult bit, because you can go on for ever otherwise.'

Their record company expects *OK Computer* to be a landslide victory and the band took their promotional duties so seriously that they even swallowed their pride and played for half an hour at the annual Weenie Roast event organised by radio station KROQ, at the Irvine Meadows open-air amphitheatre south of Los Angeles. The station wields such influence in the L.A. area that bands daren't refuse to participate, even though they don't get paid. This prompted the bizarre spectacle of Oasis and Blur on the same bill, alongside the Foo Fighters, the Wallflowers, the Cure and many more representatives of what the Americans call 'modern rock'.

I tagged myself on to the Radiohead convoy as they trundled down highway 405, aiming to arrive in plenty of time for their mid-afternoon slot. Despite rumours that Radiohead are 'big in America', their lowly position on the Weenie Roast bill was proof that they aren't yet. Once through the aggressive security cordon, we found ourselves in a glum backstage wilderness of Portaloos and tiny mobile dressing-rooms barely large enough for a medium-sized solo artist, let alone a quintet featuring two very tall guitarists. 'Welcome to hell,' said Colin Greenwood, gazing around him in saucer-eyed horror. With some difficulty, tour manager Tim Greaves had acquired canteen meal-tickets for the band, but the food was a digestion-challenging mix of polystyrene burgers and the kind of salad probably best suited to mopping up oil in your garage. Jonny Greenwood gazed down sceptically at his plate. Yorke, nursing a hangover, propped his head on his fist and glowered.

Television evidence would later prove that Radiohead were there, but their spirit wasn't. Yorke spent the afternoon in a state of sullen misery and spat and snarled at the audience even though they were trying to respond favourably. 'Are there any screaming little pigs in the audience?' he demanded, squinting malevolently at the half-full auditorium. Some girls shrieked back at him obligingly. 'This song's for you,' said Yorke, and they launched into 'Paranoid Android'. Colin wasn't needed on bass for a time and sauntered about beside his amplifier with his hands in his pockets, like a man waiting for a lift home. Then they played 'Exit Music', which seemed to go over rather well, but Yorke had convinced himself that he was at war with the crowd. 'You fucking loved that, didn't you?' he sneered, then cued Radiohead vengefully into 'The Bends'. Afterwards, the band admitted sheepishly that it hadn't been their finest hour. At least it was evidence that the group haven't succumbed to brain-dead crowd pleasing with all their performances running as predictably as a piece of computer software. You often hear that they're due to become 'the new U2', but it isn't something they seem to want. After all, it would mean making an album every four years and only playing in football stadiums.

In the end, when all the psychoanalysing and brainstorming and earnest debate is over, Radiohead still love to crank it up, rock out and hit the audience between the eyes. Maybe they should do it more often. Consider that legendary power chord that kicks off 'The Bends'.

'Oh, it's better every night live,' Yorke enthuses, suddenly animated and sitting up in his chair. 'It's always a let-down when you hear it on tape, because when you're standing in the room with all the amps on, you just remember why you want to play electric guitar. In America, I often walk on stage and go, "Hello, this is the chord of D" – BLAAAAAM! That's what it is, y'know? There's a song attached to it, but basically it's just BRRRAAAAANNNGGG!!!'

4

Band of the Year: Radiohead

Pat Blashill, *Spin*,
January 1998

he pupils of Thom Yorke's eyes zip from side to side like nervous insects. We're on the Eurostar train from Paris to London and Radiohead's singer is compulsively looking out the window at a pastoral French landscape. He doesn't see the sheep and the farms – he is keenly aware that those things out there will disappear very soon and then we will enter a tunnel and be deep, deep underneath the sea. This is significant for a man who once wrote an album called *The Bends*.

When we go under, I ask Yorke if he's claustrophobic.

'Yes,' he says matter-of-factly. 'Er, increasingly so, actually.'

A couple of days on the road have taught me that even when Thom Yorke isn't suffering from one of his various phobias, he's still more than a touch intense. He moves like a shattered little prince. He laughs a sudden, explosive, truncated laugh. His hair is short, black, and spiky. His lazy eye flutters and droops, a handicap as well as the punctuation point of his fractured charm. When he was a kid, they used to tease him about it. That may be why he's so worried that people occasionally mistake him for an arrogant prick.

Life has been like this for Yorke: his problems have become his strengths, his obsessions have fed his repulsions and his fears have inspired his music. We're on this train because Yorke hates to fly and he's positively terrified of cars. Just yesterday, someone asked him why he has written so many songs about car crashes. This was Yorke's answer: 'I just think that people get up too early to leave houses where they don't want to live, to drive to jobs where they don't want to be, in one of the most dangerous forms of transport on Earth. I've just never gotten used to that.'

Of course, because of his job, Yorke has to ride around in cars all the time. He even got inside one with a remote-control driver to shoot the video for Radiohead's latest single, 'Karma Police'. And as he sat in the backseat, lip-synching, something went wrong, and carbon monoxide fumes began pouring into the car. Yorke was terrified. And as he started to feel faint, he thought, 'This is my life . . . '

———

Radiohead may be the most uptight paranoid art-rock band presently operating on the planet. But even as such, they've been pretty lucky bastards. The group – Yorke, bassist Colin Greenwood, guitarists Jonny Greenwood and Ed O'Brien and drummer Phil Selway – began their career with a smash-hit song about being worthless. They weren't even sure they liked 'Creep' or the 1992 album it came from, *Pablo Honey* – especially after the song became a slack-rock anthem, the kind of timely hit that a band can come to regret, like a tattoo of your last girlfriend's name. So in 1995, they made a much better, much weirder second album (*The Bends*) and a bunch of very cool videos that evoked nothing so much as the finest Pink Floyd album covers. It wasn't a miracle that rock critics started loving Radiohead – it was a miracle that fourteen-year-old girls didn't stop.

'I was surprised to see what the music meant to people,' Yorke says. 'We went from being a novelty band to being the band that everyone quoted in the *NME* and *Melody Maker* "Musicians wanted" columns. After a hit like "Creep", bands don't normally survive. It can kill you. But it didn't.'

Radiohead toured behind *The Bends* for a year and a half. When Yorke returned to the band's semi-sleepy hometown of Oxford, he was full of new causes for alarm. He'd always been pretty familiar with the scary things inside his own head, but international touring had bestowed upon him a whole new world of inspirational hobgoblins. Now he knew he had to write songs about all sorts of horrible things. Domestic violence. Politicians. Cars. Bacon.

So Yorke and Radiohead went to work on an album about global hideousness. He fussed and fretted and became annoying to everyone he knew, but in the end it was all worth it. Because *OK Computer* is a gorgeous and haunting record. It's full of spindly guitars and freaked-out noise, poppy songs with Beatles in-jokes, and other numbers that ramble on for minutes before they actually become songs and it's especially full of mystery. Nothing is explained, everything is suggested. *OK Computer* is rife with terror and cynicism, but it's not particularly ironic or self-conscious. Apparently, the only thing that doesn't make Thom Yorke uncomfortable is the idea of making something quite beautiful and sincerely creepy.

'I think people feel sick when they hear *OK Computer,*' Yorke tells me. 'Nausea was part of what we were trying to create. *The Bends* was a record of consolation. But this one was sad. And I didn't know why.'

The album debuted on the *Billboard* charts at No. 21 and, fortunately for Yorke, lots of people have been eager to explain the meaning of *OK Computer.* An online correspondent for *Addicted to Noise* divined that *OK Computer* was based on Philip K. Dick's *V.A.L.I.S.,* a book that Yorke had not read. Other less excitable critics pounced on the record's title and songs like 'Paranoid Android', the bizarre first single, and decided the album was about Radiohead's fear of technology – they were unaware that Yorke and Jonny are actually quite avid Mac fans. Yorke himself didn't explain much, except to insist that 'Paranoid Android' is about the Fall of the Roman Empire.

The band showcased most of the songs on the album in two sold-out, high-profile concerts in Los Angeles and New York. In attendance were Liv Tyler, Madonna, Marilyn Manson, Courtney Love, R.E.M.'s Michael Stipe and Mike Mills, Mike D. of the Beastie Boys, three mysteriously unnamed supermodels, and, apparently, Liam Gallagher. Gallagher alone remained unimpressed, and felt the need to point out, in these pages no less, that Radiohead are 'fooking stoodents' or, in plainer English, college graduates. At least that was mostly true.

Meanwhile, MTV, a long-time supporter of the band, anointed the unsettling animated video for 'Paranoid Android' a Buzz Clip. In June, Yorke met Jonathan Glazer, the director responsible for their earlier clip 'Street Spirit (Fade Out)', on a deserted lane three hours from London, to shoot the chilling, Orwellian video for *OK Computer*'s second single, 'Karma Police'. In late

September, 'Karma Police' debuted on the music channel in heavy rotation, despite the fact that the video features lots of fire, the same element that got Beavis and Butthead into so much trouble a few years ago. It would seem that for MTV, Radiohead are above the law. The truth is weirder: the folks at the network like Radiohead videos because they don't exactly make sense.

'All their videos are intriguing,' explains Lewis Largent, MTV vice-president of music. 'Everybody has a different interpretation of them. The videos aren't cut and dried – like their video for "Just" [from *The Bends*], when the guy dies – that sort of mystery makes them watchable time and time again. You can watch "Paranoid Android" a hundred times and not figure it all out.'

For his part, Glazer thinks 'Karma Police' is about retribution, but he's not sure if that even matters. 'Radiohead are all about subtexts, about underbellies,' he says. 'Thom thinks about music in the same way that I think about film – he thinks it's a dialogue. That's why in the video he just sings the choruses – because the verses mean whatever we want them to mean.'

In fact, when Radiohead recorded *OK Computer*, Yorke was trying to make each song sound like reportage from inside twelve different brains. The record is a collection of fictions that might be true. It isn't about soul-baring or venting and it's not really about Thom Yorke either, which is just one of the things that sets Radiohead apart, not just from the last few years of alternative rock, but from our entire culture of confession.

'I just can't stand endless self-revelation,' Yorke says. 'Honesty is kind of a bullshit quality, really. Yeeaaaaaaaahh. There's honesty and there's *honesty*. Honesty about being dishonest is more healthy than professing to be honest.'

For better or worse, Radiohead arrive at a time when most

guitar bands are still labouring under the legacy of hardcore punk and Amer-indie rock and are therefore as concerned with 'realness' as most rap stars. But Radiohead aren't afraid to be a little pretentious: they make grand, sweeping rock music because they believe rock music can still be a transcendent thing. Even though their songs sometimes seem as shambling as, say, Pavement's, or as odd as Tortoise's, they more certainly conjure up the epic paranoias of Pink Floyd or the baroque grandeur of Queen. Like those bands, Radiohead really believe that they can fly. They may not have gotten around to acting like rock stars yet, but *OK Computer* is definitely a Rock Star album.

––––––––

In Paris, I meet Radiohead for dinner at a Swiss restaurant. Afterward, we spill out onto the cobblestone streets and head for the band's van.

'Paris is unbelievable, isn't it?' Jonny Greenwood asks, as we glance around at the darkening seventeenth-century block.

Yes it is, I say. And now you get to go do an interview at something called Fun Radio.

'Which means it will be everything but,' Jonny says with a smirk. Jonny is the youngest and prettiest member of Radiohead. He's the one with the cheekbones. He can tell you all about the experimental music John Cage composed for shortwave radios. When he was a kid, his older sister forced him to listen to English art-punk bands like Magazine, and the first instrument he played was violin. On *OK Computer*, Jonny plays viola, keyboards and guitar. Onstage, he wears a wrist brace (a souvenir from years of smacking around his guitar), and sometimes he plays a transistor radio.

Is there a conceptual artist inside you struggling to get out? I ask Jonny.

'I would never admit to that,' he says with a frozen smile.

The next morning, as the Eurostar finally rockets out of the darkness and back into the English sunlight, Yorke stops squirming in his seat. But only a bit. We are, after all, still talking about *OK Computer*. The band began recording the first bits of the album during the summer of '96 in their rehearsal studios, a converted apple shed. In September, Radiohead rented actress Jane Seymour's mansion, St Catherine's Court, moved in all their equipment, and began recording there. Things went well. At first.

'It was heaven and hell,' Yorke says. 'Our first two weeks there we basically recorded the whole album. The hell came after that. The house was . . . ' Yorke pauses for a quarter of a minute: 'oppressive. To begin with, it was curious about us. Then it got bored with us. And it started making things difficult. It started doing things like turning the studio tape machines on and off, rewinding them.'

The house was haunted?

'Yeah. It was great. Plus it was in a valley on the outskirts of Bath, in the middle of nowhere. So when we actually stopped playing music, there was just this pure silence. Open the window: nothing. A completely unnatural silence – not even birds singing. It was fucking horrible. I could never sleep.'

Radiohead finally finished recording and mastering in February of 1997. After they got some distance from the record, they were a little startled by it. 'At the eleventh hour, when we realised what we had done,' Yorke admits, 'we had qualms about the fact that we had created this thing that was quite revolting.' The people at Capitol Records felt the same way at first, especially since they didn't hear anything on *OK Computer* that sounded even remotely like a single, let alone like 'Creep'. But now, everyone's settled down a bit. Capitol's president Gary Gersh, when asked about Radiohead, has even said this: 'We won't let up until they are the biggest band in the world.' Actually, the only folks who are still worried about Radiohead are their fans. These days, Yorke gets a lot of concerned letters. Some suggest that maybe he should take a long vacation.

'I need to get a life of some description, at some point,' he says quietly. 'I mean, when your fans are writing to tell you to get a life, you know you need to listen.'

Do you think there's reason for people to be concerned about you when they hear *OK Computer*?

'I reckon.'

Yorke pauses for a second, and then laughs a slightly warmer laugh, one that suggests he's actually going to be just fine.

———

On the final night of the Radiohead tour, the band played a seaside arena in Brighton. They veered between moments of delicate, spacey psychedelia and shrieking, cut-up guitar flurries, from the anthemic chords of 'The Bends' to the elegant schizophrenia of 'Karma Police'.

Thom Yorke held his arms out like some sort of cubist Christ figure and occasionally made small requests of the audience. The second thing he said into the mic was, 'Don't do that thing where you move side to side, because people go under and this is not a fucking football match.' The third thing he said was, 'Please don't do that crowd-surfing shit either.' And the audience quite cheerfully obliged him. They were, by and large, boys with glasses and girls making passes. 'Stoodents.' The cute library couple next to me went into a clinch every time Radiohead played something slow, but when I tried to talk to them they just giggled nervously and discovered they could not speak.

After the show, I found myself standing on the beach under a full moon, laughing idiotically and throwing stones at the Atlantic Ocean with a couple of Radiohead fans I met backstage. One of them was Michael Stipe, and the Brighton show was the third Radiohead gig he'd seen in the last week. 'They played Reading on Friday night and a band can't really lose on a Friday, because for everyone there, it's fuck-or-fight,' he told me, 'but they were really great on top of that. When we toured with them two years ago, they played "Creep" every night. But now, they've taken that song back from the fans and they've made it really beautiful.'

Stipe was referring to *that* song, the one with the guitar that sounds like the Concorde. The big hit that made everyone think that Radiohead were a flash in the pan five years ago. And he's right: 'Creep' was great that night. It was delicious and slow and sore all over. Yorke even improvised a little. To be precise, he changed the words of the chorus from '*I'm a weirdo*' to '*I'm a winner*'.

Five: The Earnestness of Being Important

1

Karma Police

Barney Hoskyns, *GQ*,
October 2000

The posters on the ancient streets of Arles give little away. Sting is playing soon in Marseille. Upcoming is a 'Super Big Reggae Party' with U Roy and Alpha Blondy. A bullfight will take place next week in the town's ancient Roman amphitheatre. Even as one approaches the equally ancient Theatre Antique, built during the reign of the Emperor Augustus, there's scant indication that the most acclaimed group on Planet Pop is here, in Provence, to play its first live show in eighteen months. On one side of the open-air auditorium the evening sky is charcoal grey; from the other, bright golden light streams across crumbling columns and arches.

But now the old men promenading with their tiny dachshunds pause in their post-prandial tracks. For covering the railings encircling the theatre are sheets of black plastic; towering over the old brickwork is scaffolding that supports chunky klieg lights. Clustered about the theatre's back entrance is a throng of polyglot youths. A shiver of excitement ripples through the boys and girls as a slight, dark figure emerges from the doorway. No satin or sunglasses on display here; not even a tattoo. Just a guy in grey New Balance sneakers, bag slung over shoulder and head tilted into a mobile phone. Voices – French, German, Dutch, English – yap at Colin Greenwood, bass player with Radiohead, as he follows the band's producer Nigel Godrich into the sharp light. Soundcheck over, they're heading for the band's huge, lime-green tour bus to eat dinner.

Blinking and squinting behind them comes Thom Yorke, the group's tortured frontboy with his dabchick hair and wonky, lopsided eyes. Radiohead's eighteen-date summer tour of Europe hasn't even started, and already this most alternative of pinups looks vaguely defeated.

'Thom, Thom!'

'Thom, here, Thom!'

One particularly persistent German *madchen* monopolises Yorke as he tries to beat a path to the bus. He stops, poses patiently as the boys and girls capture him with tiny cameras.

And then the Creep who could be God slinks off, alone, into the sultry evening.

————

Radiohead are once again setting their controls for the heart of the rock machine, heavy weights on their slender shoulders. The weight is especially heavy on Thomas Edward Yorke, thirty-one, whose songs and lyrics and singing have made him – possibly against his own better instincts – a near superstar.

According to Colin Greenwood, 'excessive praise' for the group's third album *OK Computer* 'did Thom's head in'. Now Radiohead must follow the record up, knowing that almost anything they do may disappoint profoundly. Tonight, in Arles, the world will hear the first fruits of the band's long labours in studios in Paris, Copenhagen and England.

To understand what's expected of Radiohead is to acknowledge just how bankrupt 'rock music' has become at the dawn of the twenty-first century – as a sound, as a movement, as a pseudo-religion. ('*Oh no, pop is dead, long live pop,*' Yorke bleated back in 1993. '*It died an ugly death by back catalogue.*') Post-Cobain, R.O.C.K. has withered on the vine, discredited as a cultural force, toppled by teen pop and hip hop and even by what passes these days for 'country' music. In America, Pearl Jam struggle to stay relevant; in Britain, the embers of Ladrock barely flicker as Oasis go through their death throes.

Shining like a beacon in the midst of this morass is 1997's shimmering, densely-textured *OK Computer,* a masterpiece that took the moribund rock genre and resurrected it in thirteen astonishing tracks built around Yorke's soaring voice and melodies and the (multi) instrumental genius of Colin Greenwood's kid brother Jonny. At a point when Britrock was being shored up by lumpen cool and microwaved Beatles riffs, Radiohead dared to attempt something big and brainy and unabashedly beautiful.

In so doing they kept alive a continuum that ran from U2 through R.E.M. – the ideal of polite, slightly anguished boys reaching for meaning and anthemic transcendence through guitars and amplifiers. Radiohead revived rock's passion, its *urban hymnody,* recalling nothing so much as that post-punk period of *rockism returned* (U2, Echo & the Bunnymen, Simple Minds). Yet they also forged insistently forward, staring hard into a dystopian, over-technologised future, uninterested in peddling stadium clichés.

Significantly, the long time-lag between *OK Computer* and its successor – *Kid A* – has created a gap, a lacuna quickly filled by a spate of post-Britpop faux-Radioheads: Witness, Muse, Six By Seven, Coldplay, JJ72, Motorhomes and more. There's a quintessential Britishness about the whole crop: the self-doubt and introversion of university-educated boys called James and Dominic hand-wringing over liquid guitars. How wonderfully earnest they are, lost in dreams of Thom Yorke's ugly-duckling deity and Jeff Buckley's ecstatic grace.

Like Radiohead itself, these bands are part of a growing resistance to the paralysing pop-culture irony that's undone rock as we used to know it. Asked why people were getting so excited by his band, Coldplay singer Chris Martin offered a disarmingly simple explanation: 'It's not because of our politics or any agenda – it's because people are looking for what's important in music again.'

Yet right now the question is less whether the Muses and Coldplays will have any relevance once the masters return. The question is: are Radiohead themselves interested in trying to top the musical Matterhorn that is *OK Computer*, or are they turning defiantly away from the role of rock saviours that the world wants them to assume?

———

A Thom Yorke mix tape sends subterranean shockwaves through the lichen-covered granite of the Theatre Antique. (As a student, the singer was a revered turntablist at Exeter's Lemon Grove club.) The local *jeunesse dorée* munch on baguettes as an evening church bell peals over mangled dance beats.

The distorted digital grooves aside, the setting for tonight's show recalls nothing so much as *Pink Floyd Live at Pompeii* – or even the Grateful Dead playing the pyramids, man. Indeed, those who decry Radiohead as ersatz prog-rockers – as too earnest, too studenty, too middle-class – will have a field day mocking the choice of unorthodox venues (piazzas, more Roman theatres) on this low-key jaunt around Europe and the Mediterranean.

Swifts and swallows dart through the heavy air as, with uncanny synchronicity, the Yorke tape gives way to the Inkspots singing 'When the Swallows Come Back to San Juan Capistrano'. At 9.30 p.m., the gathering clouds burst and rain falls from a great height onto the huddled crowd.

For a cataclysmic half-hour it looks as though we may not be hearing Radiohead after all.

———

An image, frozen in pop time (or at least the early summer of 1993): a quintet of limp-haired youths unloading their 'gear' from a battered van outside a venue in Clapham Junction, south London. An unmistakable pre-gig anxiety written on their support-band faces as they heave amps through the emergency exit door. One runty little dude with big peroxide-blond locks and a glowering stringbean boy like something out of *Deliverance*.

The image comes to mind because Radiohead at this point were just A. N. Other post-grunge band, and a band who most decidedly *hadn't* been embraced by that summer's mushrooming Britpop hype. Five university-educated boys from Oxford playing sub-U2 'rock' with none of the swooning panache of Suede, Radiohead got short shrift in the cruel UK music press. At least some of the animosity came down to the entrenched anti-middle-class bias of weeklies like the *NME* and *Melody Maker*. 'Anyone Can Play Guitar', Yorke sneered on Radiohead's debut album.

But in Britain only the underprivileged are taken seriously as avatars of modern youth.

Somewhat drab as the debut [*Pablo Honey*] was, it did feature a song that put them on the map and very nearly became the albatross that finished them. A postscript to the dark abjection of grunge and its slacker offspring losercore, 'Creep' was a startling slice of self-flagellation sung in Yorke's most putrifyingly miserablist style. '*I'm a creep/I'm a weirdo*,' Thommy-boy yelped; '*What the hell am I doing here?*' When you saw him singing it – all spluttering rage and convulsion – the self-hate was toxic. This was a Kurt Cobain from the dank corridors of provincial English boarding schools.

That 'Creep' took off in, of all places, America was a double helping of irony, especially when Radiohead found themselves playing 'modern rock' radio beach parties and weenie roasts. 'When "Creep" went through the roof, Capitol Records just wanted to milk it,' *Pablo Honey*'s co-producer Paul Q. Kolderie says. 'They were doing "I'm a creep" contests and placing ads that said, "Beavis and Butthead say Radiohead don't suck".' Although a reissued 'Creep' reached the UK Top 10 in the fall of 1993, American success made the British press still more suspicious of Radiohead. It also set the terms for the band's uneasy relationship with America. On the one hand, like U2 and the Police before them, they were prepared to work hard at cracking the US market, taking several support slots on tours. On the other, Thom Yorke balked strongly at the schmoozing that was expected of him. The thorny issue of how an intelligent band retains its credibility whilst hawking its wares around the world's pre-eminent music market is one that continues to dog Radiohead (not to mention Capitol Records) as they embark on the promotion of *Kid A*.

'Bonsoir, tout le monde!'

Yorke's first words immediately endear him to the dripping Arles audience as it wrings out its T-shirts. (Would Liam Gallagher have bothered with such a gesture?) Eighteen months after the group bid *adieu* at the Stade de Bercy in Paris, Radiohead is once again a real live entity, not simply an aggregation of website rumours. Launching into 'Talk Show Host', a B-side favourite of fans-in-the-know, the band quickly makes its case. Jonny Greenwood's keyboards swirl around drummer Phil Selway's circular groove and rhythm guitarist Ed O'Brien's chopped funk-rock chords as Yorke lets rip. *'You want me?'* he bawls in the song's most transparent line. *'Fuckin' well come and find me!'*

The applause soaked up, the group turns to 'Bones', a track from their breakthrough second album *The Bends*. *'Now I can't climb the stairs,'* Yorke howls over the churning boogie riffs. *'Pieces missing everywhere/Prozac painkillers . . .'* Jonny G. is on guitar now and he's stabbing at the strings, pulling out notes that shriek and quiver in the air.

We feel it in our dampened bones. Radiohead rocks.

The Bends (1995) changed everything. Recorded in a state of semi-crisis, a point when the unavoidable tensions of sustaining a band had boiled over, it steamrollered the slovenly Britpop competition of the time.

'*The Bends* was neither an English album nor an American album,' said Paul Kolderie, who mixed the album after John Leckie (Magazine, Stone Roses et al.) had produced it. 'It really had that feel of, "We don't live anywhere and we don't belong anywhere.'"

Sonically, *The Bends* was a far richer proposition than *Pablo Honey*. Here was an art-rock band unafraid of being musos. The sheer range of textures was dazzling and came with a host of other vaguely proggy signifiers: sudden time changes, string parts written by prodigy Jonny, fractured, oblique lyrics about alienation and disease. Mix Pink Floyd with Nirvana and Jeff Buckley (who blew Radiohead away when they saw him live in London in April 1994) and you get both angst rock ('Just', 'The Bends', 'Black Star') and plangent lamentation ('High and Dry', 'Nice Dream', 'Fake Plastic Trees'). More than anything, this is where Yorke finds his voice – a voice suddenly outgrowing its Bono/Ian McCulloch origins as it built from tremulous softness to soaring intensity, supported by superhuman lungs. '[Radiohead] possess the great lyric singer of his time,' says Scott Walker, for whom the group adjusted their schedule to play the Meltdown festival in London this summer.

Radiohead weren't the only British band shooting for something more than indie cool – both the Verve and the Manic Street Preachers wanted to make big, ecstatic music – but it was *The Bends* that most mocked the Blur/Oasis spat that blew up around Britpop in 1995. 'The Britpop movement was wrong for us because it was so awash with this knowing irony,' remarked Jonny Greenwood. 'In some ways it wasn't about . . . being serious about being in a band.'

By year's end, *The Bends* had put Radiohead on the world's stage and earned them the friendship of their heroes R.E.M. When Michael Stipe took Yorke under his wing, offering pointers on how to handle success, it was as though the older band was passing on the mantle. By 1996, when they started work on *OK Computer*, Radiohead had accepted that being in a rock band didn't mean they had to behave like rock stars. 'I think what happened within the band,' John Leckie told journalist Mac Randall, 'is that they had this kind of paranoia about being polite, straight, from Oxford, never getting into any trouble or scandal, very clean, not rock'n'roll at all. That's the way they are, and yet at the time they were worried about that, about taking on a rock'n'roll career and not being rock'n'rollers. They had to learn to be themselves and to be comfortable with that.'

As they set about recording *OK Computer*, Radiohead became an entity unto itself, removed from the British music scene. Unlike the majority of groups who 'make it' in the UK, Radiohead did not up sticks and move to London. They remained in and around Oxford, where they'd all grown up, and knuckled down to work in their own rehearsal space near the village of Sutton Courtenay. Opting to produce the new album themselves with the help of *Bends* engineer Nigel Godrich, Radiohead adopted a looser, more experimental approach to their third opus. 'We weren't listening to guitar bands; we were thoroughly ashamed of being a guitar band,' Thom Yorke admitted. 'So we bought loads of keyboards and learned how to use them and when we got bored we went back to guitars.'

The bulk of *OK Computer* was recorded in a spooky Elizabethan mansion belonging to ageless actress Jane Seymour. St Catherine's Court, outside Bath, offered the right ambience for the band's bold new sound – an enveloping, almost symphonic montage of guitars and machines, loops and chorales. Into this big, open sound was poured all of Yorke's obsessions with the way technology ate into people's souls, his vocal performances comprising a single long lament for human feeling in a hyper-mediated universe. Songs like 'Paranoid Android' and 'Subterranean Homesick Alien' alternately expressed separation from society and yearning for connection.

For some, the result was a '90s *Dark Side of the Moon*; for others, it was a masterpiece that blended the Byrds and the Beatles with Can and Miles Davis, a work that gave new validity to the term 'concept album'. For Capitol, it came as something of a shock. Convinced they had the new U2 on their hands, the West Coast label had assumed Radiohead's third album would be *The Joshua Tree* to *The Bends' Unforgettable Fire*. Capitol hadn't reckoned with Radiohead's own growing suspicion of the crude brushstrokes that stadium rock required. Even *OK Computer*'s most overtly commercial track, the sublime 'Let Down', was all about the distrust of apparent sincerity. 'We're bombarded with sentiment, people emoting,' Yorke complained. 'That's the letdown. Feeling every emotion is fake.'

If Yorke's postmodern malaise was a spanner in the pop works, Capitol sounded bullish after the first drooling reviews appeared. 'There's nothing I've seen in any country in the world that's excited me as much,' the label's then-president Gary Gersh told me. 'Our job is just to take them as a left-of-centre band and bring the centre to them. That's our focus, and we won't let up until they're the biggest band in the world.'

But did such a hoary notion mean anything anymore? Not to Radiohead, who in an earlier era might have been Pink Floyd or even the Beatles but who'd surfaced at a *zeit* when the *geist* was all about questioning and subverting the fake plastic pillars that supported the rock mythos. In her book *I'm a Man: Sex, Gods and Rock'n'Roll*, poet Ruth Padel calls rock 'a theatrical dream of being male . . . full of male teenage selfishness, contradiction, violence, misogyny, narcissism, supremacism, resentment, anger, darkness and fantasies of omnipotence'. For Radiohead, as for R.E.M. before them, rock has become an exhausted cartoon, an arena of empty exhibitionism.

Shattered by the *OK Computer* tour, which took them through to the end of 1998, Radiohead finally regrouped to begin work on a new record at the beginning of 1999. As with *The Bends* and *OK Computer*, painful false starts – this time in studios in Paris and Copenhagen – were the order of the day. Ed O'Brien's often painfully honest 'diary' on the band's website radiohead.com kept fans abreast of the maddeningly uncertain process by which they were writing new material. At the root of the band's uncertainty was a central loss of faith: the faith in rock itself.

———

'This is a new song . . . '

Here are the words we've been waiting Thom Yorke to say all day, and now he's said them. Tomorrow they'll be on the net and rock's global villagers will be e-gabbling about 'the new songs'. Radiohead play seven new songs at the Theatre Antique and most of them leave the crowd looking bemused. Are they songs at all? Or are they mere experiments, fragments worked up to resemble finished pieces?

'Optimistic' is moody and muted, as is the warmer 'Morning Bell', sung mainly in falsetto and arranged in 5/4 time. Neither appears to possess a chorus, and both suggest Yorke is aiming for the shapeless, post-triphop sound of 'Rabbit in Your Headlights', his mesmerising cameo on U.N.K.L.E.'s *Psyence Fiction* album. 'Dollars and Cents' is more spacious, opening out into long vocal lines on its chorus, but it's hardly 'The Tourist'. Later comes the monochordal grunge-fuzz of 'Everyone – The National Anthem', with Jonny Greenwood miking the 'found sound' of a transistor radio and the others grinding away over Phil Selway's pounding sixteenths. 'In Limbo' is formless but pleasingly dreamy, with Ed O'Brien at the keyboard and Selway playing splashy jazz fills, but 'Everything In Its Right Place' – based around electric piano chords that sounded like old Steely Dan or Stevie Wonder out-takes – is nothing more than an ascending motif masquerading as a song. Doubtless it's a precautionary measure to make the last new number, 'Knives Out', the most accessible. With Yorke strumming an acoustic and O'Brien harmonising nicely, this Smithsy item could almost be Travis.

What stirs the youth of Arles, of course, is the majestic megaballads ('Lucky', 'Exit Music', 'No Surprises', 'Climbing up the Walls') and the post-grunge blasts of angst ('Bones', 'Just', 'My Iron Lung'). 'Oh, you know this one,' Yorke says as he introduces 'Street Spirit', then adds, '*Phew!*' 'Thank you for being so nice on our first gig back,' he grunts after penultimate encore 'Nice Dream'.

What chance a backlash when *Kid A* is released next month? Already knives have glinted in the British press. 'Why would a band with such a rare gift for combining sonic invention with memorable, emotive songs give up half its winning formula?' asked the *Observer*. 'Prog rock for dullards,' sneered the *Guardian* of Radiohead's Meltdown appearance in July.

———

On the eve of the Meltdown show, Thom Yorke posts a typically cryptic note on radiohead.com. It's a direct quote from Malcolm

Lowry's *Under the Volcano* and begins thus: 'Or is it because there is a path, as Blake well knew, and though I may not take it, sometimes lately in dreams I have been able to see it? . . . I seem to see now, between mescals, this path, and beyond it strange vistas, like visions of a new life together we might somewhere lead.'

With *Kid A*, Radiohead are taking the road less travelled, a winding track that makes a sharp exit off rock's superhighway. Modern music may be about to experience its most dramatic rebirth.

2

Kid A:
Revolution in the Head

Simon Reynolds, *Uncut*,
November 2000

What went wrong with British rock? Surveying the current panorama of mediocrity, it's hard to recall a more barren time. The last four years' output of UK guitar-based music makes the early '70s – that fabled hiatus of stalled stagnation between '60s supernova and punk renewal – seem like a period of astonishing abundance and diversity. (Which it actually was, if you think about it: the official rock history gets it wrong, as it so often does.)

What happened to the culture that produced bands like Roxy Music, Joy Division, the Fall, the Banshees, the Specials, the Associates, the Human League, the Smiths, My Bloody Valentine (and this to-name-just-a-few litany includes neither obvious greats nor the mavericks that brighten the corners of Brit rock's pantheon)? Bands who each created their own aesthetic universes and singular pop languages. Now steel yourself and scrutinise the standard-bearers of recent years: Gomez, with their amiable pastiches of bygone Americana: Manic Street Preachers, the People's Choice after years of dogged slog, peddling overwrought new wave melodrama alarmingly redolent of the Boomtown Rats; Catatonia, Stereophonics, Gay Dad and other inkie cover faves offering what apparently passes for star quality, singing and songcraft in this blighted isle. The sense of doldrums, of living through undistinguished times, is completed by the steady drizzle of solo albums and post-break-up projects from the debris of Madchester and Britpop – Butler, Squire, Brown, Coxon, Ashcroft.

Why does British rock continue to come up empty? Obviously, Britpop shoulders much blame – for its jingoism and nostalgic flight from contemporary multiculture; for sanctioning derivativeness and grave-robbing necrophilia; for its anorexic, anachronistic fetish for the snappy three-minute ditty (as if the seven-inch single was still the culture's prime format). Most pernicious of all is the damage done to the ideal of independent music by Britpop's Make It Big At All Costs ethos, which made the pursuit of innovation for its own sake unfashionable, even faintly ludicrous. If the Stone Roses started this tendency (citing only the most obvious influences, like the Beatles, as mark of their ambition and self-regard) and the Manics turned it into ideology (so that having obscure influences or experimental impulses became the sign of defeatism and elitism), it was Oasis who made it orthodoxy. Their sole *raison d'être* was to be big, to create a sense of size that we could all bask in. And so empty boasts about seeing no reason why this band shouldn't be as big as the Beatles became compulsory for the kind of groups that exist to fill up one-page features in the weekly music papers.

Since major labels alone have the clout to make bands that big, the result was a massive withdrawal of energy and interest from the independent sector. Look at the indie charts now and you'll find a motley coalition of drum'n'bass and techno records, death metal albums and other micro-genre niche-markets and pop stars who happen to go through independent distribution. The kind of diverse but unified independent music culture that in 1988 could sustain an AR Kane album at No. 1 for four weeks doesn't exist anymore.

By now, though, there should have been the backlash, seeds of regeneration budding if not blooming. Britpop's bubble burst quite a while back (*This Is Hardcore*'s unexpected shortfall, the bloat and crapulence of *Be Here Now*) and the gold-rush A&R blunders have issued their dismal debuts and in many cases already been downsized from the rosters. But apart from the odd cult-figure-in-waiting (your Badly Drawn Boys) and veteran shape-shifters (your Primal Screams, Saint Etiennes and so on) this unprecedented inspiration-drought continues.

Why?

Dance culture done it. Dance culture was the worst thing that ever happened to British rock. Not just because its unparalleled enticements permanently hijacked the greater portion of rock's potential audience (even in its lamest, most edge-less form – trance and hard house – clubbing beats gigging by an unbeatable margin). But because the electronic arena has sucked up a good ninety per cent of the musical intellect available, Brit rock ails because this country's sharpest musical minds are dedicated to making instrumental, non-band music. Why should the Eno-style inspired non-musicians bother with all the friction and hassle of being in a band when they can implement their ideas quickly via compliant, near infinitely flexible machines? Dance culture and its home-listening-oriented adjuncts even hold out the possibility of making a few bob. As a result, rock has been left to people with the worst motivations: fame, exhibitionism, the desire to make music like they did in the good old days (the '60s, punk/new wave). Or it's left rock to people with something to 'say': the quote machines, the would-be poets. 'All mouth, no trousers' has been Brit rock's cardinal liability since the post-punk era, when attitude, self-salesmanship and music paper-friendly gift of the gab became more valued than instrumental skill or sonic vision.

For most of the '90s, the ferment of post-rave music made the mounting failure of Brit rock easy to ignore. So why not just dispense with rock and be done with it? Because dance has its own downside – what you might call 'all trousers, no mouth'. The problem with funktional ravefloor fodder and *Wire* magazine-type abstraction alike is that it is so sheerly sonic, about the materiality of rhythm and texture and nothing else. Whereas the genius of British pop has always been the way that sonics and discourse, music and ideas about music, have meshed and cross-catalysed each other. It's not that dance music is meaningless. It can even 'say' stuff about the world outside the club's walls, through vocal samples, rhythmic tension, bass pressure, atmospherics. But the feelings dance music communicates tend to come in primary colours, without shading or ambivalence. Mostly, it has the vicarious quality of the drug experiences it's generally designed to enhance: blasts of euphoria, impersonal force-fields of energy that you can plug into. It can be hard to connect the weekend's sensation rides and artificial highs with everyday life.

Which is why the late '90s saw lots of people who'd been through the rave adventure suddenly feeling stranded in an emotional void. I really noticed it in 1997: friends hitherto exclusively of the electronic persuasion were suddenly listening to albums by bands like the Verve and Spiritualized. Above all, they were listening to *OK Computer*. That album had the ravishing textural splendour required to seduce ears used to electronica's lavish sonic palette, but it also contained the complicated emotions, spiritual nourishment and solace that rock at its best has always provided.

In a sense, dance music has been Britpop's accomplice, its partner-in-crime – together they have created a fatal split in British pop culture, separating musical innovation from all the other stuff that the UK has always excelled at (stylisation, attitude, arty pretentiousness) and without which music is 'just' music. A great British rock record in the Y2K would have to fuse the severed halves, reconnect sound and significance, get the balance right between trousers and mouth. A great, fully contemporary rock record would have to rival the vivid colours, spatial weirdness and rhythmic compulsion routinely available in the realm of electronic music but combine them with the kind of interiority and potential for individualised response that surface-and-sensation oriented, collective-high-inducing dance rarely reaches.

Kid A is such a record. On 'Everything in its Right Place', the lead vocal is just one strand in a shimmering tapestry of multi-tracked and treated Thom Yorke voice-goo, whose pulse-riffs and rippling patterns simultaneously recall Robert Wyatt's *Rock Bottom* and contemporary avant-electronica outfits like Curd Duca. On 'Kid A', a drastically processed and illegible Yorke vocal nestles amid a honeycomb of tweeting'n'cooing space-critters and enchanting music-box critters – again, the track would be right at home in the world of 'glitch techno' labels like Mille Plateaux or Mega. The jack-knifing two-step beat that powers 'Idioteque' explicitly nods towards contemporary dance, but leeches the joy out à la PiL's 'Memories' or Joy Division's 'She's Lost Control' – call it death garage. At the opposite extreme, the beat-less 'Treefingers' – a miasma of glistening vapours and twinkling haze – could be an eerie dronescape from Aphex Twin's *Selected Ambient Works Vol II* or Eno's *On Land*. Now you too can own your own miniature of eternity.

Elsewhere on the album, the coordinates are less electronica and more the remotest extremities of the rock tradition. All wincing and waning atmospherics, 'How to Disappear Completely' is the missing link between Scott Walker's desolate orchestral grandeur and the swoonily amorphous ballads on My Bloody Valentine's *Isn't Anything*. The grind-and-surge bass-riff, cymbal-splashy *motorik* drums and asteroid-belt-debris guitars of 'The National Anthem' initially recall Faust or Loop at their most *kosmische*, until the free-blowing entrance of the Art Ensemble of Chicago-style horns takes the song to another outer zone altogether. 'Optimistic' combines the noble pure-rock drive of the Bunnymen circa *Heaven Up Here* with the gnarly, swarf-spitting graunch of Gang of Four. 'In Limbo' would be *Kid A*'s most old-fashioned sounding song (imagine a fey, fatalistic castaway from Eno's solo albums trapped in the treadmill churn of Led Zep's 'Four Sticks') if not for its dazzling sound: a shimmer-swirl of dense overdubs, as if the song's swathed in a cloud of hummingbirds.

Kid A's sound is astounding throughout: warm, smudgy, the instruments seeming to bleed through and mingle with each other uncannily. Colin Greenwood's bass is a particularly powerful presence, often seeming to throb from inside your own body, hip hop-style. On 'Morning Bell', it's like the rest of the music is the outer crust or husk of the monstrously swollen but tender bass-pulse.

Revealing fact: most Radiohead websites provide 'guitar tabs' so that fans can copy the three guitarists' every last fret fingering, chord progression and tone-bend. Something tells me there won't be too many tabs transcribed from *Kid A*, though. (Tabs ingested, Christ yeah!) The use of effects like sustain and delay, in tandem with the signal-processing and disorientating spatial potential of the mixing desk, is frequently so drastic that the guitars function as texture-generators rather than riff-machines. They're just another means of sound-synthesis. Indeed, it's often impossible to tell where a sound originated – it could be from guitars, keyboards/synths, orchestral/acoustic instruments or from digital effects/samples/mixing board malarkey.

Kid A is the return-with-a-vengeance of a phenomenon that had seemingly petered out: post-rock. This highly contested genre dates back to 1993–94, when various smart operators began to notice the glaring and ever-widening gap in sonic vividness between guitar-based music and 'sampladelia' (the whole area of digital music that encompasses dance, atmospheric electronica and hip hop). The result was a loosely connected network of artists engaged in closing that innovation gap, a semi-movement I had the temerity to christen 'post-rock'. At its utmost, post-rock delivered an aggregation of psychedelias: the original psychedelic cosmonauts (especially the Krautrock contingent), the Jamaican psychedelia of dub, the neo-psych resurrection of the late '80s (Spacemen 3, Sonic Youth, MBV and so on), the digital psychedelia of '90s electronic dance. What all these phases had in common was their partial or total abandonment of live performance as the model for recording: the willingness for music to be unrealistic, anti-naturalistic, a studio-spun figment.

Despite its early promise, though, the reality of post-rock rarely lived up to the dream. Too much post-rock failed to supply what people get from trad rock (the singer's charisma/neurosis, big riffs, something to look at onstage, tunes you can hum in the bath, the whole apparatus of identification and catharsis), without ever really rivalling what full-on dance offers either (groove power, surrogate drug-sensations, the rush). What you got was mood music – not necessarily emotionless but tending to elicit admiration rather than involvement. I always thought post-rock would languish on the hipster margins until an Established Band took on its ideas – an R.E.M., Pearl Jam, U2 (who came close, and nearly whittled away their superstardom in the process). Now Radiohead have embraced post-rock (if not the concept, then certainly its techniques and its intent) but brilliantly merged it with all that indispensable trad-rock stuff like Emotion and Meaning.

Kid A is the kind of record that makes you want to curl up in a foetal ball inside your headphones, immerse yourself utterly – not just to catch all the loving sonic details, but because it's a record for wallowing. Yorke may resent the hack stereotype of himself as 'tortured artist', but his words and delivery do little to resist it. The song-moods run the gamut of dismal D-words: despondency, dis-association, dejection, discomfort, and (on the Floyd *Animals*-redolent 'Optimistic') broader cultural themes of decline and de-evolution. Ian McCulloch hyped his first solo album back in 1989 by saying that it was time for 'some bleak' (the context being Madchester's Day-Glo positivity). Against a similar backdrop of vacant, boom-time optimism, Radiohead bring the bleak in a thousand shades of lustrous grey.

What's striking about *Kid A* is how perfectly the colours of Yorke-as-instrument fit with the band's palette. Sometimes he gets a little help from technology – effects lend a wincing toothache edge to his voice on the solar-wind howl of 'The National Anthem', while on 'Everything in its Right Place' and 'Kid A' Yorke offers himself up as raw material to be slice'n'diced, played backwards. On 'In Limbo', the chorus (either '*in a fantasy*' or '*your inner fancy*': diction is deliberately imprecise throughout, adding to the sense of Yorke as an ensemble player rather than frontman) crumbles and disappears into the band's wall of sound.

You can learn a lot about bands through their fans: one of the top Radiohead websites has a section called Song Interpretations, where fans email in their own private and widely divergent readings of lyrics that are either opaque or so indistinctly enunciated they enter ''*Scuse-Me-While-I-Kiss-This-Guy*' territory. As with any classic rock band, Radiohead's music musters the aura of gravity that puts fans into this interpretive mode – a sensation of deep-and-meaningful that's as important as any actual statements being made. Although this kind of approach can be reactionary in that perennial sixth form/undergraduate/music paper-reader middlebrow way, it has a certain oppositional value at this precise moment because it goes against the grain of the pop culture – teen pop's ascendance, dance at its most complacent and non-utopian (trance, garage, R&B, all basically accept reality as it is). Radiohead's re-invocation of art-rock seriousness, at a time of compulsory triviality and pseudo-camp cynicism, is a reminder that people once believed music could change minds, could have profound, life-shaking impact.

This earnestness of being important is one reason why the Pink Floyd comparison dogs Radiohead, although Joy Division would be just as appropriate. *Kid A* is the kind of record that would have come out on Harvest or Virgin in the early '70s, on Factory or 4AD in the early '80s. Today, if this was an unknown band's debut, you'd have to say Domino or Kranky. (Often the record sounds like lo-fi on a *Dark Side of the Moon* budget, lo-fi for audiophiles.)

Kid A is also an album in the bygone sense of the word. The immaculate aesthetic logic of the track sequencing (something of an obsession for Radiohead) lends *Kid A* the sort of shape and trajectory that lingers in your mind. Rather than reprogramming the CD into micro-albums of favourite bits, people will want to play and replay it in its entirety. Smart, too, of Radiohead to resist the temptation to release a double or even use the CD's full capacity, and instead go for a 50-minute duration, just a little longer than the classic vinyl elpee.

How groundbreaking is *Kid A* really? Committed margin-walkers will argue that if you like the title track, you'll find more wildly warped and deranging stuff on tiny glitch-techno labels out of Cologne or will claim that freaks in Japan or New Zealand are unleashing more out-there space-rock jams than 'The National Anthem'. They might be right (I couldn't tell you). But the fact is, in pop music context is everything. It matters that this is Radiohead, who didn't have to go out on such a limb, but did. Radiohead are shoving all this strangeness, hitherto the preserve of hipster snobs, down the earholes of the Q readership – not exactly a vanguard of listeners. And the fact that the band's slightly middlebrow following will, out of sheer loyalty, learn to love it, is exciting. (Q readers are often mocked for picking *OK*

Computer as the Greatest Album of all Time – but why not? Who says the Best LP Ever couldn't occur in rock's fourth decade rather than its first?)

Context is everything and it makes a mighty difference that this is an awaited record. There's a momentousness that – unjustly, inevitably – will never pertain to the next effort by Labradford or Mouse on Mars. The sense of a Major Band on a Journey that is exceeding expectations recalls the giant steps made with each successive album by the Beatles or the way that certain art-rock luminaries progressed by taking the weirdest elements of their previous record and making them the blueprint for their next (for example, the sequence that climaxed with Talking Heads's *Remain in Light*) or just springboarded into a strange beyond of their own imagining (for example, Kate Bush's *The Dreaming*). Radiohead could have easily, profitably, remade *OK Computer*. But instead they've made a record where every track sounds 1) unlike each other and 2) unlike anything they've done before, yet still 1) works as a glorious whole and 2) has a distinct Radiohead signature.

Saviours of Brit rock? Don't know about that, but *Kid A* is a shining example and stinging reproach to the rest of the Brit rock pack for their low horizons and underachievement.

3

'Kid A's . . . Alright'

John Harris, *Select*,
November 2000

The band are in a big top, the burger van is admirably non-corporate, the new songs are . . . well, new. And the audience is utterly bewildered: Radiohead, it would appear, are back.

'This is for the band,' says Thom Yorke, just before Radiohead play a song called 'I Might Be Wrong', the recorded version of which will not appear until summer 2001 (at least). ''Cos we had the bloody stupid idea of playing in a tent.'

In all fairness, the idea seems sane enough. As a gig venue, the tent easily passes muster: Radiohead promised an upgrade in sound quality vis-à-vis the run-of-the-mill outdoor event, and they have delivered. The visuals are a little rudimentary and the three lasers outside that beam a pyramid into the night sky are a bit Pink Floyd, but that's a relative trifle. Most importantly, the tent is a 'non-branded environment'. That, more than a love of fresh air and a wish to see unremarkable fields on the outskirts of British cities, is why everyone is standing in the mud-strewn grounds of Tredegar House, Newport, Gwent. Naomi Klein's anti-capitalist bible *No Logo* is Radiohead's *livre du jour*; the tent means they are doing their bit.

In a corner of tonight's field, just along from Ultimate Burger and to the left of the admirably non-corporate toastie van, there is the only beer outlet: a compact and bijou version of your average festival bar. Its queues are about ten people deep. It takes twenty minutes to get a drink. 'It's bloody Radiohead, though, isn't it?' groans one wag. 'You're not meant to have a good time.'

The wait, however, is not the main issue. The bar, as it turns out, is selling nothing other than Budweiser. (Actually, you can also get Virgin alcopops, but that's hardly the point.) The beer is served from the can into big red cups – and the cups, of course, are branded. With a dirty Budweiser logo. *Select* doesn't want to be picky or anything, but this really doesn't seem right. So, if only for the sake of conversational sport, we sidle up to Ed O'Brien at the brief after-show soirée. It's being held in an old farm outhouse that rather suggests the kind of room where you once had breakfast on a geography field trip. Everyone, incidentally, is drinking bottled Kronenbourg.

So, Ed. Why are Budweiser doing all the beer?

[Genuinely shocked] 'Are they?'

Oh, yes.

'Isn't it the Workers Co-op? [i.e. the Workers Beer Company]?'

No, you can only get a Budweiser. In a branded beer cup.

'Beer cup? OK. We'll sort that out. That'll change. I didn't know that. You carry on learning. [In humorous voice] We haven't changed the beer cups! We've failed!'

Enough about 'branding'. The key reason for the current clamour around Radiohead is the imminent appearance of *Kid A*, aka Radiohead's Unfathomably Experimental Electronica

Album, aka The Record That Will Save British Rock as a Viable Creative Force. Naturally, it is neither of these things. Ed O'Brien calmly informs *Select* that *Kid A* is 'just a collection of songs that fit well together on a record, that we made in the last year and a half.' The description fits Radiohead's ironically blank aesthetic to perfection – their video collection, let us not forget, was called *Seven TV Commercials*; the passes on their last tour were labelled 'Generic Sticky Pass'. Perhaps *Just a Collection of Songs that Fit Well Together on a Record that We Made in The Last Year and a Half* would have made the ideal title.

Radiohead, after all, are currently in the business of deflating expectations. Though Ed O'Brien's internet diaries initially looked like a simple matter of fan-friendly warmth and admirable spontaneity, they also shed enough light on Radiohead's travails to show that they were merely a five-piece group having problems with their fourth album. And the fact that they quietly began touring a good three months ago speaks volumes: the intention is obviously to avoid the grisly fate documented in the tour film *Meeting People is Easy*. The problem was simple: walking to the world's stages after thousands of publications had claimed that *OK Computer* was a work of twenty-four-carat genius. 'A few people write in specific magazines that are really influential,' Thom told *Select* in December 1997, 'and everyone just reiterates it again and again and again. And whatever the sentiment was in the original review turns into this garbled echo . . . Expectations got really high. I had a real crisis. We all did.'

'This feels very different from *OK Computer*,' says Ed. 'It feels more like *Bends*-era in terms of our attitude onstage and where our heads are. There's just not that big cloud over our heads that we had doing *OK Computer*. There are expectations, but it's like,

"We're going to do this on our terms." Round the time of touring *OK Computer* was dark. And there were little things, like the fact that it rained the whole time we toured. Which you might not think makes a difference, but actually . . . And that was a heavy record. And this isn't.'

Long-term, Radiohead want to avoid the 'Here we are with our brand-new album' scenario completely. Colin Greenwood has talked about his dislike of 'having this massive dump every two-and-a-half years, with fanfares and clarion calls'. Fortunately, technology is on their side: more visionary minds within the music business know that the hour[ish]-long CD is as transient a notion as the forty-five-minute LP and online distribution will eventually kill it. Groups will release two songs here, five songs there and eighteen songs when the fancy takes them. Their subscribers will pay on a track-by-track basis and everyone will be much happier. Simple.

For now, however, Radiohead are stuck with the stone-age ritual of promoting their new album via a spurt of British tour dates. In the light of their recent pronouncements, the whole enterprise feels distinctly transitional, a little uncomfortable even. There is also the fact that the gig doesn't mutate into your usual frenzied exorcism – thanks to Radiohead's timing, this is an altogether cagier affair. Out of the twenty-three songs they play tonight, ten have only been heard by band insiders and – thanks to leaks on the web – hard-bitten internet apostles. Just to make things even more interesting, three of those ['You and Whose Army', 'Dollars and Cents', 'I Might Be Wrong'] aren't even on *Kid A*. You begin to suspect, in fact, that the new album won't make complete, coherent sense until its sister record – which the band have hinted will be released pretty quickly – sees the light of day.

Rather inevitably, the audience flits between loud abandon and a mixture of curiosity, nodding appreciation and where's-the-bar bafflement. Radiohead begin with 'The National Anthem', one of the album's more adrenalised songs, and then play 'Bones'. That, in turn, is followed by the altogether more obtuse, pared-down 'Morning Bell'. And so the pattern is repeated: 'My Iron Lung' is succeeded by 'You and Whose Army'; 'No Surprises' by 'Idioteque', 'Airbag' by 'Everything in its Right Place' – for the most part, just Thom and his electric piano. As with most of *Kid A*, it lies several light years from strait-laced, four-four rock.

There is something deeply ill-at-ease about a world in which 'alternative' music is recurrently played to forty thousand people and used to soundtrack the goals of the week. Blur discovered it when they played the entirety of *13* to nonplussed festival audiences in the summer of 1998. 'This is not the idea at all,' you could hear the crowd's mind thinking. 'Stop it now! Get the Stereophonics on!' Needless to say, the spectacle of Radiohead playing their new material in front of eight thousand people in a huge tent explodes the contradiction completely. Most of the new songs singularly fail to suit their surroundings. They'd be much better off in a place about a third of the size. And maybe, just maybe, that's the whole point.

'When you're playing to eight thousand people,' says Ed O'Brien, 'there are going to be people who just want you to play out-and-out rock, but people hopefully know us better now, know that we won't do that. We might do a little bit: we played "The Bends" tonight, which we haven't played for two years . . .'

'People going to the bar during the new stuff?' muses Jonny Greenwood. 'I don't know about that. I'm not sure. Were they leaving? [Fatalistically] Oh, well. Maybe that happens.'

It's now 11 o'clock. Radiohead have long since played their last song, the distinctly anti-climactic 'Motion Picture Soundtrack'. Phil Selway, Colin and Jonny Greenwood and Ed O'Brien are bouncing around the aforementioned after-show gathering. (Thom, in keeping with his own brand values, is nowhere to be seen.) Things have obviously gone pretty well; they give off a relaxed aura no doubt heightened by the fact that there is no gargantuan world tour looming. This trek lasts a mere five weeks, after that they'll decide on their next step. Naturally, all conversations quickly hurtle towards the new record: its obtuseness, its disdain for orthodoxy, the fact that even the most slavish Radiohead disciple will initially get a headache trying to understand it. Have they played it to their friends? What do they think?

'Well,' says Ed O'Brien, 'I played it to my old man. For me, he's always the benchmark. 'Cos he hated *Pablo Honey* – "Couple of good tracks on there, 'Creep' and 'Blow Up' and that's about it." And he was right, I think. And when I gave him *The Bends*, I didn't hear anything for a couple of days and he loved it. Played him *OK Computer*, didn't hear from him for a week and he came back and said, "I think it's amazing." This is a Pink Floyd fan from the '70s! And with this one, he came back and said, "I don't know whether I understand some of the sounds, but I think it's got a quality that someone who's fifty-five can understand." But, generally, he thinks it's more for our generation – ours and sort of sixteen-year-olds. The sounds are a bit too perverse for him.'

About eighteen months ago, when the album's creative hind legs were dragging, it seems that Radiohead came perilously close to splitting up. This was around the time that Ed's diaries took on a tone of something approaching despair and when he asked the not-at-all-rhetorical question, 'Are we moving into Stone Roses territory?'

So – how close was a split?

'I don't know. I mean . . . basically, the questions will always be asked, "Are we still enjoying it? Are we actually doing something different? Are we gaining from doing this?" If we're going over old ground, there's no point doing it. We're obviously not doing it to maintain some kind of lifestyle, because we don't have those kind of lifestyles. You've got to keep learning. And the other thing is, you've got to enjoy it. It was like, "Fucking hell – you get to thirty-two years old, and if you're not enjoying it . . ."'

When Colin Greenwood's problems with the bi-yearly 'dump' are mentioned, Ed's eyes light up. He talks about online opportunities with the kind of visionary zeal that's usually the preserve of internet entrepreneurs. He has seen the future, it seems. It's best described with a rather prosaic word, but that doesn't diminish the excitement. 'Subscription, mate,' Ed froths. 'Subscription. Things are going to change. I think there's an analogy between what's happened with football and what's happened with music. I'm not having a go – you make a good living doing this – but basically bands get screwed by record companies. That's a fact. And that's all going to change: with the onset of online distribution, the whole way that music is made will change. Seventy-eights dictated the way music was made, then 45s, then 33s, then CDs – it's all changed. Now, wouldn't it be great to do a track a month, and do it on subscription and people could download it? And two years down the line, you could do a compilation for those who wanted one. So, ten years down the line, bands could be in the same place that footballers are now – your Coldplays could be on forty grand a week.'

Jonny Greenwood, by contrast, isn't quite so messianic about the whole subject: 'I'm not sure about that. It'd be nice to get things out really quickly, release them as we do them, but where does the specialness go? I remember getting Smiths albums and the whole package, the whole idea, being really amazing. So I'm in two minds about all that.'

Now, of course, we are standing in a completely brand-free environment, finally free from even Ultimate Burger and the toastie van. With no less enthusiasm, Ed is happily manoeuvred towards his fondness for anti-corporate bible *No Logo*. It obviously got to him . . .

'Oh, very much so. It put into words what I was feeling. And I liked the way there was some optimism at the end; the fact that she talks about this growing global mood.'

You reportedly went on a demo recently . . .

'The May Day one. The one in London where they daubed the cenotaph with paint.'

Did you, er, see any action?

'Not really. I remember standing underneath Churchill, with the green Mohican. Was it scary? No. It was a little bit hairy up the front, I suppose.'

The crowd in the outhouse slowly thins out, as the fridge runs dry and their taxis arrive. The youth (and middle-youth) of Newport have long since departed, to either excitedly await the arrival of *Kid A* or quietly wonder what on earth has happened to the group who wrote 'Fake Plastic Trees'.

At around midnight, a diminutive figure scuttles through the dregs of the party. It's Thom Yorke, wearing a mischievous smile. 'Alright?' he says.

'Alright?' replies *Select*.

THE EARNESTNESS OF BEING IMPORTANT

And then he disappears, leaving his guests to pick their way home, through thousands of Budweiser cups.

Six: Whose Army?

1

Review of *Amnesiac*

R. J. Smith, *Village Voice,*
26 June 2001

The prop plane circled the ballpark, trailing the type of banner you might also see at the beach. The message, though, was not what you usually see at LA's Dodger Stadium. 'Radiohead *Amnesiac*' it read, orbiting lazily in the afternoon heat. The guy beside me looked up and pondered. 'I wonder who they think their audience is,' he said.

'You and what army,' I should have answered.

A quick summary before the plane runs out of fuel: in 1997 Radiohead issued *OK Computer,* a panoramic wall of datapanik that critiqued new tech through dazzling use of some very old technology – electric guitars. They sold about 1.5 million US copies, influenced indie rockers and turntablists and a few brave rappers, made a documentary where they begged the world to go away like they were vampires melting in the sunlight. And then they really freaked out. Last year they released *Kid A,* which, besides having really bad cover art, freaked out Radiohead's *fans* – with basically no guitars, no science-fiction narratives, and plenty of emergency-room blips that sounded creepy, downsized, evasive. Radiohead came back from success by basically turning into another band.

The whole record arrived as a statement about what they were not (rockers or pop stars) and what they would not do (tour, advertise, do interviews, shoot videos, enjoy themselves). *Kid A* confused everyone and sold about 800,000 US copies. Most important, with Thom Yorke ready to spontaneously combust, *Kid A* chewed out some negative space, turned down the buzz, and let them get on with making music. The shock is that what the reaction to *Kid A* gave them the courage to do after all – besides reach out to their audience with interviews, videos and airplanes – was release a better *Kid A*. Or maybe that should be said another way. *Kid A* introduced us to their new intentions and what a year ago seemed like a gesture now sounds like – hey! – music.

Amnesiac's songs are taken from the very same sessions that produced *Kid A* and the basic outline is the same: verse-chorus song structures only when the mood hits, texture as important as melody and all over the place the same electronic poptones – the sound of dead brain cells bouncing down an incandescent hospital stairway. Where *Kid A* couldn't help but be seen as a reaction to fame and intense scrutiny, *Amnesiac* illuminates what Radiohead are now and will likely be for a long time: an evasive, wilfully experimental rock band who feel uncomfortable in their own skins.

Which isn't to say that there aren't some subtle distinctions between the two records. If *Kid A*'s songs seem rooted in a pitched battle over the future, *Amnesiac*'s feel recorded the moment after. The songs are obsessed with achieving a sense of peace, a release from a world that's power-mad, polluted and obsessed with technology. *Amnesiac* feels like the first post-WTO record, its anti-globalism so deep at the core of the music that it feels intuitive. This should be no surprise from a band that has plugged Naomi Klein's *No Logo* from the stage, and a singer who has spoken out for third-world-debt forgiveness.

Where the end-of-the-world dread was once framed in slightly corny sci-fi narratives, it now just *is*. Events have conspired to make this music mean more – events and symbols, like the black-clad messengers marching down urban centres all over the world, trashing McDonald's and questioning globalism. And the music has changed too and I bet will continue to change for records to come. They are wrestling with a sound that eschews tension and release and instead mimics processes – decay, disruption, memory.

Yorke is a particularly English sort of social critic: even when he's singing about the end of the world, his words are modestly few. '*While you make pretty speeches/I'm being cut to shreds*,' he croons on 'Like Spinning Plates' and that's about as direct as he gets; he doesn't trust pols ('You and Whose Army' has been described as a slap at Tony Blair), but even less does he trust the confessional mode. So how he conveys his themes ends up a little round-the-way, a strange strategy when your subjects include the heat-death of the universe. Except maybe it's not a strategy after all. It's just him.

He's stubborn in a passive kind of way. Last year he drove journalists crazy by refusing to answer questions except through odd, shattered online dispatches; the truly twisted thing about this was that driving journalists crazy didn't even seem to provide much pleasure. Thom doesn't know from fun. He doesn't seem to get pleasure, either, from telling Radiohead fans in 'Knives Out' that guitars are never to fully return. '*I want you to know/He's not coming back/He's bloated and frozen*', he sings at half the tempo the band is playing. But then: '*Still there's no point in letting it go to waste.*'

And the rest of the band? They hang with him. Yorke once described his relations with his bandmates as akin to the UN, where he's the United States. He's a behemoth more equal than others, but if the other guys have strong feelings about that, they hide them well. They hide themselves well, too, when the music requires it – drummer Phil Selway replaced by a hard drive in one cut, re-emerging on 'Pyramid Song' with a head-bobbing full trap set flourish. These UN delegates craft a sound that takes in the stubbornly passive techno of the Warp label and folk-rock as embraced by R.E.M. and Sigur Rós, a sound that wants to embrace '60s big-band jazz but doesn't quite know how – 'Life in a Glass House' is like Mingus produced by George Martin, a great way to end the record.

They must have voted as a bloc to come up with 'I Might Be Wrong', which sports a fat blues guitar line lodged like a mote in God's eye. Here they are a band in the pre-industrial sense: you know, with guitars and a drummer and stuff. But then they flip the script and the chip skips and they become a symphony or a hard drive.

It might get a little random, without the ten-ton prude at the microphone. But as long as Thom Yorke sings with a disengaged voice that seeps out of the muck like swamp gas and as long as his lyrics continue in their current clipped mode, he and Radiohead might just remain brilliant, strong-willed and downright clammy. The kind of people who will smash a Starbucks and then embarrassedly excuse themselves and withdraw into the dust.

2

How Radiohead Learned to Loathe the Bomb

Peter Murphy, *Hot Press*,
11 October 2001

In the days following the terrorist attacks on New York, the Pentagon and Pittsburgh on September 11 2001, Radiohead were not the kind of band anyone wanted to listen to. As news networks broadcast raw hand-held footage shot by bystanders – film that probably cost a couple of dollars to process but looked like scenes out of *Independence Day* – and as surrealist montage and reportage fused into one, this writer had to force himself to play their last three albums. Too emotional. Too paranoid. Too aware.

Thom Yorke, a singer plagued by *'unborn chicken voices'* – the Chicken Licken of rock'n'roll, in fact – might've wondered if it wasn't an acorn that hit him on the head but a piece of the sky, a chunk of American Airlines Flight 11 from Boston, slicing through a stitch in time. As far back as *OK Computer*, you could find eerie pre-echoes in songs like 'Airbag' (*'In the next world*

war/In a jack-knifed juggernaut/I am born again'), which m.
been written by Jeff Bridges' character in *Fearless*, a guy
walks away untouched from an air accident with delusions of
immortality. In 'Idioteque' off *Kid A*, stray lines escape the cold
Kubrick surfaces of the music like interplanetary SOS signals: '*Ice
age comin', ice age comin'*... *We're not scare mongering*... *This
is really happening*...'

Of course, Radiohead couldn't have predicted any of this, but
sometimes the arts have an uneasy relationship to ESP. We've all
heard about the cover art of hip hop act the Coup's *Party Music*
and its eerie resemblance to the mutilated Twin Towers. Primal
Scream have been playing a new song called 'Bomb the Pentagon'
all summer. New York resident David Bowie posted a message on
his website saying no one could've imagined what happened on
9/11, seemingly forgetting his own doomsday soothsayings on
'Five Years' and *Diamond Dogs*. Mere days after the disaster,
Martin Amis wrote that 'the temperature of planetary fear has
been lifted toward the feverish; "the world hum", in Don DeLillo's
phrase, is now as audible as tinnitus.'

Your reporter didn't want to be catching a train to Belfast; he
wanted to be under the table in the nearest tavern. If the purpose
of terrorism is to inflict terror, then I didn't want to give the
perpetrators the pleasure. I wanted to be frivolous. I wanted to
forget.

But Radiohead wouldn't let me.

When the world goes to war, the weird turn pro. Throughout the
last century, creative minds of every discipline have attempted to
make sense of war by making war on sense. The responses to the

social traumas of the times – not just international conflict but industrial revolution, racial tension, technological convulsions – took the form of a whole prism of isms: cubism, surrealism, dadaism, modernism, post-modernism, abstract expressionism, vorticism. After World War I, representational art couldn't hack it as a means of conveying The Horror. Strapping young boys went into battle and came back in cubist bits and pieces. T. S. Eliot's *The Waste Land* was one of the first of the strange new twentieth-century visions, a panorama of echoes with its texts edited – or rather, cut up – by father of modernism Ezra Pound. Joyce and Beckett followed. Sergei Eisenstein's *Battleship Potemkin* found its image in Francis Bacon. Fritz Lang's *Metropolis*, Charlie Chaplin's *Modern Times* and Lorca's *Poet in New York* dwelled on the dehumanising forces at work in urban societies.

Elsewhere, Schoenberg and Stravinsky punched holes in classical music for Stockhausen, Cage and Riley to peer through and even folk tunes like 'I Wish I Was a Mole in the Ground', a strange ditty recorded by Bascom Lamar Lunsford in the late 1920s, corresponded with Breton and Buñuel's surrealist manifestos. A decade later, milestones such as Picasso's *Guernica* and Dali's *Autumn Cannibalism* refracted the ravages of the Spanish Civil War. After bearing witness to the slaughter of innocents, neither painter could ever see the human form in the same way again. Similarly, in 1939, Billie Holiday recorded Abel Meeropol's 'Strange Fruit', written about lynchings in the deep south, a song full of strange and grotesque images of bodies hanging like fruit for the crows to pluck and the wind to suck.

Rock'n'roll itself was born in the shadow of the bomb: that crazy cowboy riding the missile in *Dr Strangelove* could've been Sam Phillips or Jack Clement. Ginsberg, Kerouac, Burroughs,

Pollock and Charlie Parker tried to expel through their work the dread that entered the species' nervous system at Hiroshima–Nagasaki, 1945. Thirty years after World War II, Captain Beefheart's 'Dachau Blues' from *Trout Mask Replica* attempted to translate the unspeakable truths of the death camps – the 'Bluebeard's castles of our century' in the words of critic George Steiner – through dada blues and spasmodic jazz.

The 1960s brought their own shit-storms. Bob Dylan wrote 'A Hard Rain's a-Gonna Fall' in '63 as a spooked response to the Cuban missile crisis. It was, in the words of biographer and folk expert Robert Shelton, a 'poetic cosmos whose extremes of horror and lost tenderness somehow match the hells and heavens of modern reality'. At Woodstock 1969, at the height of the Vietnam war, Jimi Hendrix made a napalm painting out of the 'Star Spangled Banner'.

Neil Young reprised this act with Crazy Horse in 1991, taking Sonic Youth on tour during the Gulf War and saturating songs like 'Blowin' in the Wind', 'Powderfinger' and 'Cortez The Killer' with white-hot hails of feedback. U2 hauled their Zoo TV extravaganza across America soon after, parodying the madness of a conflict that for many seemed to exist only in the hysterical nightmare mind of CNN.

And in the last years of the century, Radiohead perfected their own form of comic-paranoiac expressionism, a sound that encapsulated, in the word of one writer, 'what it's like to feel terrified by the times'. In September 2001, in the wake of those attacks on a no-longer-impregnable Fortress America, Radiohead were the last band you'd want to see live, but maybe the one that mattered most. The night of the eleventh, they were on stage in Berlin, Thom Yorke dedicating 'You and Whose

Army' to US President George Bush. As the world entered a period of queasiness on a par with the Bay of Pigs, the band journeyed on to Belfast, opening that show with 'The National Anthem' and sounding like – well, there's no other metaphor for it – a war machine being cranked into life. The pre-show tape selection of crooned ballads and doo-wop tunes only added to the eerie 1930s' atmosphere. Over two hours and ten minutes, Radiohead played a taut set, with songs like 'Morning Bell', 'Paranoid Android', 'Pyramid Song' and 'Exit Music (For a Film)' all taking on chilling new meanings, until eventually the tension dissipated into 'How To Disappear Completely' and everyone left the building feeling no better but perhaps a little less alone.

———

Anybody want a drink before the war? Champagne in a plastic tumbler, in a too-bright room. It's an hour or so after that show in Belfast's Odyssey Arena and I've just been asking Radiohead guitarist Jonny Greenwood if there'd been any talk of how to approach the night's set in the light – or darkness – of the week's events.

'No, none at all,' he says. 'I think everyone in the room had gone through the same week. You lose the will to be upbeat, obviously.'

Was he tuned into the resonances in songs like 'Airbag' and 'Idioteque' on stage?

'Yeah, obviously, but that happens all the time, I suppose, resonances with what's going on. Although, let's face it, the last week was the biggest event of the century.'

He's picking listlessly at the subject rather than getting his teeth into it. I take it to be the infamous Radiohead reticence or a guitarist's prerogative. Only later do I hear that his wife can't get a flight out of Israel. As Jonny's bassist brother Colin enters the room, I'm talking about how the *Kid A* and *Amnesiac* albums reminded me of the consparanoia TV shows that prevailed from the late '70s to the mid-'80s, as unease in the Middle East infected another generation of post-bomb babies. I'm thinking of *Quatermass*, *Edge of Darkness* . . .

'*Threads*,' remembers Colin, referring to the documentary style projection of a nuclear winter that put the fear of God into every schoolchild old enough to understand its implications.

Jonny: 'I remember going into primary school and everyone saying, "There's going to be a nuclear war today."'

'The paranoia,' continues Colin, 'and *Day of the Triffids*. It's weird playing these shows at the moment. You play some of the songs and it just feels too much. But playing Berlin was really good two nights ago, Tuesday night. Eleven thousand people had bought tickets and they all came and there were like forty walk-ups.'

Earlier, as Thom jerked like a wired-up rag doll to his band's relentless *motorik* during 'Idioteque', singing '*Women and children first*' in a shrill, panicked voice, I kept thinking of Martin Amis's nuclear war essays, written under the influence of terrified new-fatherhood in the mid-'80s. Some men find in the role of parent new survival mechanisms, reasons to be cheerful parts one, two and three. Others become susceptible to all manner of survival phobias. A week after the Twin Towers, Amis was reprising those essays in a *Guardian* feature entitled 'The First Circle of Hell'. 'The illusion is this,' he wrote. 'Mothers and fathers need to feel that they can protect their children. They can't, of course, and never could, but they need to feel that they can. What once seemed more or less impossible – their protection – now seems obviously and palpably inconceivable. So from now on we will have to get by without that need to feel.'

Thom Yorke became a father some months ago – one wonders how it affected him?

'I think with him it's definitely the former rather than the latter,' Colin says. 'It's really interesting, 'cos it's obviously been so good for him as an experience. I think now with Noah he definitely has that pragmatism of having a child and that's what's important. I was talking to him about it in Berlin. If you're not gonna be with your kid, then you might as well make sure it's worthwhile being away. And that's been great, I think. He's been less obsessing about the potential perils of the future and more thinking about making the moment worth it and making time matter. It's fucking great, 'cos all you wanna do is see everyone happy that you've been working with for fifteen years. And you can see with Thom and Phil, they're really enjoying making this work *because* they want to be home as well.'

Jonny: 'I think it makes you aware of what's important about making music and what's not worth wasting – all that pain and the unproductive side gets avoided.'

Flashback to another moment from the Belfast show: the refrain of 'You and Whose Army' struck a chord with the crowd for obvious reasons, but was offset by the rather amusing premise of Yorke inviting '*the Holy Roman Empire*' outside for a scrap. On the night, it sounds like a guy arguing both ends of the sectarian divide in one song.

'It's a good example of what I love about his lyrics,' observes Colin, 'that combination of direct involvement and aggro and that sublimation at the end of it, taking it somewhere else and elevating it at the end. That's a mark of his great gift as a songwriter, to make you feel things viscerally and transport you from that point to somewhere else.'

Of course, the inverse of that is 'Exit Music (For a Film)', the tale of two lovers fleeing from peril, ending with the softly sung line 'We hope that you choke'.

'That's true,' Colin concedes, 'his voice always jars for me at the end, when he's singing that and people are singing along with it as well, but in a good way, it's a good dissonance.'

One thing about Radiohead in 2001 – they've become almost an amorphous organism. Anyone who saw the grim documentary *Meeting People is Easy* will understand exactly why the musicians and Yorke in particular have grown so wary of the kind of Best Band in the World hoopla that accumulated around them between *The Bends* and *OK Computer*. These days, they infiltrate the culture in more insidious ways. In an interview last year, Brad Pitt compared them to Beckett. There's a veiled reference to 'Exit Music (For a Film)' early in Chuck Palahniuk's novel *Choke*. Neil Jordan wanted to use their music in *In Dreams* but couldn't because he feared the sounds would overpower the visuals. Strange bedfellows until you consider the inevitable connections between the work of all concerned and recent events. Pitt starred in the film of Palahniuk's *Fight Club*, whose premise centred on the notion of domestic lo-tech terrorism. Palahniuk's novel *Survivor* is a tale narrated into the black box recorder of a crashing plane by Tender Branson, the last living member of the Creedish Death Cult. Neil Jordan, for his part, explored the doomsday atmospheres of the Cuban missile crisis in his adaptation of Patrick McCabe's *The Butcher Boy*.

Mind you, all this is news to Jonny Greenwood – he still has trouble getting his head around hearing Radiohead's music disseminated through mass media. 'You see it on trailers for television shows, from football to documentaries about Concorde,' he marvels. 'It's strange how it seeps through and doesn't get heard that often in other ways. The first time you hear your music on the radio, it's really weird that it's coming out of a box where nothing's moving. I still can't get over the shock of it. And most times people don't know that it's Radiohead, in a way.'

The Radiohead on stage tonight are the end product of a process of deconstruction that began shortly after the *OK Computer* campaign. When the quintet reconvened to record a follow-up to that album in Paris and Copenhagen at the start of 1999, they were a band of blind men holding different parts of the elephant. Yorke, the group's benevolent dictator (he once likened Radiohead to the UN, with himself as America), seemed to be fighting shy of melody, choruses, even lyric. Under the influence of Krautrock and the Warp label back catalogue, his strategies were radical to the point of advocating that the players abandon their chosen instruments. Guitarist Ed O' Brien, on the other hand, figured they should record an album of straight-ahead three-minute tunes. Jonny Greenwood didn't necessarily agree with either, being in thrall to composers like Olivier Messiaen – one of the pioneers of the ondes Martenot, an instrument that would feature largely on the new sounds alongside a whole battery of black boxes and analogue synthesisers – and Charles Mingus.

Jonny: 'The Mingus thing started with the excitement of discovering those big-band records that weren't how big bands are normally perceived. Suddenly there's this chaotic, dark, really vicious music. But then we had to obviously hire in a brass section and try and get them to play like that, and me and Thom were in the room trying to conduct and there's not many gestures you can do! But they were amazing, and really young as well.'

———

The *Kid A* sessions were strained affairs as the band groped to find common reference points. There were echoes of U2's *Achtung Baby* and R.E.M.'s *Monster* traumas: different configurations of personnel fighting to reconcile melody with experimentalism.

'It's also the relationship between all the people involved as well,' Colin reflects. 'It's like a mid-life crisis, whether you still like each other or are you happy making compromises and stuff like that. We were trying to find another way of doing what we do without ending up in a similar sort of space as *OK Computer*, where there was this feeling that you were being fast-tracked into being processed as the next R.E.M. or U2 type thing. I'm not slagging them off, but in terms of how they're perceived by people. But I think it was also just a fear of putting a record into a shop. I think we had to definitely rethink a lot of things. They were studio albums as well, which was the first time we'd done that in a way, because before we'd always recorded music we'd played live, like *OK Computer* and *The Bends*.'

When *Kid A* was released in October 2000, its abandoning of guitar-based song structures was received with some incomprehension by not just the band's critics, but many of their peers. The album got guardedly positive reviews, but one often suspected this was because the writers were too chicken-hearted to admit they didn't get it. In retrospect, *Kid A* was as misunderstood as *OK Computer* was overrated. It wasn't even that much of a departure, especially if you figured the intervening *Airbag/How Am I Driving?* extended EP into the equation.

'It's very interesting, that whole diffusing a sticky situation,' Colin says. 'Nick Hornby wrote that thing in the *New Yorker* where he thought we were terrible because we'd sort of betrayed the faith that people had after *The Bends*, that sort of nostalgic way of writing. But I think that record is really fantastic, and *Amnesiac* is more a sort of echo of what we'd done with *Kid A*. It was a fine line of wanting to do something that was creative and also wanting to try and back away from all the media nonsense. And I think it's a sideways thing; looking back on it, *Kid A* was really strong, it wasn't just avoiding people who wanted us to do another *OK Computer.*'

I put it to Jonny that a lot of the *Kid A* criticism was like football commentary, as in 'they're not fielding their best players' or 'they're not playing to their strengths': Thom's tunes and Jonny's guitar.

'It's as though lots of people who really liked us heard a few bands coming out who sounded similar,' he considers, 'and they were thinking, "Oh, Radiohead are going to show us how to do it!" They wanted us to sound like the bands who sound like us, but better!'

'It was spurned-lover stuff,' adds Colin. 'I think it was a real fight in the studio as well. There was that conflict between wanting to do something that was good, but also wanting to do something that was unexpected. That was the big tension. You have to deal with the concept that you have to put a record out into the public arena and if you read the papers you're obviously aware of where other people want you to go. And if that's not where Thom is comfortable, it causes a lot of tension and it can impact upon the creativity as well. You feel that the tools you have to do your music have been taken away from you and sort of appropriated and debased.'

Jonny: 'I remember a version of "Motion Picture Soundtrack" that we recorded that had the kick and the snare and it just had no magic to it and the other version was far better. The point is, we played both versions to our managers and they said, "Yeah, it's better but it's not going to sell as much!"' Of course, the version without the backbeat made the final cut. But interestingly enough, American audiences, long ridiculed for their conservatism, welcomed *Kid A* and its sister album *Amnesiac* with open arms.

'We've had the most support in the world from America on the last two records,' Colin says. 'And this last touring that we've done in America, playing those open-air concerts, the references we always like to make are bands like the Grateful Dead, some concerts like Phish did, Neil Young I guess, a sort of roaming festival, open air, recording bootlegs vibe. And it was really a privilege to be able to play open-air in Chicago or in Seattle or Liberty Park right next to the Trade Towers for two nights; it was the most beautiful setting. What we mean in America is completely different to anywhere else in the world. You can lose a lot of baggage halfway across the Atlantic and you can go to America and take them on their terms, not English press terms. And we've definitely relished that.'

So what next for Radiohead? Contrary as ever, they seem freed up and optimistic in a world that feels anything but. The forthcoming *I Might Be Wrong* mini-album will showcase the band's robust live arrangements of material from the last two albums. After that, Colin talks about a return to premiering new songs live before re-entering the studio.

'I think we're in a very similar situation now as we were going into *OK Computer*,' he suggests. 'I think we had to do two records and take time out to get back to that point, 'cos definitely, by the end of touring *OK Computer*, you felt you were being *propelled*. And because a lot of the structures on *Kid A* and *Amnesiac* were a lot looser, you have to improvise and make up things a tiny bit, so there's more room for random accidents. Whereas with *OK Computer* we'd honed it to this stadium-fulfilling thing, every song had the same thing played every night and it stopped being musical and became more about repetition and less about performance. It's very interesting, the body language of people on stage. [With Thom] it's all from his body. His dad was a boxer and he taught Thom how to do some boxing when he was a kid and you can see that sort of physical, brawling, punching quality. He's got such amazing, rhythmic. intuitive drive.'

———

After the show, Thom's not doing press but he *is* hanging out in hospitality. Wearing a scrub of beard, he looks, as ever, like a man on leave from the Carter Family's country noir classic 'Worried Man Blues', the story of a guy who lays down to sleep by a river and wakes up in chains. A couple of hours earlier, he'd dedicated 'Street Spirit' to 'all the Americans who can't get home' and I was reminded of what it must have felt like watching Neil and Crazy Horse on that Gulf war campaign. Elsewhere in the show, as I scouted for a line that might make sense amidst images of a traumatised fireman breaking off from digging in the Manhattan ruins to speak to a priest, or of exhausted medics cutting themselves and putting salt on the wounds to stay awake, the refrain from 'Lucky' seemed to hang in the air long after it was uttered.

'Pull me out of the air crash . . . we are standing on the edge.'

3

Review of *I Might Be Wrong* – *Live Recordings*

Stephen Dalton, *Uncut*,
December 2001

D rawing a line under *Kid A* and *Amnesiac*, this eight-track mini-album performs an efficient job of reminding us that Radiohead remain powerful live performers.

The duty of concert recordings to re-invent studio blueprints is conscientiously applied, with off-kilter arrangements, extraneous noise and frothing psycho-jabber galore. Thus 'The National Anthem' is a brutalist riot of dirty scuzz-bass and radio static, 'Idioteque' a ragged post-junglist meltdown, 'Everything in its Right Place' a chattering menagerie of self-sampling vocal fragments on an infinite fractal loop. Rock'n'-frugging-roll, dude.

Thom Yorke builds to a fiery freak-out in almost every song, spitting death-rattle bile in 'I Might Be Wrong' and 'Dollars and Cents'. But there are moments of pure, unforced beauty, too, notably the queasy piano reading of 'Like Spinning Plates' and a debut airing of the lusty, much-bootlegged acoustic rarity 'True

Love Waits'. Anyone still hammering the flagrantly untrue 'no tunes' argument against Radiohead should start their re-education here.

All the same, a vague air of missed opportunity hangs over this frustratingly short snapshot. Many stand-outs from the live shows have been overlooked: the luminous 'You and Whose Army', say, or the exquisitely sour 'Knives Out'. The pointed lack of material from before *Kid A* also seems perverse, denying the historical and sonic framework that these incendiary concerts provided. The scaling-down of ambition which some dissenters detected in these albums is thus reinforced, when actually their live presentation proved the opposite.

But for all their self-imposed limitations, at least Radiohead prove here that they can conjure blazing intensity, visceral physicality and raging rock dynamics from even wilfully opaque jazzoid chuffing. No surprises, then, but some grandly fucked-up old friends.

Seven: The Most Gigantic Lying Mouth of All Time

1

Review of
Hail to the Thief

Will Hermes, *Spin*,
26 June 2003

I t's all right – you can admit it. When the bedroom lights are
out and all you can see are the shooting stars on your screen
saver, you've heard yourself whisper: 'It's so not OK, computer.
You mediate our work, our play, even our sex lives. Do you have
to mess with our rock bands, too?'

It's an understandable response to the dystopian blip pop of
Radiohead's 2000–01 tag team, *Kid A* and *Amnesiac*. But it's a
misguided one. Electronic music has informed the band's
approach ever since singer Thom Yorke was a club DJ in college
during the early '90s. And anyone who's caught them in concert
during the last few years – or heard 2001's *I Might Be Wrong: Live
Recordings* – has felt how bone-shaking those two albums are at
their core. If anything, *Kid A* and *Amnesiac* have improved with
time; if they don't rival the passive-aggressive guitar grandeur of
OK Computer, they're logical extensions of it.

Anyway, *Hail to the Thief* obscures the are-we-rock-or-not? debate from the get-go. '2+2=5' opens with an electronic sputter that turns out to be the crackle of a guitar amp, not a laptop. A sly digital beatbox gives way to drummer Phil Selway's very human pounding; the song itself is a schiz-out that mixes the tantrums of the Pixies with the sad dreamscapes of Sigur Rós, two of Yorke's most beloved bands. From track to track, *Thief* seesaws between the chill of sequencers and the warmth of fingers on strings and keys, like roommates having a stereo war. Yet the tension somehow holds things together – when the piano rises from the loop quicksand of 'Backdrifts' or jostles with the clipped beats of 'Sit Down. Stand Up', it feels more like a band playing to a multitude of strengths than the formal wrestling of *Kid A*.

But like all their records, *Hail to the Thief* is driven by psychic stress – in this case, the strain placed on people of conscience by a world in which so-called democracies bum-rush the electoral process and attack nations in lieu of practising diplomacy. Beginning with its title (a common Bush-dissing protest-poster slogan), the record is filled with war-haunted narrators ready to sandbag and hide ('2+2=5') or lie down in a bunker ('I Will'). Some of them imagine walking amid bullets ('Scatterbrain') and dragging out their dead ('A Wolf at the Door'); others want to suck your blood or eat you alive. And naysayers are powerless. '*We tried, but there was nothing we could do*,' croons Yorke on 'Backdrifts', a conspiracy blues riding antsy digital beats. '*All tapes have been erased.*' The record's most lacerating track, 'Myxomatosis' – named after a virus used to curb rabbit populations in Europe – asserts that even those brave enough to speak out are '*edited, fucked up, strangled, beaten up*' by a news media whose gatekeeping policy Yorke nails: 'No one likes a smart-ass/But we all like stars'. (Word to Michael Moore.)

But Hail to the Thief is too impressionistic to be reduced to a political screed. Like even Radiohead's most abstract work, it's strewn with the burnished, elongated melodies that have made them the most diversely covered band since the Beatles: see classical pianist Christopher O'Riley (True Love Waits), jazzman Brad Mehldau ('Exit Music (For a Film)'), the Flaming Lips ('Knives Out'), and the surprisingly hot Strung Out on OK Computer: The String Quartet Tribute to Radiohead.

It's also a reminder of the group's key paradox: no other band makes fear and sorrow seem so empowering. 'We're not an indie band,' Yorke once insisted; Radiohead refuse to disappear up their aesthetic arses. Instead, they pitch a big – if strangely decorated – tent and invite a crowd, on their own terms. Because as grim as things may get, there's still strength in numbers.

2

Make Rock Not War!
An Interview with Thom Yorke

Will Self, *GQ*,
July 2003

─────────

In the medieval trench that's Turl Street in Oxford, Thom Yorke, the city's most famously and aggressively diffident son, rocks back and forth in his blue-and-white basketball shoes, howling with derision.

'Oh no!' he yelps, 'I can't stand this stuff! I used to walk past this window and see if I could pick out just one thing – one thing I could wear.'

He moves on from the dummies wearing waxed jackets, grey flannels and tweeds, to the shoe shop next door. 'These aren't so bad,' I say. 'Couldn't you cope with at least a pair of shoes?' He scrutinises the rows of Church's handmade boots and brogues with some care, before conceding that if he had to, he'd be prepared to don 'those up there'. And what were they, the proverbial glass slippers that the Cinderella of rock would be bespoken for? Why, suede loafers, of course.

Yorke was looking both suede-coloured and a loafer when I'd found him in the coffee lounge of the Randolph hotel an hour or so earlier. The Randolph is the kind of four-square hotel you'd expect to find in the centre of Oxford. It has an air of solid eighteenth century prosperity about it: a few bewigged burghers wouldn't look out of place, stuffing their faces with boiled beef before climbing into their broughams for a drive round this immemorial seat of learning. Yorke was drinking black coffee from a half-plunged cafetiere and glancing at the headlines of that morning's *Guardian*. His state of modish *deshabillé* – open-necked blue-and-white striped shirt, flared jeans and a curious, round-necked nylon zip-up waistcoat – combined with a couple of days' gingery stubble and mussed hair, to give him an anachronistic feel: twenty-first-century bedsit-boy cut and pasted on to the coaching house's sepia interior.

Yorke began talking politics without any preamble, and so our encounter was immediately and incontrovertibly datelined: 25.4.03. The fall of Baghdad happened only sixteen days previously and its shattered brick and mortar was on his mind more than other kinds of rock. Yorke has been drifting into more and more explicitly political waters for the past three years. Together with Bob Geldof and Bono, he took up cudgels on behalf of the Jubilee 2000 campaign to 'drop the debt' of the developing world and, while he hasn't exactly taken the hypocritical step of embracing the anti-capitalist movement, he's been making quite a few noises-off about greed and rapaciousness. On the first Sunday of the Anglo-American attack on Iraq, both of us had attended the demonstration at RAF Fairford in Gloucestershire, the airbase from which the B52 bombers set off with their bunker-busters, daisy-cutters and all the other horrible exploded euphemisms of warfare.

And now there was *Hail to the Thief*, Radiohead's first album in three years, and surely its title alone was a provocative tilt at the government of George W. Bush? Certainly, Yorke was concerned to put his seriously bitter credentials on the coffee table. 'Did you hear John Humphrys interviewing Geoff Hoon on the radio this morning?' he asked me. 'He was pushing Hoon hard on the issue of weapons of mass destruction and basically Hoon didn't have an answer for any of it, couldn't justify why it is that they won't let the UN weapons inspectors back in.'

I asked him if he was politicised when he was at Exeter University and Yorke displayed his trademark diffidence. 'On and off. I didn't like all the factionalism and the language you have to adopt. But I was involved a bit, we managed to ban some of the Young Conservatives from the student union and I was proud of that.'

His time at university wasn't exactly formative for Yorke; instead I think it probably confirmed him as a stayer more than a goer. In previous interviews he's waxed disconsolately about his discombobulated childhood, the frequent changes of school and the bullying at those schools because of his paralysed eye (a congenital defect that's left him with an oddly profound monocular stare). But to me he seemed emotionally grounded and secure. He conceded – albeit uneasily – that his had been a happy – if profoundly unmusical – family. 'My parents didn't even have a hi-fi until I got one, they had one of those radio-cassette things.'

His father, a salesman for a company that made mass spectrometers and other equipment used in the nuclear industry 'spent the 1960s walking around with a test tube of plutonium in his hand'. There was Thom and his younger brother, who ended up attending Oxford University. 'He was at Hertford College.

I hung around a bit with his friends. What I remember most was that, however trashed the place got the night before, these people would come and clear it all up in the morning.'

Yorke was a musical prodigy of sorts, and by the age of thirteen he was strumming a guitar and composing lyrics. A half-generation too young for punk, his early influences – he confessed with a wry smile – included naff Japan ('I loved David Sylvian's voice') and the predictable R.E.M..

Yorke's earliest musical forays were deconstructive. 'You always have that "I can do better than that" impulse and more specifically you want to find out a way of doing it.' But pretty soon he was gigging at weekends, with the support of his parents. 'They heard the music all the time coming from above their TV, because that's where my room was. But they were pretty good – they could've been a lot worse. They bought me amps and shit.'

I asked him if he got a major buzz out of that early gigging, but he seemed nonplussed. 'It's difficult to remember what it was like before we made records, but I do remember being surprised that people liked it. When you're on stage you feel you've got something, but you're not sure that it will last. I get much higher off of it now that I'm better at it.'

My Struggle wouldn't be a good title for Thom Yorke's autobiography. Far from being forced to hump their equipment around the small club circuit, Yorke and his boyhood jamming friends – then tentatively named On A Friday – had a record deal within months of going at it full time. These were the very same geezers who kept returning to Oxford at regular intervals throughout their various college careers to rehearse. In fact, the reason why I think Yorke is so grounded is that he's always stayed so decisively put, either geographically in Oxford or emotionally within the same cliques of friends and colleagues. Twelve years on, he's still playing with the same band of brothers and he's still with the partner he met at college in Exeter.

Rachel was one of the group of friends Yorke met at the art college where he did the fine art half of his degree. Another friend from this era does the artwork for Radiohead's albums and he told me that he was still in touch with the rest of the art students he hung out with at that time. Long-lasting relationships with friends and his lover, regular contact with his parents – particularly now that Yorke has given them a grandson, Noah – and a rootedness in Oxford that's reminiscent of his friend Michael Stipe's commitment to Athens, Georgia. None of this speaks of a particularly tortured soul and, while I don't doubt that his much-flagged breakdown after the worldwide success of *OK Computer* was traumatic, Yorke seems to have come through the psychic proving ground of rock stardom with his head screwed on both tight and right.

Still, there was a hint of paranoia as we walked out into the slightly gloomy noontime in the rain-splattered heart of England.

Reaching the junction of Broad Street, the Cornmarket and George Street – the very commercial hub of the city – Yorke pointed to a row of bars and said, 'That's where they herd everyone on a Saturday night now. The police post patrols at both ends of the street, and if it all goes off they shut the place down. Oxford can be pretty heavy on a Saturday night.'

Next off it's the surveillance cameras – which are mocked up to look like old fashioned street lamps – that claim his attention. Later in our ramble, Yorke talks about the aggro on the train up from London (a case of *KO Commuter*?). And when I call his attention to how preoccupied he appears by random acts of senseless violence, he admits that he was involved in a fight as recently as two years ago. 'This guy said something as I went by, he obviously recognised me and stupidly I followed after him and asked him to repeat it. Next thing I know he's swinging on me, kicking me and all these people are just walking past, totally ignoring it.'

A slight, five-foot seven-inch man, it's easy to see why Yorke's boyhood sense of vulnerability has been carried forward into adulthood, preserved in the aspic of fame and emolument. Yorke obviously hated the notoriety that went with the massive commercial success of *OK Computer*, and to me he said that 'I don't want to do that stadium-rock thing'. He said that he was no longer recognised in the street and that Stipe had taught him how to make himself 'invisible', just by assuming the correct and confident mental attitude as he walks down a street. I dare say I must've been queering Yorke's incognito – with our disparity in heights and our obviously purposeless trawl about the teeming streets we must've appeared an odd couple – but during the three hours I spent with him he was recognised four times and asked for autographs. By the time we were walking back across the centre of town he suggested we avoid the busiest streets, clearly fed up with being spotted.

Earlier, propped on the high wall of one of the college gardens, we looked down on the immaculate lawns surrounding the Radcliffe Camera, one of those domed Renaissance Oxford buildings which give the city an almost oriental air. Yorke pointed to one of the alcoves let into the Camera and said, 'That's where we did a lot of drinking when we were teenagers.' A remark that led us inevitably on to the subject of drugs and intoxication in general. 'I was always advised not to do acid,' Yorke said. 'My friends thought that what with everything that was going on in my head already it wouldn't be a good idea.' I observed that I hadn't ever read or heard him make any comment on intoxication, whether in connection with his own creativity or simple hedonism. 'I've never wanted it to colour the music,' he said, 'that's why I leave it open.' When I pressed him he said, 'Obviously it's important not to stay like this' – he swept a hand over his sober mien – 'all the time. You get it with music anyway, but alcohol is grotesquely inappropriate for making the required change . . . '

'And what would be better?' I pressed him again.

'Oh, I dunno, something prescribed, I s'pose.'

'What, Prozac?' I quipped, but this was as far as Yorke would go on the matter.

He doesn't go much further down the road to rock excess in any other direction either.

A long-time vegetarian, he 'gave up meat in the early '90s; touring was playing havoc with my digestion'. Smoking roll-ups also had to go. 'It was destroying my voice, I'd make it halfway through a gig and then it'd crack.' But Yorke was happy to confess to getting badly snake-bitten in the past. 'The first time I drank them I had to go to the doctor the next day because I was still seeing double and he told me that I had alcohol poisoning.' But he conceded that this kind of heavy drinking had also been jettisoned. Yorke seems to have entered the detached house of common sense through practising this kind of restraint, rather than pressing on to the illusory palace of wisdom offered by class As.

Achingly sensible chap.

As we walked down the passageway that leads between Merton

and Corpus Christi Colleges and out on to the green expanse of Christ Church meadow, I began to feel a little like the decadent Sebastian Flyte in Evelyn Waugh's *Brideshead Revisited*. Yorke was coming on so cuddly and sexless that he could've been Flyte's teddy-bear Aloysius. What about groupies? I wheedled. Wasn't it part of your perception of rock stardom when you were plonking away on your guitar in your bedroom? Yorke laughed raucously. 'Ha-ha, yeah, man, it never happened. I'm just too bloody-minded; if I see other people doing it, then I just don't want to do it. It's as simple as that. I remember being at the Brits one time and Oasis were doing their Oasis thing and it was all very amusing and everyone was very amused in their tolerant manner. It made me want to do the exact fucking opposite. That's just me.'

This English reticence extended into Yorke's money talk. Presumably, I pointed out, he had cartloads of wonga? 'Probably not as much as you'd think, but yeah, it's all right.'

But d'you live an expensive lifestyle or what?

'I consider it to be slightly too expensive, yeah. But that's mostly wrapped up in the two houses that I've bought.'

You're not into larging it, are you, you're not that kind of person?

'I'm almost pathologically the opposite. I ring up my bank manager to ask him if it's all right for me to buy a Mini.'

And does he laugh?

'Yeah.'

Do you give it away?

'What?'

The money.

'What, *charity*?' Yorke affected a twee tone.

Yeah. Will you be divvying it up for Iraq?

'Well, I keep cutting out those Red Cross ads, so I guess I'll do that, but fucking hell, the Americans should be forking out for that.'

This was a rare flash of contentiousness and, when the two of us sat down for lunch at a Thai restaurant just off the High Street, Yorke's remarks about the very meat of *Hail to the Thief* were as vegetarian as his pak krua noodles. 'I'm not quite sure how we arrived at that title, we had lots and lots of ideas kicking around, and that was the one where everybody said "Yes" . . . but I don't think it's highly antagonistic, because out of this week's current context it sounds to me something from a fairy tale. I think the reason the others were into it was because it fitted the way the record sounded. The political stuff is only there because of the lyrics and the lyrics are only written that way because that's the way they came out. It wasn't like I sat down to write something political, but my mindset is more immersed in that than it was four or five years ago. There are a lot of reasons for that: a lot of it comes from listening to the radio compulsively because it coincides with my son's eating times.'

But the political climate in the States had definitely been hardening to opponents of the war and so I was interested in whether Yorke thought the album's title would affect its reception in America. Would Radiohead be touring? 'Oh yeah – well, hopefully.'

I've only done one American interview, but the interesting thing is that it really isn't as bad as you might assume.

'Obviously this is something we've been talking to our press people over there about, and they say, don't worry about it, it doesn't mean shit. This debate is throughout the whole country, it's not like you see it from the other side of the river. The whole thing is kicking off so badly in America, even in *The New York*

Times every day of the week now. I brought it up four times with the band and said, look, this may kick off, but they were confident that it wouldn't happen and that it wasn't the main point.'

Even if the US reaction isn't as anodyne as Yorke expects, he's got his creative get-out formulated: 'When something works, it works and you just have to leave it. With this, when I was typing up the lyrics at the end, it suddenly dawned on me that this was like – oh, shit! But I hadn't had that at all while making it, it was only at the end when it was too late to do anything about it . . . that's the point at which it's not yours anymore anyway.'

Can you let go of your work once it's finished?

'This one was really fucking hard, we had massive arguments about how it was put together and mixed. Making it was a piece of piss; for the first time it was really good fun to make a record . . . but we finished it and nobody could let go of it. 'Cause there was a long sustained period during which we lived with it but it wasn't completely finished, so you get attached to versions and we had big rows about it.'

Was it very emotionally draining?

'For me it was the last straw.'

But if this makes Yorke out to be po-faced about his own creative process, at other times in our conversation he was bizarrely irreverent and self-deprecatory. Of *OK Computer* he said that 'even when we were making that record it was quite a weird thing for us, because we were thinking, "They're going to fucking hate this" . . . Everything was one big wind-up, especially for the press, because we wanted to make what we thought was a really over-the-top record and I remember feeling like we were taking the piss and they swallowed it whole. It was actually a good record, so that was fine, but it was a real shock. "Paranoid

Android", I just thought it was really funny, but everybody was talking about it, hmm, like a serious song, and I was, "C'mon, it's a fucking joke!" Anyway . . . ' And he lapsed into noodling.

There was also a certain mildly schizoid cast to Yorke's peregrinations. On the one hand he conceded to 'becoming the CEO of a major company' every time Radiohead brought an album out and having – especially with *Kid A* – taken a fanatical interest in the minutiae of sales and marketing, but at the same time he inveighed against the way the major record labels were vertically integrating production and distribution, with the end result that they 'put out shit'. He'd told me he was through with the big gigs and yet he also admitted that he was doing a big-venue tour for the new album. He told me that he never ever read his own reviews, and yet once the tape was off he gave a trenchant and impassioned critique of how low pay in the music press meant that critics had to review albums on the first play.

I suspect that I met Yorke in that feel-good zone before the public reception of *Hail to the Thief* got under way, and that were I to be allowed time with him after a blip in the steadily-mounting acclaim his music has received over the past decade, then I'd see a distinctly more paranoid android.

Still, why complain? Yorke proved a thoughtful and grounded companion for a saunter around the dreaming spires. With his literary references ranging from e.e. cummings to Philip Larkin to Dante, and his musical from Charlie Mingus to Thelonious Monk to Bruckner (as we'd dallied in a college chapel he suggested we might thieve an antique spinnet), he's cultured, but not oppressively so.

I also don't think his demitasse radicalism is anything but the truth as he sees it. I asked him why, unlike Robert del Naja of

Massive Attack and Damon Albarn of Blur, he hadn't been a more vocal opponent of the Iraq war. 'I totally bought it. I thought that if this [the existence of weapons of mass destruction] is true then we obviously have to do something about it. I was trying not to believe that our glorious leader is misguided in his political allegiance but, as time went on, the way the current American administration was behaving made it so fucking obvious that it was nothing to do with anything except what they wanted.'

Yorke emphatically rejects the role of being a spokesman for a generation. 'It's fucking tits!' he spat when I tried the hat on him, but with his vague environmentalism and hazy anti-establishment pronouncements he seems tailor-made for the job, or at any rate he would be if he could just get it together to visit a decent tailor. He had conceded – as I'd forced him to contemplate the suiting and booting in Turl Street – that he'd recently bought a handmade pair of Chelsea boots from a shoe shop in Jermyn Street, but then he spoiled even this excessive act by saying: 'But you'd have to have a proper suit to wear with them and I haven't, so they're just sitting in my cupboard.'

Back outside the Randolph hotel, Yorke and I parted and he shuffled off to rehearse with his band. He'd admitted that Oxford could sometimes seem a little on the small side and that, while he couldn't face the sleeplessness that the metropolis engendered in him, he might like to live in a city where there was a bit more of a scene, like Bristol. But watching the back of his khaki jacket recede down Beaumont Street, it occurred to me that he'd be a fool to move anywhere but another university town. Because despite his multi-platinum album sales and his thirty-seven years and his alleged prickliness, Yorke faded into the afternoon throng with nary a ripple, just another student type with a CND lapel badge to prove it.

3

The Story of Tchocky

Ian Gittins, Q, summer 2003

O n 27 February 2002, Radiohead designer Stanley Donwood mounted the stage at the Staples Center, Los Angeles, to receive a Grammy for Best Recording Package for his work on the curious, book-like sleeve on their *Amnesiac* album. With him was his closest colleague and creative sidekick, Tchocky. One of the worst-kept secrets in Radiohead circles was thus blown wide open: Tchocky was none other than Thom Yorke.

Possessed of a strong interest in the visual arts and graphic design, Yorke has adopted the Tchocky alter ago to work alongside his former college friend Donwood on the band's striking sleeve art ever since 1995's *The Bends*. With his name extended to the even more whimsical Dr Tchock, he also scores a co-credit for 'cartography' for the complex map of abstract symbols that accompanies new album *Hail to the Thief.* Donwood has long been acknowledged as the prime creator of the abstruse, tangential cover art that complements Radiohead's equally cerebral music, but Tchocky's role is somewhat more nebulous. How did this bizarre persona originate? Yorke, typically contrarily, declines to elucidate, but the character is clearly closely derived from *Chocky*, a 1968 sci-fi novel by *Day of the Triffids* author John Wyndham.

The Wyndham book tells the story of Matthew, an ingenuous eleven-year-old who is 'possessed' by the spirit of Chocky, a missionary sent from a distant, declining galaxy to investigate the potentialities of Earth. It's easy to imagine this tome appealing to an adolescent Yorke, particularly as it pre-empts a staple Radiohead lyrical theme: think, for example of the '*Aliens [who] hover, making home movies for the folks back home*' from *OK Computer*'s 'Subterranean Homesick Alien'.

Yorke's notorious control-freak tendencies lead him to habitually insert several digits in every area of Radiohead's singular pie, and Donwood himself freely admits the singer's extremely hands-on role in the band's artwork. 'Dr Tchock does pretty much everything while I drink Martinis in the cocktail lounge,' he sarcastically told one questioner in a rare webchat interview two years ago. In truth, the pair work in close tandem on a host of creative ventures.

Donwood's first Radiohead project was the sleeve for *The Bends*. Its abstracted, jagged images and plaintive slogans ('It's so beautiful up here . . . I don't ever want it to end') appear relatively primitive next to the complexities of the artwork on the later albums, and Tchocky doesn't receive a credit. However, it was on the artwork of 1997's seismic *OK Computer* that Donwood really came into his own.

Donwood decamped to actress Jane Seymour's palatial mansion outside Bath with the band as they made the album, and Yorke would frequently leave recording sessions to pore over a laptop with the designer as the pair attempted to create visuals which reflected the fractured, abstracted music that Radiohead were crafting.

'There was a lot of time spent in the vast library, a computer in a corner and an old armchair in front of it,' Donwood told Q two years ago. 'Someone was screaming into a microphone outside at night. For me, everything was about being erased, like taking snapshots then scraping away the surface to reveal the bones.'

'We were both obsessed by the idea of noise,' concurred Yorke. 'Background noise. Everything is background noise. Our whole lives, how our minds work. And the whole album is about that – levels of mental chatter.'

The resultant sleeve was a masterpiece of modern urban paranoia akin to T. S. Eliot's *The Waste Land*, with dislocated, random phrases of varying levels of profundity and banality emerging at angles from striking graphics. 'Jump out of bed as soon as you hear the alarm clock!' one motto ordered. 'Authorities here are alert,' proclaimed another. 'When we were finished, I was incredibly happy with it,' reflected Donwood. 'But then I had grave doubts.'

This was beguiling and provocative sleeve art, though, and inevitably websites sprang up dedicated solely to deciphering the quantum mass of cryptic, gnomic symbols. Fans on www. followmearound.com pointed out phrases in Hebrew and Esperanto; somebody translated a Greek motto: 'Don't throw unnecessary objects in the sea.' 'The lyrics for "Airbag" are shaped just like a tank,' mused one dogged seeker after truth. 'Perhaps it has to do with the line *"In the next world war"".'

As *OK Computer* revived the great lost *Sgt. Pepper* art of stoned students theorising over the meaning of album sleeves, Donwood and Tchocky raised the bar again with 2000's *Kid A*. Where *OK*

Computer's cover was blanched and erased ('bound up with the idea of white noise,' as Yorke had it), *Kid A*'s was rich, febrile and utterly compelling. As Radiohead's querulous, questing music spiralled off into more freeform and esoteric terrain, Donwood ensured the graphics were equally far-out. *Kid A*'s cover depicted what looked like an Alpine landscape from a distant galaxy. Inside, geometric shapes loomed over blasted vistas: a nuclear family stared into a glacial abyss. A sheet of tracing paper carried detailed sketches of what looked like a viaduct caught in a dinosaur's mouth and Radiohead's trademark cartoon bears danced on a mountain top. The effect was of a saturated, overloaded collage: the credit ran 'Landscapes, knives and glue by Stanley & Tchock'.

It's standard critical practice to bracket *Kid A* and 2001's *Amnesiac* together as the two constituent parts of Radiohead's headstrong, musically wilfully 'difficult' phrase. This has always been a dubious critical device: as Yorke once despairingly noted, 'If *Kid A* is "difficult", there really is no fucking hope for us.' Nevertheless, whatever the musical similarities, the Donwood/ Tchocky-generated library book that housed the album represented a quantum leap for Radiohead's visuals. Donwood regarded it as vastly different from its predecessor. '*Amnesiac* was in close-up and *Kid A* was wide-angle,' he explained. 'Same goes for the artwork – *Kid A* was rural, and *Amnesiac* urban. There was a break between making the two sleeves and I had *Amnesiac* on a CD player all the time we were doing the pictures. It's a headfuck, really – if the music is intense and constant, then the accompanying artwork is sort of automatic.'

Inside a red, hardback cover depicting a sobbing cartoon figure, a riot of images proliferated. Radiohead's talismanic bear dissolved into tears: stern letters over a modern cityscape declared 'The Decline and Fall of the Roman Empire Volume II'. A sketched drawing depicted the presidents of AOL and Time Warner hugging as their monolithic corporations merged, while ghostly trees appeared to mourn the death of the planet. The aggregation of semi-captured, glancing images of waste and decay seemed to combine in a nightmare depiction of a world living on borrowed time. The degree of detail and the intensity of the apocalyptic imagery were stunning – an idea shared, in early 2002, by the Grammy Awards committee.

Unsurprisingly, Donwood and Tchocky failed to use the stage of the Staples Center to gush effusive thanks to their A&R men and corporate paymasters. 'I felt pretty stupid,' claimed Donwood afterwards. 'Awards ceremonies are simply corporate occasions that exist to raise the profile of various products, though the limos were nice – and the champagne and the hotel. All that stuff was a lot of fun, but the Grammy thing itself was in the Staples Center, which exists because Mr and Mrs Staple sold a fuck of a lot of office supplies. Go figure, as they say in the States.'

The most recent manifestation of Donwood and Tchocky's visual creative juices was the sleeve to *Hail to the Thief*, with its puzzling, intricate map of phrases and slogans ('Plague Pit', 'Dog Lashes', 'Succubus') that will have geeks and computer techies across the planet pondering and decoding for decades. Is it really a 'non-alphabetical index to honeycomb roadmap, labyrinthine catacombs, &c'? Or is it just a series of portentous modern buzz-words, artfully arranged? 'We just do what we do,' offers a deadpan Donwood. 'They make songs and I draw pictures.'

Yet Donwood and Tchocky's creative collaborations stretch well beyond Radiohead's sleeve art. Yorke's alter ego is a frequent contributor to the designer's website, www.slowlydownward. com, an intriguing collection of abstract art, short stories and impressionistic nuggets of prose. Tchocky and Donwood are currently offering visitors the chance to take part in their slyly satirical NO DATA survey.

Definitively Yorke-like, the survey, 'covering consumer life-styles, personal habits, sexual preferences, looming terrors and crushing humiliations' invites readers to supply information to NO DATA, 'a division of Anonymous Industries, which in turn is part of a huge transnational corporation that you don't need to know about, apart from the fact that it's more powerful than a Government, but less accountable, unelected and possibly even unscrupulous.' There follows a range of statements with which you are invited to agree to disagree:

All participation is a myth
I have been manipulated and permanently distorted
There is no justice in road accidents
I am being paid to act weirdly

Once the reader has woven his way through this maze of provocative statements, s/he is thanked for their co-operation and told: 'The information has been stored on our database. Your secrets are our secrets.' You can almost hear Yorke's sardonic, reedy laugh as you read the words.

Anybody seeking a fantastic visualisation of Radiohead's ascetic, troubled ethos is also pointed towards Radiohead TV, Donwood and Tchocky's recent innovation on the band's official website, www.radiohead.com. Subtitled 'The Most Gigantic Lying Mouth of All Time', the arch, beautifully designed programming consists of snatches of tracks, videos, blipverts and subliminal sloganeering and a handful of faultlessly arty mini-movies by Donwood, Dr Tchock and collaborators. The staple themes of alienation, paranoia and creeping globalisation are, you won't be surprised to hear, all present and correct.

'Would I still do art for Radiohead if they became shit? Not only that, but I'd become shit too, in solidarity,' Donwood commented recently in interview, and there is no doubt that his status as the visual realisation of Radiohead's muse outstrips that of any other band and designer: only Joy Division/New Order and Peter Saville really come to mind. His graphics are as intrinsic an element of Radiohead as Yorke's existential howl or Ed O'Brien's plangent guitar arabesques.

In John Wyndham's novel, Chocky exits his corporeal home when he is discovered and probed by scientists. His privacy is crucial. By contrast, Yorke uses Tchocky as a means of communicating with the band's fans. Journalists and band followers can lob questions towards Radiohead at their spin-off website, www.spinwithagrin.com; most answers, when they sporadically appear, are credited to Tchocky. 'We are not little rag dolls you play with but say nothing and go back in the box when your [sic] finished with us,' he recently indignantly told a hack who mildly questioned the band's ideals.

Finally, Tchocky also makes sporadic appearances on fan websites, verbally sparring with delighted disciples who unexpectedly suddenly find themselves debating with their hero. An afternoon visit to Radiohead's official chatroom, the oddly-monikered The Byzantine Ziggurat, finds devotees in full flow deconstructing the minutiae of the *Hail to the Thief* sleeve. Tchocky is not in attendance.

'He hardly ever comes in,' explains a chatter by the rather prosaic name of Sock. 'He's like the rest of the band. They only really log on nowadays and come in here when they're drunk. Have I ever spoken to Tchocky? Yes, just once. It was on Christmas Day. There were only three of us in here, then suddenly Tchocky came in to talk to us.'

And what did he say?

'He said, "Merry Christmas, you fucking cunts."'

4

Radiohead, or the Philosophy of Pop

Mark Greif, *n+1*,
autumn 2005

I've wondered why there's so little philosophy of popular music. Critics of pop do reviews and interviews; they write appreciation and biography. Their criticism takes many things for granted and doesn't ask the questions I want answered.

Everyone repeats the received idea that music is revolutionary. Well, is it? Does pop music support revolution? We say pop is of its time and can date the music by ear with surprising precision, to 1966 or 1969 or 1972 or 1978 or 1984. Well, is it? Is pop truly of its time, in the sense that it represents some aspect of exterior history apart from the path of its internal development? I know pop does something to me; everyone says the same. So what does it do? Does it really influence my beliefs or actions in my deep life, where I think I feel it most, or does it just insinuate a certain fluctuation of mood or evanescent pleasure or impulse to move?

The answers are difficult not because thinking is hard on the subject of pop, but because of an acute sense of embarrassment. Popular music is the most living art form today. Condemned to a desert island, contemporary people would grab their records first; we have the concept of desert-island discs because we could do without most other art forms before we would give up songs. Songs are what we consume in greatest quantity; they're what we store most of in our heads. But even as we can insist on the seriousness of *value* of pop music, we don't believe enough in its seriousness of *meaning* outside the realm of music, or most of us don't or we can't talk about it or sound idiotic when we do.

And all of us lovers of music, with ears tuned precisely to a certain kind of sublimity in pop, are quick to detect pretension, overstatement and cant about pop – in any attempt at a wider criticism – precisely because we feel the gap between the effectiveness of the music and the impotence and superfluity of analysis. This means we don't know about our major art form what we ought to know. We don't even agree about how the interconnection of pop music and lyrics, rather than the words spoken alone, accomplishes an utterly different task of representation, more scattershot and overwhelming and much less careful and dignified than poetry – and bad critics show their ignorance when they persist in treating pop like poetry, as in the still-growing critical effluence around Bob Dylan.

If you *were* to develop a philosophy of pop, you would have to clear the field of many obstacles. You would need to focus on a single artist or band, to let people know you had not floated into generalities and to let them test your declarations. You'd have to announce at the outset that the musicians were figures of real importance, but not the 'most' anything – not the most avant-garde, most perfect, most exemplary. This would pre-empt the hostile comparison and sophistication that passes for criticism among aficionados. Then you should have some breathing room. If you said once that you liked the band's music, there would be no more need of appreciation; and if it was a group whose music enough people listened to, there would be no need of biography or bare description.

So let the band be Radiohead, for the sake of argument, and let me be fool enough to embark on this. And if I insist that Radiohead are 'more' anything than some other pop musicians – as fans will make claims for the superiority of the bands they love – let it be that this band was more able, at the turn of the millennium, to pose a single question: how should it really ever be possible for pop music to incarnate a particular historical situation?

Radiohead belongs to 'rock' and, if rock has a characteristic subject, as country music's is small pleasures in hard times (getting by) and rap's is success in competition (getting over), that subject must be freedom from constraint (getting free). Yet the first notable quality of their music is that even though their topic may still be freedom, their technique involves the evocation, not of the feeling of freedom, but of unending low-level fear.

The dread in the songs is so detailed and so pervasive that it seems built into each line of lyrics and into the black or starry sky of music that domes it. It is environing fear, not antagonism emanating from a single object or authority. It is atmospheric rather than explosive. This menace doesn't surprise anyone. Outside there are listeners-in, watchers, abandoned wrecks with deployed air bags, killer cars, lights going out and coming on. 'They' are waiting, without a proper name: ghost voices, clicks of tapped phones, grooves of ended records, sounds of processing and anonymity.

An event is imminent or has just happened but is blocked from our senses: *'Something big is gonna happen/Over my dead body.'* Or else it is impossible that anything more will happen and yet it does: *'I used to think/There is no future left at all/I used to think.'* Something has gone wrong with the way we know events and the error leaks back to occurrences themselves. Life transpires in its representations, in the common medium of a machine language. (*'Arrest this man/He talks in maths/he buzzes like a fridge/He's like a detuned radio.'*) A fissure has opened between occurrence and depiction, and the dam bursts between the technical and the natural. These are not meant to be statements of thoughts *about* their songs or even about the lyrics, which look banal on the printed page; this is what happens *in* their songs. The technical artifacts are in the music, sit behind our lips and slide out when we open our mouths – as chemical and medical words effortlessly make it into the lyrics ('polystyrene', 'myxomatosis', 'polyethylene').

Beside the artificial world is an iconography in their lyrics that comes from dark children's books: swamps, rivers, animals, arks and rowboats riding ambiguous tracks of light to the moon. Within these lyrics – and also in the musical counterpoint of chimes, strings, lullaby – an old personal view is opened, a desperate wish for small, safe spaces. It promises sanctuary, a bit of quiet in which to think.

Such a pretty house
and such a pretty garden. No alarms and no surprises . . .

But when the songs try to defend the small and safe, the effort comes hand in hand with grandiose assertions of power and violence which mimic the voice of overwhelming authority that should be behind our dread-filled contemporary universe but never speaks – or else the words speak, somehow, for us.

> *This is what you get*
> *when you mess with us.*

It just isn't clear whether this voice is a sympathetic voice or a voice outside – whether it is for us or against us. The band's task, as I understand it, is to try to hold on to the will, to ask if there is any part of it left that would be worth holding on to, or to find out where that force has gone. Thom Yorke, the singer, seems always in danger of destruction and then he is either channelling the Philistines or, Samson-like, preparing to take the temple down with him. So we hear pained and beautiful reassurances, austere, crystalline, and delicate – then violent denunciations and threats of titanic destruction – until they seem to be answering each other, as though the outside violence were being drawn inside:

> *Breathe, keep breathing.*
> *We hope that you choke,*
> *that you choke.*

And the consequence? Here you reach the best-known Radiohead lyrics, again banal on the page, and with them the hardest mood in their music to describe – captured in multiple repeated little phrases, stock talk, as words lose their meanings and regain them. 'How to Disappear Completely', as a song title puts it – for the words seem to speak a wish for negation of the self, nothingness and nonbeing:

For a minute there
I lost myself, I lost myself.

I'm not here. This isn't happening.

A description of the condition of the late 1990s could go like this: at the turn of the millennium, each individual sat at a meeting point of shouted orders and appeals, the TV, the radio, the phone and mobile or cell, the billboard, the airport screen, the inbox, paper junk mail. Each person discovered that he lived at one knot of a network, existing without his consent, which connected him to any number of recorded voices, written messages, means of broadcast, channels of entertainment and avenues of choice. It was a culture of broadcast: an indiscriminate seeding, which needed to reach only a very few, covering vast tracts of our consciousness. To make a profit, only one message in ten thousand needed to take root; therefore messages were strewn everywhere. To live in this network felt like something, but surprisingly little in the culture of broadcast itself tried to capture what it felt like. Instead, it kept bringing pictures of an unencumbered, luxurious life, songs of ease and freedom and technological marvels, which did not feel like the life we lived.

And if you noticed you were not represented? It felt as if one of the few unanimous aspects of this culture was that it forbade you to complain, since if you complained, you were a trivial human, a small person, who misunderstood the generosity and benignity of the message system. It existed to help you. Now, if you accepted the constant promiscuous broadcasts as normalcy, there were messages in them to inflate and pet and flatter you. If you simply said this chatter was altering your life, killing your privacy or ending the ability to think in silence, there were alternative messages that whispered of humiliation, craziness, vanishing. What sort of crank needs silence? What could be more harmless than a few words of advice? The messages did not come from *somewhere*; they were not central, organised, intelligent, intentional. It was up to you to change the channel, not answer the phone, stop your ears, shut your eyes, dig a hole for yourself and get in it. Really, it was your responsibility. The metaphors in which people tried to complain about these developments, by ordinary law and custom, were pollution (as in 'noise pollution') and theft (as in 'stealing our time'). But we all knew the intrusions felt like violence. Physical violence, with no way to strike back.

And if this feeling of violent intrusion persisted? Then it added a new dimension of constant, nervous triviality to our lives. It linked, irrationally, in our moods and secret thoughts, these tiny private annoyances to the constant televised violence we saw. Those who objected embarrassed themselves, because they likened nuisances to tragedies – and yet we felt the likeness, though it became unsayable. Perhaps this was because our nerves have a limited palette for painting dread. Or because the network fulfilled its debt of civic responsibility by bringing us twenty-four-hour news of flaming airplanes and twisted cars and blood-soaked, screaming casualties, globally acquired, which it was supposedly our civic duty to watch – and, adding commercials, put this mixture of messages and horrors up on screens wherever a TV could only be introduced on grounds of 'responsibility to know', in the airport, the subway, the doctor's office and any waiting room. But to object was demeaning – who, really, meant us any harm? And didn't we truly have a responsibility to know?

Thus the large mass of people huddled in the path of every broadcast – who really did not speak but were spoken for, who received and couldn't send, were made responsible for the new Babel. Most of us who lived in this culture were primarily sufferers or patients of it and not, as the word had it, 'consumers'. Yet we had no other words besides 'consumption' or 'consumerism' to condemn a world of violent intrusions of insubstantial messages, no new way at least to name this culture or describe the feeling of being inside it.

So a certain kind of pop music could offer a representative vision of this world while still being one of its omnipresent products. A certain kind of musician might reflect this new world's vague smiling threat of hostile action, its latent violence done by no one in particular; a certain kind of musician, angry and critical rather than complacent and blithe, might depict the intrusive experience, though the music would be painfully intrusive itself, and it would be brought to us by and share the same avenues of mass intrusion that broadcast everything else. Pop music had the good fortune of being both a singularly unembarrassed art and a relatively low-capital medium in its creation – made by just a composer or writer or two, or four or six members of a band, with little outside intrusion, until money was poured into its recording and distribution and advertising. So, compromised as it was, music could still become a form of unembarrassed and otherwise inarticulable complaint, capturing what one could not say in reasonable debate and coming from far enough inside the broadcast culture that it could depict it with its own tools.

A historical paradox of rock has been that the pop genre most devoted to the idea of rebellion against authority has adopted increasingly more brutal and authoritarian music to denounce forms of authoritarianism. A genre that celebrated individual liberation required increasing regimentation and coordination. The development could be seen most starkly in hard rock, metal, hardcore, rap metal – but it was latent all along.

Throughout the early twentieth century, folk musics had been a traditional alternative to forms of musical authority. But amplification alone, it seems, so drastically changed the situation of music, opening possibilities in the realm of dynamics and the mimesis of other sounds, that it created avenues for the musical representation of liberation that had nothing to do with folk music's traditional lyrical content or the concern with instrumental skill and purism. Specifically, it gave pop ways to emulate the evils that liberation would be fighting against. Pop could become Goliath while it was cheering David. One aspect of amplification by the late 1960s stands out above all others: it opened up the possibility, for the first time, that a musician might choose to actually hurt an audience with noise. The relationship of audience to rock musician came to be based on a new kind of primitive trust. This was the trust of listeners facing a direct threat of real pain and permanent damage that bands would voluntarily restrain – just barely. An artist for the first time had his hands on a means of real violence and colluded with his audience to test its possibilities. You hear it in the Who, the Doors, Jimi Hendrix. In the 1960s, of course, this testing occurred against a rising background of violence, usually held in monopoly by 'the authorities', but being manifested with increasing frequency in civil unrest and police reaction as well as in war overseas. All of which is sometimes taken as an explanation. But once the nation was back in peacetime, it turned out that the formal violence of rock did not depend on the overt violence of bloodshed, and rock continued to metamorphose. The extremity of its dynamics developed toward heavy metal during the 1970s – and some connected this to industrial collapse and economic misery. Later it was refined in punk and post-punk, in periods of political defeat – and some connected the music's new lyrical alternations of hatred of authority with hatred of the self to the political, economic and social outlook.

Maybe they were right. But this is perhaps to give too much automatic credence to the idea that pop music depicts history almost without trying – which is precisely what is in question.

To leap all the way into the affective world of our own moment, of course, might require something else: electronic sounds. To reproduce a new universe, or to spur a desire to carve out a life in its midst, a band might need a limited quantity of beeps, repetitions, sampled loops, drum machines, noises and beats. 'Electronica', as a contemporary genre name, speaks of the tools of production as well as their output. Laptops, Pro Tools, sequencers, and samplers, the found sounds and sped-up breaks and pure frequencies, provided an apparently unanchored environment and a weird soundscape that, though foreshadowed in studios in Cologne or at the Columbia-Princeton Electronic Music Center, didn't automatically fit with the traditions of guitars and drums that pop knew. But the electronic blips the music used turned out to be already emotionally available to us by a different route than the avant-gardism of Stockhausen or Cage. All of us born after 1965 had been setting nonsense syllables and private songs to machine noise and then computer noise, since the new sounds reached our cradles. Just as we want to make tick and tock out of the even movement of a clock, we wanted to know how to hear a language and a song of noises, air compressors and washer surges, alarm sirens and warning bells. We hear communication in the refined contemporary spectrum of beeps: the squall of a microwave, the chime of a timer, the fat gulp of a register, the chirrups of cell phones, the ping of seat belt alerts and clicks of indicators, not to mention the argot of debonair beeps from the computers on which we type.

Radiohead, up until the late 1990s, had not been good at spelling out what bothered them in narrative songs. They attempted it in their early work. One well-known and well-loved but clumsy song sang about the replacement of a natural and domestic world by plastic replicas ('Fake Plastic Trees'). That account was inches away from folk cliché – something like Malvina Reynolds's 'Little Boxes'. Its only salvation may have been the effect observed rather than the situation denounced: '*It wears you out*', describing the fatigue human beings feel in the company of the ever-replaceable. *The Bends,* the last album produced before their major period, had this steady but awkward awareness, as the title implies, of being dragged through incompatible atmospheres in the requirements of daily life. But the band didn't yet seem to know that the subjective, symptomatic evocation of these many whiplashing states of feeling – not overt, narrative complaint about them – would prove to be their talent.

On the first mature album, *OK Computer,* a risk of cliché lingered in a song of a computer voice intoning '*Fitter, happier, more productive*' – as if the dream of conformist self-improvement would turn us artificial. But the automated voice's oddly human character saved the effect. It seemed automated things, too, could be seduced by a dream of perfection equally delusory for them. Then the new commensurability of natural and artificial wasn't a simple loss but produced a hybrid vulnerability when you had thought things were most stark and steely. The band was also, at that time, mastering a game of voices, the interfiling of inhuman speech and machine sounds with the keening, vulnerable human singing of Thom Yorke.

Their music had started as guitar rock, but with the albums *Kid A* and *Amnesiac* the keyboard asserted itself. The piano dominated; the guitars developed a quality of an organ. The drums, emerging altered and processed, came to fill in spaces in rhythms already set by the front-line instruments. Orchestration added brittle washes of strings, a synthetic choir, chimes, an unknown shimmer or bleated horns. The new songs were built on verse-chorus structure in only a rudimentary way, as songs developed from one block of music to the next, not turning back. And, of course – as is better known, and more widely discussed – on the new albums the band, by now extremely popular and multimillion-selling, 'embraced' electronica. But what precisely did that mean? It didn't seem in their case like opportunism, as in keeping up with the new thing; nor did it entirely take over what they did in their songs; nor were they particularly noteworthy as electronic artists. It is crucial that they were not innovators; nor did they ever take it further than halfway – if that. They were *not* an avant-garde. The political problem of an artistic avant-garde, especially when it deals with any new technology of representation, has always been that the simply novel elements may be mistaken for some form of meanings of 'revolutionary' – one, forming an advance in formal technique; the other, contributing to social cataclysm – are often confused, usually to the artist's benefit, and technology has a way of becoming infatuated with its own existence.

Radiohead's success lay in their ability to represent the feeling of our age; they did not insist on being too much advanced in the 'advanced' music they acquired. The beeps and buzzes never seemed like the source of their energy; rather, they were a means they'd stumbled upon of finally communicating the feelings they had always held. They had felt, so to speak, electronic on *OK Computer* with much less actual electronica. And they did something very rudimentary and basic with the new technologies. They tilted artificial noises against the weight of the human voice and human sounds.

Their new kind of song, in both words and music, announced that anyone might have to become partly inhuman to accommodate the experience of the new era.

Thom Yorke's voice is the unity on which all the musical aggregations and complexes pivot. You have to imagine the music drawing a series of outlines around him – a house, a tank, the stars of space or an architecture of almost abstract pipes and tubes, cogs and wheels, ivy and thorns, servers and boards, beams and voids. The music has the feeling of a biomorphic machine in which the voice is alternately trapped and protected.

Yorke's voice conjures the human in extremis. Sometimes it comes to us from an extreme of fear, sometimes an extreme of transcendence. We recognise it as a naked voice in the process of rising up to beauty – the reassurance we've alluded to in the lyrics – or being broken up and lost in the chatter of broadcasts, the destroying fear. In the same song that features a whole sung melody, the vocals will also be broken into bits and made the pulsing wallpaper against which the vulnerable, pale voice of the singer stands out. Only a few other popular artists build so much of their music from sampled voice rather than sampled beats, instrumental tones, or noises. The syllables are cut and repeated. A 'wordless' background will come from mashed phonemes. Then the pure human voice will reassert itself.[1]

A surprising amount of this music seems to draw on church music. One biographical fact is relevant here: they come from Oxford, England, grew up there, met in high school and live, compose and rehearse there. Their hometown is like their music. That bifurcated English city, split between concrete downtown and green environs, has its unspoiled centre and grey periphery of modest houses and a disused automobile factory. Its spots of natural beauty exist because of the nearby huge institutions of the university, and if you stand in the remaining fields and parks you always know you are in a momentary breathing space, already encroached upon. But for the musically minded, the significant feature of Oxford is its Church of England chapels, one in each college and others outside – places of imperial authority, home to another kind of hidden song. The purity of Yorke's falsetto belongs in a boys' choir at evensong. And then Yorke does sing of angels, amid harps, chimes, and bells: *'Black-eyed angels swam with me/. . ./ And we all went to heaven in a little row boat / There was nothing to fear and nothing to doubt.'*

---

1 Stanley Cavell used to say that the first impulse opera evokes is to wonder where in the physical singer the immaterial song can be located. In live performance, the striking thing about Thom Yorke is how small a person he is. Not only is his voice excessive, beyond human averageness, it is moored to a smaller-than-average body and onstage persona that seem to dramatise the question, in his music, of where voices come from – from individual people or the techniques that surround and overmaster them.

And yet the religion in the music is not about salvation – it's about the authority of voices, the wish to submit and the discovery of a consequent resistance in oneself. It is anti-religious, though attuned to transcendence. The organ in a church can be the repository of sublime power: a bundling of human throats in its brass pipes or all the instruments known to man in its stops. You can hear your own small voice responding, within something so big that it manifests a threat of your voice merely being played mechanically and absorbed into a totality. To sing with an organ (as Yorke does at the end of *Kid A*) can be to discover one's own inner voice in distinction to it and at the same time to wish to be lost, absorbed, overwhelmed within it. A certain kind of person will refuse the church. But even one who refuses the church will not forget the overwhelming feeling.

Sublime experience, the philosophical tradition says, depends on a relation to something that threatens. Classically it depended on observing from a point of safety a power like a storm, cataract or high sea, that could crush the observer if he were nearer. (By compassing the encompassable power in inner representation, it was even suggested, you could be reminded of the interior power of the moral faculty, the human source of a comparable strength.) Radiohead observe the storm from within it. Their music can remind you of the inner overcoming voice, it's true. But then the result is no simple access of power. This sublime acknowledges a different kind of internalisation, the drawing of the inhuman into yourself and also a loss of your own feelings and words and voice to an outer order that has come to possess them.

The way Yorke sings guarantees that you often don't know what the lyrics are; they emerge into sense and drop out – and certain phrases attain clarity while others remain behind. This de-enunciation has been a tool of pop for a long time. Concentrating, you can make out nearly all the lyrics; listening idly, you hear a smaller set of particular lines, which you sing along to and remember. It is a way of focusing inattention as well as attention.

The most important grammatical tic in Radiohead lyrics, unlike the habitual lyrical 'I' and apostrophic 'you' of pop, is the 'we'. *'We ride'*, *'We escape'*, *'We're damaged goods'*, *'Bring down the government/. . ./They don't speak for us'*. But also: *'We suck young blood'*, *'We can wipe you out/. . ./Anytime'*. The pronoun doesn't point to any existing collectivity; the songs aren't about a national group or even the generic audience for rock. So who is 'we'?

There is the scared individual, lying to say he's not alone – like the child who says, 'We're coming in there!' so imagined monsters won't know he's by himself. There's the 'we' you might wish for, the imagined collectivity that could resist or threaten, and this may shade into the thought of all the other listeners besides you, in their rooms or cars alone, singing these same bits of lyrics. There's the 'we', as I've suggested, of the violent power that you are not: the voice of the tyrant, the thug, the terrifying parent, the bad cop. You take him inside you and his voice spreads over all the others who – somewhere singing these words for just a moment – are like you. You experience a release at last, so satisfying does it feel to sing the unspoken orders out loud to yourself, as if at last they came from you. You are the one willing the destruction – like Brecht and Weill's Pirate Jenny, the barmaid, washing dishes and taking orders, who knows that soon a Black Ship will come for her town, bristling with cannons. And when its crew asks their queen whom they should kill, she will answer: *'Alle!'* So the characteristic

Radiohead song turns into an alternation, in exactly the same repeated words, between the forces that would defy intrusive power and the intrusive power itself, between hopeful individuals and the tyrant ventriloquised.

It has to be admitted that other memorable lyrics sing phrases of self-help. Plenty of these important lines are junk slogans from the culture and of course part of the oddity of pop is that junk phrases can be made so moving; they do their work again. In a desperate voice: *'You can try the best you can/If you try the best you can/The best you can is good enough.'* Or: *'Breathe, keep breathing/Don't lose your nerve.'* Or: *'Everyone/Everyone around here/Everyone is so near/It's holding on.'* On the page, these lyrics aren't impressive, unless you can hear them in memory, in the framing of the song. Again, one has to distinguish between poetry and pop. The most important lines in pop are rarely poetically notable; frequently they are quite deliberately and necessarily words that are the most frank, melodramatic, and unredeemable. And yet they do get redeemed. The question becomes why certain settings in music and a certain playing of simple against more complex lyrics, can remake debased language and restore the innocence of emotional expression. (Opera listeners know this, in the ariose transformations of *'Un bel dì'* ('One fine day') or *'O mio babbino caro'* ('Oh, my dear papa'). But then opera criticism, too, has a long-standing problem with lyrics.) In the midst of all else the music and lyrics are doing, the phrases of self-help may be the minimal words of will or nerve that you need to hear.

The more I try to categorise why Radiohead's music works as it does, and by extension how pop works, the more it seems clear that the effect of pop on our beliefs and actions is not really to create either one. Pop does, though, I think, allow you to retain certain things you've already thought, without your necessarily having been able to articulate them, and to preserve certain feelings you have only intermittent access to, in a different form, music with lyrics, in which the cognitive and emotional are less divided. I think songs allow you to steel yourself or loosen yourself into certain kinds of actions, though they don't start anything. And the particular songs and bands you like dictate the beliefs you can preserve and reactivate, and the actions you can prepare – and which songs and careers will shape your inchoate private experience depends on an alchemy of your experience and the art itself. Pop is neither a mirror nor a Rorschach blot, into which you look and see only yourself; nor is it a lecture, an interpretable poem, or an act of simply determinate speech. It teaches something, but only by stimulating and preserving things that you must have had inaugurated elsewhere. Or it prepares the ground for these discoveries elsewhere – often knowledge you might never otherwise have really 'known', except as it could be rehearsed by you, then repeatedly reactivated for you, in this medium.

But is the knowledge that's preserved a spur to revolution? There is no logical sense in which pop music is revolutionary. That follows from the conclusion that pop does not start beliefs or instil principles or create action *ex nihilo*. It couldn't overturn an order. When so much pop declares itself to be revolutionary, however, I think it correctly points to something else that is significant but more limited and complicated. There is indeed an antisocial or countercultural tendency of pop that does follow logically from what it does. That is to say, there is a characteristic affect that follows from a medium that allows you to retain and reactivate forms of knowledge and experience that you are 'supposed to' forget or that are 'supposed to' disappear by themselves – and 'supposed to' here isn't nefarious, it simply means that social forms, convention, conformity, and just plain intelligent speech don't allow you to speak of these things, or make them embarrassing when you do. Pop encourages you to hold on to and reactivate hints of personal feeling that society should have extinguished. Of course, this winds up taking in all classes of fragile personal knowledge: things that are inarticulable in social speech because they are too delicate or ideologically out of step, and things that should not be articulated because they are selfish, thoughtless, destructive and stupid. That helps explain how these claims for 'What I learned from pop' can go so quickly from the sublime to the ridiculous and back to the sublime. It explains why we are right to feel that so much of what's promised for pop is not worth our credulity. But, again, risking ridiculousness, I think the thing that pop can prepare you for, the essential thing, is *defiance*. Defiance, at its bare minimum, is the insistence on finding ways to retain the thoughts and feelings that a larger power should have extinguished.

The difference between revolution and defiance is the difference between an overthrow of the existing order and one person's shaken fist. When the former isn't possible, you still have to hold on to the latter, if only so as to remember you're human. Defiance is the insistence on individual power confronting the overwhelming force that it cannot undo. You know you cannot strike the colossus. But you can defy it with words or signs. In the assertion that you can fight a superior power, the declaration that you will, this absurd overstatement gains dignity by exposing you, however uselessly, to risk. Unable to stop it in its tracks, you dare the crushing power to begin its devastation with you.

Power comes in many forms for human beings and defiance meets it where it can. The simplest defiance confronts nature's power and necessity. In the teeth of a storm that would kill him, a man will curse the wind and rain. He declares, like Nikos Kazantzakis's peasant Zorba, 'You won't get into my little hut, brother; I shan't open the door to you. You won't put my fire out; you won't tip my hut over!' This will is not Promethean, simply human.

In all forms of defiance, a little contingent being, the imperilled man or woman, hangs on to his will – which may be all he has left – by making a deliberate error about his will's jurisdiction. Because the defiant person has no power to win a struggle, he preserves his will through representations: he shakes his fist, announces his name, shouts a threat and above all makes the statements 'I am', 'We are'. This becomes even more necessary and risky when the cruel power is not natural, will-less itself, but belongs to other men. Barthes gives the words of the French revolutionist Guadet, arrested and condemned to death: 'Yes, I am Guadet. Executioner, do your duty. Go take my head to the tyrants of my country. It has always turned them pale; once severed, it will turn them paler still.' He gives the order, not the tyrant, commanding necessity in his own name – defying the false necessity of human force that has usurped nature's power – even if he can only command it to destroy him.

The situation we confront now is a new necessity, not blameless like wind or water and yet not fatal as from a tyrant or executioner. The nature we face is a billowing atmospheric second nature made by man. It is the distant soft tyranny of other men, wafting in diffuse messages, in the abdication of authority to technology, in the dissembling of responsibility under cover of responsibility and with the excuse of help – gutless, irresponsible, servile, showing no naked force, only a smiling or a pious face. The 'they' are cowardly friends. They are here to help you be happy and make fruitful choices. ('*We can wipe you out anytime.*')

At its best, Radiohead's music reactivates the moods in which you once noticed you ought to refuse. It can abet an *impersonal* defiance. This is not a doctrine the band advances, but an effect of the aesthetic. It doesn't name a single enemy. It doesn't propose revolution. It doesn't call you to overthrow an order that you couldn't take hold of anyway at any single point, not without scapegoating a portion and missing the whole. This defiance – it might be the one thing we can manage and better than sinking beneath the waves. It requires the retention of a private voice.

One of the songs on *Hail to the Thief* has a peculiar counter-slogan:

> *Just 'cause you feel it*
> *Doesn't mean it's there.*

To sense the perversity of the appearance of these words in a pop song, you have to remember that they occur inside an art form monomaniacally devoted to the production of strong feelings. Pop music *always* tells its listeners that their feelings are real. Yet here is a chorus that denies any reference to reality in the elation and melancholy and chills that this chorus, in fact, elicits. Yorke delivers the lines with an upnote on 'feel' as he repeats them, and if anything in the song makes your hair stand on end, that will be the moment. He makes you feel, that is, the emotion

244

he's warning you against. Next he sings a warning not to make too much of his own singing: 'There's always a siren/Singing you to shipwreck.' And this song, titled 'There There', was the first single released off the album, pressed in many millions of copies; it was played endlessly on radio and MTV.

The purpose of the warning is not to stop feelings but to stop you from believing they always refer to something, or deserve reality or should lead to actions or choices or beliefs – which is, of course, what the messages you hear by broadcast like you to make of them. The feelings evoked by a pop song may be false, as the feelings evoked by all the other messages brought to you by the same media as pop songs may be false. You must judge. If leading you to disbelieve in broadcast also leads you to disbelieve in pop, so be it; maybe you believed in pop in the wrong way. You must distinguish. The broadcast messages are impersonal in one fashion. They pretend to care about you when actually they don't know or care that you, as a single person, exist. Impersonal defiance is impersonal in another way; it encourages you to withdraw, no longer to believe that there is any human obligation owed to the sources of messages – except when they remind you, truly, of what you already have subtly sensed and already know.

You can see a closed space at the heart of many of Radiohead's songs. To draw out one of their own images, it may be something like a glass house. You live continuously in the glare of inspection and with the threat of intrusion. The attempt to cast stones at an outer world of enemies would shatter your own shelter. So you settle for the protection of this house, with watchers on the outside, as a place you can still live, a way to preserve the vestige of closure – a barrier, however glassy and fragile, against the outside. In English terms, a glass house is also a glasshouse, which we call a greenhouse. It is the artificial construction that allows botanical life to thrive in winter.

Radiohead's songs suggest that you should erect a barrier, even of repeated minimal words, or the assertion of a 'we', to protect yourself – and then there proves to be a place in each song to which you, too, can't be admitted, because the singer has something within him closed to interference, just as every one of us does, or should. We'll all have to find the last dwellings within ourselves that are closed to intrusion and begin from there. The politics of the next age, if we are to survive, will include a politics of the re-creation of privacy.

4

Thom Yorke, Free Agent

Ann Powers, *Los Angeles Times*,
28 June 2006

Last year, Thom Yorke was supposed to unwind. Radiohead, the band whose decade-long ascent has turned the singer into pop's definitive reluctant visionary, was on hiatus after a protracted cycle of recording and touring.

Yorke was savouring the retreat from what he wryly calls 'making RECORDS, in big capital letters' and the chance to reacquaint himself with his Oxford home, his longtime partner Rachel Owen and two young children. But instead of clearing a space for calm, Yorke found himself up to his neck in new thoughts.

'At my house, there's a room about this size,' Yorke said, gesturing at the spacious suite in San Francisco's Clift hotel where he sat discussing *The Eraser*, the album he's releasing on 10 July. 'The entire room was just covered – the whole floor, with notes and scraps of paper. A friend of mine came by just before we started recording and he was just looking through it, laughing his head off, saying, "How are you going to piece this together?"'

Yorke's workroom mess, mirrored by the sonic 'bits and bobs and shreds of all sorts of random chaos' on his laptop, gave him a sense of freedom he'd momentarily lost within Radiohead, which lands in LA for two nights at the Greek Theatre starting Thursday. In league with two long-time collaborators, the visual artist Stanley Donwood and producer Nigel Godrich, Yorke enclosed himself amid these fragments, shutting out other influences. 'That's how you get that thing where a project has its own universe,' he explained. 'You say, well, everything in this room, that's all there is, that's all I've got.'

The fruitful little island of disarray contrasted radically with the high-stakes mood surrounding Radiohead's most recent chart-topper, 2003's *Hail to the Thief,* which left the band seriously in need of some elbow room. Made quickly, during a time when Yorke was becoming deeply involved with the environmentalist group Friends of the Earth, *The Eraser* is a return to focus for Yorke, whose energy had flagged under the weight of his band's outsized reputation. 'It was done in the context of Radiohead,' he said, adding that he initially dreaded telling his bandmates he'd embarked on the effort. 'The best thing about it was that it wasn't a problem. Of course it was fine. Why wouldn't it be?' That the band dynamic 'is a liquid thing is very important'.

On its current tour, Radiohead is playing a wide swath of favourites plus some exciting new material, perhaps enriched by the confidence Yorke says he's regained by making *The Eraser,* which will be released on the super-hip independent label XL. Radiohead is one of pop's highest-profile free agents, having parted with EMI, the conglomerate that released its previous seven albums. *The Eraser* could be viewed as part of a larger move toward independence.

Asked whether Radiohead would consider distributing its next album independently, Yorke unhesitatingly said yes. 'We have two or three options and that's one,' he said. 'Once we finish whatever we think is good enough to put out, then we'll start thinking about it. We haven't discussed it a great deal. I would love for us to drop a chemical weapon within the music industry. But I don't see it as our responsibility, either.'

In the meantime, there's *The Eraser* – a project the label-resistant Yorke hates to label 'solo'. What began as a side trip into the abstract electronic music he loves became, to the singer's surprise, forty minutes of remarkably powerful and direct music. Sure to be one of the year's critical and cult favourites, *The Eraser* is an evocative portrait of life made slippery by urban sprawl, murky political alliances and global warming – and given hope through individual and communal resistance – with the blips and bleeps of Yorke's laptop excursions coalescing into soulful, politically charged songs.

'It started out with loads and loads of beats and la la la,' Yorke said, mocking his own obscurantist tendencies. 'It was pretty intense and very, very heavy.' Yorke's busman's holiday gave his producer a chance to highlight Yorke's poignant tenor and melodic sense. 'In the midst of it all there were two or three things that made Nigel and me go, "Ooh, there's something really direct here. Someone might even understand it the first time around."'

'In the band he's always finding ways to bury himself,' Godrich said in a phone interview. 'Being a big fan of his voice and his songs, I wanted to push that. It would have been sad if he'd just made an oblique record. But because it was predominantly electronic, I had a really good excuse to make his voice dry and loud.'

The leap beyond the band context might easily have led Yorke into murky territory. A fan of experimental electronica, the singer first came up with a collection of tracks that didn't really reach out. 'It made complete sense to me, but there wasn't enough there for anybody else,' he said of these early efforts. But the desire to meld his voice with the computer's led to unexpected intimacies. 'The music, no matter what way you look at it, is coming out of a box,' said Yorke, noting that even the acoustic sounds of piano, guitar and bass samples on *The Eraser* are computer-processed, and he cites Bjork's 1997 electro-torch suite *Homogenic* as a primary reference point. 'It has its own space. We consciously decided to not expand it beyond that. The vocals are exactly the same, right there in the speakers. The record was built to be listened to in an isolated space – on headphones or stuck in traffic.'

The traffic reference is no casual one for Yorke, whose concern about the environment nearly caused him, at one point, to 'flip my lid'. Its songs send up warning flares that are cosmic in scope, yet movingly personal – the sonic equivalent of a hand held up to a tidal wave. That's an image Donwood included in *London Views*, the 'apocalyptic panorama' inspired by *The Eraser* that makes up the album's cover art. One of the linotype's most powerful segments depicts King Canute, the legendary English monarch who proved the limits of kingly power by trying and failing to command the ocean. The tale inspired Yorke's flood of lyrics too.

'In the paper one day, Jonathan Porritt was basically dismissing any commitment that the working government has toward addressing global warming, saying that their gestures were like King Canute trying to stop the tide,' Yorke said of the British environmentalist. 'And that just went "ker-ching" in my head. It's not political, really, but that's exactly what I feel is happening.

We're all King Canutes, holding our hands out, saying, "It'll go away. I can make it stop." No, you can't.'

Such 'not really political' talk has become tough for Yorke to resist, despite his desire to stay in the artist's traditional spot above the fray. *The Eraser*'s most controversial song is 'Harrowdown Hill', named after the Oxfordshire neighbourhood where authorities found the body of Dr David Kelly, a whistleblower who allegedly committed suicide after telling a reporter that Tony Blair's government had falsely identified biological weapons in Iraq.

'I called it "Harrowdown Hill" because it was a really poetic title,' he said. 'To me it sounded like some sort of battle, some civil-war-type thing. Finishing the song, I was thinking about the 1990 poll tax riots – another of England's finest moments, when they beat . . . protesters, and you know, there were old ladies there and kids with families. I didn't expect that many people to realise that Harrowdown Hill was where Dr Kelly died. I'm not saying the reference isn't there, but there's more to it.'

'Harrowdown Hill' makes its point through startling sounds and shards of emotionally charged speech; it's as political as a private – even secret – moment can be. Its startling beauty is typical of *The Eraser* – which, like all of Yorke's best work, finds its strength in the spaces where words and music dissolve, only to form something new. Literary types might call it poetics. For Yorke, it's all about hearing the world through the individual voice.

'I have friends who were involved in the tsunami,' he said. 'Talking to them, you realise that no matter how huge or terrifying an event is, you're not going to grasp it from the newspaper; it doesn't even matter if you see the wave on television. The only way you can actually relate to it is when someone explains their experience, one to one.'

Eight: Present Tense

1

OK Computer: Why the Record Industry is Terrified of Radiohead's New Album

Andy Gill, *Independent*,
5 October 2007

Ever since a cadre of politicised hippies tore down the fence at the 1970 Isle of Wight Festival, the more anarchically-inclined of rock fans have demanded that music be 'free', contending that pop's position under the entertainment-industry umbrella fatally compromises its aesthetic and political freedom. Now, as Radiohead offer their album *In Rainbows* to the world potentially for as little as a penny apiece, that revolutionary ambition is upon us.

Ironically, it has been triggered not by penniless hippies in some inner-city squat, nor by indie-label firebrands, but by one of the biggest bands in the world, whose rise occurred under the stewardship of EMI, the UK's bastion of corporate entertainment for over three-quarters of a century. And, piling irony upon irony, far from having their aesthetic and political freedom compromised by the relationship, Radiohead have actually grown more artistically adventurous with each successive album and remain one of the industry's most politically engaged acts.

Under the new set-up, fans will be offered the chance to buy the band's album for whatever they deem appropriate. Most will pay between one pound and five pounds, which seems reasonable. Those desperate for a more physical artefact are offered a high-quality vinyl double-album package, with lavish artwork and an extra CD of otherwise unavailable tracks, for forty pounds – and even at that price, the band will sell shedloads. The CD version of the downloads, it's reported, will creep out sometime next year.

The move has been widely viewed as the inevitable corollary of the rise of digital downloading, which in less than a decade has all but demolished the old retail sector. It's shocking to consider that Napster, the website that established the notion of free access to music via file-sharing, was only started in 1999 but, by 2001, had a worldwide user base of more than twenty-six million fans, all looting whatever music they could find. The mainstream industry, unable or unwilling to see beyond the hardware forms – vinyl, CD, cassette – that were the backbone of their business, was blindsided by the file-sharing boom, and instead of seeking some form of accommodation with downloaders, initially reacted by trying to criminalise them: acts such as Metallica and Dr Dre instigated legal action against Napster in 2000, and the following year A&M Records sought an injunction preventing its copy-righted recordings from being offered via the website.

The RIAA (Recording Industry Association of America) began suing individual alleged file-sharers, an aggressive policy that backfired somewhat when the organisation appeared to be bullying victims including a twelve-year-old girl, a sixty-six-year-old woman allegedly downloading gangsta rap, and, in 2005, a woman who had died the previous year, aged eighty-three. To date, they have instigated over twenty thousand cases.

But not everyone believed Napster was entirely damaging to a record's sales potential. Some felt the opposite was true in many cases – that the exposure afforded by file-sharing could stimulate sales. This was proven in 2000 when tracks from Radiohead's *Kid A* appeared on Napster three months before the album's official release. An unflinchingly experimental album, significantly different in style from *OK Computer* and featuring no obvious singles, it was a challenging work, yet despite the millions of free downloads, it still became the band's first American chart-topper. Previously, their best placing had been the lowly 21 achieved by *OK Computer.* Clearly, Napster had not harmed its prospects, and it could be argued to have provided invaluable promotional assistance.

The industry came to realise that the larger war was lost and started developing relationships with 'legal' download services such as Apple's iTunes, belatedly tapping into the revenue stream facilitated by the popularity of the iPod. The effect on retailers, however, has been catastrophic. The big chains, such as Virgin, struck deals allowing them to sell CDs at a more competitive price, but the smaller-volume operators – the independent shops that sustained the indie fringe – have been unable to compete and are disappearing. Record labels, meanwhile, are struggling to find a new role within the industry, with many forced into the current, seemingly endless, round of mergers.

Radiohead are not the only act to embark on this strategy – their announcement was followed by a similar offer from Alan

McGee on behalf of the Charlatans' next album – but they are the biggest. In recent years, however, their sales have declined; after *Kid A*, the *Amnesiac* and *Hail to the Thief* albums could only manage gold certification in America, which has led some to speculate that the new strategy may be a means for the band to compensate for declining popularity by keeping a larger proportion – indeed, one hundred per cent – of sales revenue, rather than the small share previously offered by Parlophone.

The band, originally called On A Friday, signed a six-album deal with Parlophone in 1991 after a chance meeting between the label's Keith Wozencroft and guitarist Jonny Greenwood in the Oxford record shop where the latter worked. They changed their name to Radiohead (after a track on Talking Heads' *True Stories*) and began recording their debut album *Pablo Honey*. Their first single, 'Creep', a double-edged exercise in ironic self-deprecation, reflected the band's admiration of the Pixies, but was poorly received on its first release; Radio 1 considered it 'too depressing' to play. But the song built a following in America, where its smouldering dynamic and cathartic chorus slotted neatly into the prevailing grunge aesthetic. It remains their biggest hit and helped hoist *Pablo Honey* to a respectable chart position, just outside the Top 30.

But as their American promotional tour stretched into its second year, the band grew bored with playing the songs they had written years before and almost broke up. Keen to distance themselves from 'Creep', their follow-up album *The Bends* featured the kind of artistic volte-face that sends chills down label bosses' spines, with the band re-establishing themselves as an arena-rock outfit with the ability to inject powerful emotional content into complex musical structures. 'When *The Bends* came out,' drummer Phil

Selway later said, 'everyone went on about how uncommercial it was. Twelve months later, it was hailed as a pop classic. The record company were worried there wasn't a single on it, and we ended up with five Top 30 hits from it.'

The Bends might have scared their label, but its unprecedented blend of melodic prog-rock and soul would serve as the template for a generation of lesser talents, most notably Coldplay. Their stature was also rising among their peers, with R.E.M.'s Michael Stipe – whose idealism and idiosyncratic appearance made him an obvious role model for singer Thom Yorke – admitting that he was scared by how good they were. 'Thom Yorke, with "My Iron Lung", that's just an amazing metaphor to put into a song,' Stipe gushed to me in 2001. 'Stuff like that just makes me want to work harder and write another song that's as good as that.'

The reception accorded *OK Computer* in 1997 suggested that Stipe's admiration was shared by millions, as this complex work became their most popular album. Yorke admitted he was surprised at the reception, saying that 'what really blew my head off was the fact that people got all the things, all the textures and the sounds and the atmospheres we were trying to create'. The subsequent world tour was filmed for a fly-on-the-wall documentary, *Meeting People is Easy*, a film that revealed the band's growing distaste for the music business as they laboured through a gruelling year of concerts. In the year after the tour's conclusion, their only public appearances would be at a couple of benefit concerts for Amnesty International and the Tibetan Freedom Movement, indications of the growing political engagement of Yorke.

Since then, Yorke has used his rock-star profile to bring good causes to his fans' attention, advising them to read books such as

Naomi Klein's anti-corporate tract *No Logo* and Alastair McIntosh's *Soil and Soul: People Versus Corporate Power*, an account of the author's campaigns to prevent industrial despoliation of Scotland's Western Isles. More recently, the singer has bitten the bullet avoided by most stadium-rockers, criticising the 'ridiculous' amount of energy needed to fuel large-scale concert events – even threatening to cease touring the more far-flung destinations unless steps were taken to reduce carbon emissions.

After *OK Computer*, Radiohead came close to splitting up. Yorke suffered severe depression, which led to writer's block, and the members' different ideas as to their future direction seemed to presage solo careers. But again they reinvented themselves, turning from guitar-based rock and creating music heavily influenced by jazz, electronics and the avant-garde. The sessions furnished two of the most unusual albums ever to top the album charts, 2000's *Kid A* and, a year later, *Amnesiac*. Sales were understandably lower than those of *OK Computer*, but the return of their familiar, crowd-pleasing guitar-rock style alongside the more recent electronic passages and experimental developments on 2003's *Hail to the Thief* restored a certain equilibrium to their progress.

Hail to the Thief was the final album delivered under Radiohead's original Parlophone contract, and more cynical observers saw its restoration of relative sonic normalcy as an attempt to bolster the band's commercial appeal to suitors, which for a gold-chip act like Radiohead would include virtually every major label. But as the years passed, no deal was done. The band was clearly in no hurry to get into bed with the corporate world again, as Yorke and Greenwood took time out to make solo albums. Then, suddenly, the announcement that *In Rainbows* would be sold directly by the band, cutting out the various middlemen and the cosy industry practices weighted so heavily in the labels' favour. And one can only imagine the trauma wrought in record-label boardrooms by their decision to charge whatever purchasers deemed appropriate.

Radiohead's decision is only the latest, if the most damaging, nail in the coffin of the mainstream music business. Not that the labels' clients will be wasting their tears; for decades, artists have complained about the inequity of contracts, with their in-built skimming of ten per cent to cover 'returns' of damaged copies (even on supposedly indestructible CDs), and the way that instead of receiving the same percentage of revenue from the higher-priced CD as from vinyl, artists were routinely offered the same sum. And for decades, all but the most powerful artists were unable to do anything about it. At the other end of the scale, naive young bands who accepted huge advances would discover, when they were less successful than expected, that they were heavily in debt to their label and prevented from releasing material elsewhere until it was paid off.

A spendthrift, short-term culture prevailed at many labels, in which vast sums were expended promoting singles acts who would never recoup it in album sales, while longer-term prospects were deprived of the support that might help their careers blossom. Back in the '60s, even a lower-division journeyman rock band like Budgie got to make a handful of albums before they were dumped; by the '90s, successful indie acts with hit singles were being cut adrift prematurely, often because label bosses were 'slimming down' the artist roster to just a few stars and steady sellers to make their company more attractive to potential purchasers.

It was a climate that bred waves of artist disaffection. When the likes of Prince and George Michael declared themselves little more than 'slaves', the general reaction was one of incredulity; but if stars of that magnitude felt hard done by, just imagine how demoralised and crushed the ranks of lesser earners must have felt. And when artists such as Bob Dylan, Paul McCartney and most recently Joni Mitchell would rather do business with a company like Starbucks than with the established labels, something is drastically rotten in the state of Denmark Street.

Digital downloading has turned the entire industry on its head. Facing sharp falls in album sales, established acts have re-thought their approach. Until recently, a band would tour primarily to encourage sales of their album. Now, the Stones, for instance, make vastly more money out of concert tickets and merchandising than from record sales. For Prince, it's well worth giving away his new album to promote his profitable run of shows at the O2 Centre.

But Radiohead's decision to, in effect, give away their album hoists the whole issue on to a much higher level, prompting a slew of thus-far-unanswerable questions. Such as: won't fans expect to get all music for free, even that made by penniless acts? How does a small act establish and develop itself, without sales income or label assistance? Indeed, why bother making records at all, when the promotional effect on club gigs results in such low returns? What happens to the staff laid off when record shops close? And doesn't this simply establish a new class division, between those who are able to own and operate computers and those who are denied access – how do they get to enjoy *In Rainbows*?

I've no idea but, for the moment at least, the pay-what-you-like strategy affords punters the opportunity to make sharp critical assessments where they really hurt: right there in the musicians' pockets. So: shrewd or stupid? You be the judge.

2

Review of *In Rainbows*

Robert Sandall, *Daily Telegraph*,
9 October 2007

Not since 1998, when Oasis delivered *Be Here Now*, their feverishly anticipated sequel to *What's the Story (Morning Glory)?*, has a rock album generated as much heat ahead of its release as Radiohead's *In Rainbows*.

The fuss over the past week has centred on the band's decision to offer it, in the first instance, as an MP3 download from their own website for which fans can choose to pay whatever they like. But this was only the last drama in a saga which has rumbled on for the best part of three years. Out of contract with their old label Parlophone in 2003 after finishing *Hail to the Thief*, and with only themselves now to please, Radiohead have dallied over *In Rainbows* like no other record in their sixteen-year career. On the face of it, this is not good news. Extended, unsupervised periods in the recording studio are notoriously bad for rock bands and tend to result in overblown stillborns like Fleetwood Mac's cocaine opus *Tusk* and the inconsequential doodlings that dominate the Stone Roses' sadly mistitled *Second Coming*.

But in Radiohead's case, the delays and the false starts have had a happy ending. Maybe it was a good thing that Jonny Greenwood, who was appointed the BBC Concert Orchestra's composer in residence in 2004, was distracted by his first commission ('Super Het Receiver') when the band began work on their seventh album in early 2005. Thom Yorke's abrupt departure later that year to work on a solo album clearly didn't do any harm either. Perhaps it was the very fact that their two most restlessly experimental members have been able to let off steam away from Radiohead meant that when the band finally reconvened last year they set about recording their most straight-forwardly enjoyable album since *OK Computer*.

Here, back at last, is the magic ingredient that has been lacking, or at least hiding, on Radiohead records ever since a highly-disgruntled Thom Yorke came off the road exhausted in 1999 and announced that he had 'had it with melody'. What a sad day that was, coming from the man who dreamed up 'Fake Plastic Trees' and 'Karma Police', to name but two of the sublimely original tunes that turned Radiohead into a much-loved, multi-million selling global draw. Say what you like about *Kid A*, *Amnesiac* and *Hail to the Thief* – and there is much that can be said, for and against – none of the group's twenty-first-century offerings boasts a melody that can hold a candle, let alone a lofted cigarette lighter, to the best of Radiohead in the 1990s.

Though *In Rainbows* puts that to rights, it takes its time to show its full hand. The opening track 'Step 15' finds Yorke doing his impersonation of a ghostly choirboy over a mildly autistic, *Kid-A*-flavoured hip-hop beat. 'Bodysnatchers' continues in a vein familiar to fans of the band's recent work, with a fuzzed guitar riff having a fight with a competing time signature from the rhythm section while Yorke wails over the top. Everything changes with track three, 'Nude', a song that sounds like a classic old soul ballad with some slightly strange sonic edges. This reminds you instantly of the widescreen, emotionally coloured splendour that Radiohead used to evoke on a regular basis before the urge to unsettle listeners usurped the desire to offer them something more cathartic.

In Rainbows doesn't really put a foot wrong from then on in. The band can't resist a dash of dissonance and random distortion here and there, but then again they wouldn't still be Radiohead if they had edited that out of the mix; and for every nod to weirdness for its own sake there is a string arrangement that's more up George Martin's street than Messiaen's.

Likewise, a few of Thom Yorke's lines still retain that truculently tetchy undergraduate air, particularly when he starts bemoaning the 'collapsing infrastructure' on 'House of Cards'; but Yorke has never written a more direct love song than the bell-strewn 'All I Need', or penned a catchier singalong anthem than 'Jigsaw Falling into Place'. Radiohead aren't obviously trying to reclaim ground they surrendered after their world conquest with *OK Computer*: their guitar arrangements here tend to favour acoustic strums and delicate arpeggios rather than the thunderous twang of old.

They've done epic, for the time being anyway. For all that, their seventh album sits far closer to their third than it does to their sixth. With a less unconventional outfit, you would have to call *In Rainbows* a return to form. With Radiohead it feels more like the band have finally solved a problem that only they would ever have thought needed solving in the first place.

3

Review of Phil Selway's
Familial

Wyndham Wallace, bbc.co.uk,
August 2010

Guaranteed worldwide coverage because of his day job as Radiohead's drummer and signed to Bella Union, a UK indie label currently at the top of its game, Phil Selway is in an enviable position.

It's hard not to wonder what his fate might be were he not part of one of the world's most successful rock bands, however. Singer-songwriters serving up softly spoken whimsy aren't exactly in short supply, after all, and *Familial* certainly breaks few boundaries. In fact, even the most fervent of Radiohead fans might lack the patience to get excited about this humble collection. But therein lies its charm.

Distancing himself as much from the oblique lyrical tendencies favoured by Thom Yorke as from Radiohead's complex approach to alternative, occasionally experimental rock, Selway here restricts himself mainly to acoustic guitars, barely perceptible rhythm tracks and whispered sincerity. Indeed, the most striking aspect of its production is his modesty: rather than gathering together famous friends, he turned to Lisa Germano, an artist whose profile has dwindled so far since her 1994 4AD debut that she barely qualifies for cult status, and to Wilco's Glen Kotche and Patrick Sansone.

Instead of Nigel Godrich's expansive studio techniques, Selway hired engineer Ian Davenport and recorded in his management company's studios. Forsaking oblique angst at the world's injustices, moreover, he writes as a man in his mid-forties about, as the title suggests, domestic matters, inspired by the 2006 death of his mother. Consequently *Familial* initially seems timid, even half-hearted, but persistence reveals an album full of sweet sentiment and honest meditations. Opener 'By Some Reflection' dwells in hushed tones on the familiar artistic problem of depression, 'The Ties That Bind Us' is full of references to '*the family man*' and his desire to '*shield*' his son '*from my mistakes*', and 'Broken Promises' addresses the loss of his mother in universal, touching terms.

Whether this understated, almost folksy collection is easily distinguished from the endless stream of sensitive types pouring out their hearts onto tape, however, is hard to say. But 'Don't Look Down', with its subtle background drone, is as soothing as chamomile tea, and 'A Simple Life' boasts a startling, haunting brass arrangement.

If Selway's fame can help encourage people to explore the more refined subtleties of music like this, then he's served himself and his fellow songwriters well.

4

Review of
The King of Limbs

Mike Diver, bbc.co.uk,
February 2011

<hr />

Radiohead's sense of timing is quite something. Just when it looks like Arcade Fire, on a high after victory at the Grammy and Brit awards, are set to become The Biggest Band In The World, the Oxford five-piece confirm that their eighth album isn't only done, but yours for a few bucks in mere seconds – no need to get dressed, let alone leave the house.

When it looks like teenage hip hop crew Odd Future are going to send Twitter into meltdown on the back of an alarming video, these old-timers position their own promo clip online, sit back and watch social networks collapse under the weight of a million thumbs-in-a-frenzy sorts expressing their adoration.

Their grasp of timing, in an arrangements-versus-attention sense, is equally remarkable. Just as 2007's *In Rainbows* shaved several minutes from the run-time of the preceding *Hail to the Thief*, so *The King of Limbs* cuts their full-length form down to a concise eight tracks and thirty-seven minutes. It's the band's shortest ever album, perfectly tuned to the listener of the twenty-first-century – perhaps more likely to listen to music on the way in or out of work, on a commute, than at their leisure with a nice glass of red. Of course, the digital distribution of the band's previous LP was so successful that this set was sure to follow a similar release pattern – something tangible will follow in March – but this is a remarkably neat and tidy package. Perhaps it wasn't sequenced with succinctness in mind; but that it does its job in a short space of time is important.

Because if *The King of Limbs* dragged its limbs for too much longer, the impression left might be very different. For five tracks this album unfolds in a manner very similar to *In Rainbows'* memorable array of electro-chirrups and synth-sweeps, all glitches and groans where, a decade previous, Radiohead were very much A Guitar Band. The staggering, off-kilter step of opener 'Bloom' might not click with those holding a candle for The Return of the Gallagher a week from this record's release, but to anyone with even half an ear tuned to *In Rainbows* it'll seem very (although not over-) familiar indeed.

'Morning Mr Magpie' plucks its way into a Foals-ian spin, the masters seemingly taking on board a few tips from their hometown pupils. 'Lotus Flower' – the source of #thomdance Twitter activity once its video was unveiled – is another piece that looks backwards rather than projecting into bold, new sonic territories. It flails and flaps, but in a manner entirely in keeping with its makers' predilection for the metronomic; to the wrong ears, it's five minutes of the same beat, utterly unremarkable.

But that's the beauty of Radiohead – they've never, certainly not since the breakthrough days of 'Creep', been a band for the people. They're too idiosyncratic for that, and even though there are moments aplenty here that suggest the band hasn't furthered their vision, subtle differences to a tested formula ensure *The King of Limbs* is another great album from Britain's most consistently brilliant band. And come 'Codex', it truly strikes the listener dumb. Like 'Motion Picture Soundtrack', 'Street Spirit', 'Sail to the Moon', 'Nude' – insert your own favourite slow-paced Radiohead number here – it's a piece of rarefied beauty. Thom says something about dragonflies, something else about nobody getting hurt; the words blur and blend, though, as beneath them the simplest, most strikingly gorgeous piano motif bores its way into the heart.

And it's here, not any of your limited-character blogging or video-sharing sites, that Radiohead trump all comers, again.

5

Jonny Greenwood:
'What do I do? I just generally
worry about things . . .'

Rob Young, *Uncut*,
April 2011

The car pulls into the courtyard of a small complex of offices in the middle of a housing estate on the fringes of Didcot, an Oxfordshire railway town. There are two doors into this unit and we take the right-hand one at first, which leads, like the proverbial rabbit hole, into a warren of cramped rooms.

Here's a drum kit, now a stack of guitar amps and, finally, as the air becomes muggier, even slightly fetid, we reach the control room, a windowless space piled high with effects racks, keyboards, a crumpled black leather sofa and mixing desk. This is where Jonny Greenwood has been lurking, putting the finishing touches this damp January morning to his soundtrack for Lynne Ramsay's adaptation of Lionel Shriver's *We Need to Talk about Kevin*, made for BBC Films and starring Tilda Swinton and John C. Reilly.

Despite being enthused by the outcome – mainly music played by Jean Kelly on a seven-string Irish harp – Greenwood seems eager to get out of this lightless place and, after manager Bryce Edge hands him a plastic bag of victuals from the local Waitrose, suggests we retire to the awards-lined lounge of his management's offices up the left-hand staircase. Looking at the shiny discs, trophies and statuettes Radiohead have picked up for *OK Computer*, *Kid A* and others over the years, one can't help but wonder: how is work progressing on the follow-up to 2007's *In Rainbows*?

'It seems to be slow, but there's lots of work going on,' Greenwood explains. 'We've been with each other an awful lot. It's more about working out which is the right path to go down for each of the songs and ideas. I don't think people appreciate what a mess most bands' records are until they're finalised, the songs are in order and you've left the right ones off and put the right ones on and suddenly it has something. We're quite incompetent, I think, and always have been.'

Right now, Greenwood is representing his parallel side, his composerly career which has run alongside (and fed into) Radiohead for several years. This month his music – introspective orchestral stuff – graces the soundtrack of Tran Anh Hung's *Norwegian Wood*, a stately, melancholy, period-detail-soaked adaptation of Haruki Murakami's coming-of-age novel. At just over two hours, the film's hazy, atmospheric evocation of late-'60s' Tokyo is strangely static and for much of the first hour the only music that's heard is a sprinkling of early Can tracks.

'I told him about Can,' claims Greenwood, 'because originally, he had lots of Doors, and I had the Oliver Stone heebie-jeebies about "This is the '60s", Jimi Hendrix and so on. I thought, Can, they had a Japanese singer, it sort of fits . . . '

Greenwood's music for films began in 2003 with *Bodysong*, a wordless documentary about human motion and activity with antecedents in films like *Koyaanisqatsi*.

'Jonny always wanted to go against the grain, mess with expectations,' recalls *Bodysong*'s director, Simon Pummell. 'At one point he was looking into the possibilities of soundscapes of extinct languages. The way the percussion in the "Violence" section slowly shifts into a more synchronised, obsessional beat – and moves from excitement to something oppressive, as the images escalate from brawling to genocidal brutality – is an example of the music really telling the story together with the images.'

He moved from art-house to mainstream theatres with Paul Thomas Anderson's *There Will Be Blood* in 2007, with a harsh catgut accompaniment – 'music about the characters and the landscape', he says – that scaled the movie's epic peaks and troughs with atonal introspection and wide-horizon scrape. Partly derived from a stand-alone commission he'd written for the BBC Concert Orchestra called 'Popcorn Superhet Receiver', it was a musical language of understatement.

'It's recurring textures,' explains Robert Ziegler, who conducted the orchestra on both soundtrack recordings. 'Certain clusters that he used, especially in *There Will Be Blood*, just nailed the quality of the film. And some of the new music he wrote – propulsive, rhythmic things – worked out wonderfully. He got that menace; on one of the most brilliant cues, "Open Spaces", he played the ondes Martenot [an eerie-sounding early electronic instrument] and the whole conception of it was perfect. Those huge Texas landscapes and it was just this little cue, but it lifted the whole film.'

I ask Greenwood whether he needs something visual as a starting point. 'Yeah,' he replies, 'I enjoy having something to write the music for that's concrete, but at the same time the luxury of it not being that concrete, more an excuse to write music. My most exciting days ever are the morning of recording a quartet or an orchestra or a harp player, and knowing they're coming, and setting up the stands and mics and putting music out for them. And then after four hours it's all over and you've got something. I've had a real soft ride. Traditionally film composers are way below the make-up people in the pecking order. It's not seen as important, unless you find enthusiastic directors. And I've been lucky three times in a row.'

Is that excitement greater than coming out on stage in front of thousands at a Radiohead gig? 'Yeah, I think it is,' he says. 'Because you've got weeks of preparation, and it's just on paper and wondering what is going to happen. These great musicians are coming in and you can hand them something that's fairly lifeless and they can make it very musical. That's been a big discovery for me: you realise how much they put into it . . . they can make things sound musical even if it's just a C major chord. It can sound far more exciting than you thought it was going to. It's a big secret, but you don't realise how much input comes from these people. "I can do this four or five different ways – which way would you like it?" Or "You can get this kind of effect from the strings" and so on.'

Robert Ziegler is in no doubt of Greenwood's talents as a composer, citing Polish modernist Penderecki as an antecedent. 'Obviously he's got the same attraction to masses of sound and big clusters of orchestral sound. As a film composer you have to be careful not to "frighten the horses" and the producers . . . '

There Will Be Blood led directly to Greenwood's next commission, as Tran Anh Hung used some of it as guide music on
early cuts of *Norwegian Wood*. 'When I saw *There Will Be Blood*,'
says Hung, 'I was completely seduced by Jonny's music. It was a
"new sound" with a profoundness that I have not heard elsewhere
in films. The emotions coming from his music were so . . . right,
so mysterious and yet so obvious. No doubt for me that Jonny's
music would give a dark, deep beauty that *Norwegian Wood*
needed.' Eventually Greenwood adapted another piece,
'Doghouse', for the finished film. 'Doghouse' is a triple concerto
for violin, viola and cello, inspired by thoughts of Wally Stott's
scores for Scott Walker songs like 'It's Raining Today' and
'Rosemary' languishing in the BBC library. On a structural level,
'As a toddler 1 was once shown that the note D on a piano is
between the two black notes, and that's D because it is in a kennel,
and that piece is written with this symmetrical pattern that
started on that note,' Greenwood explains.

————

The hands-on business of composing music might seem diamet-
rically opposed to rock's spontaneity. But since 2000's *Kid A*,
Radiohead have been moving away from the sound of five men
in a room playing live to a more laboriously constructed, digi-
tally processed approach. The forces of group and orchestra were
combined on the group's most recent offering, 'Harry Patch (In
Memory Of)', a tribute to the last surviving WWI veteran (who
died in 2009, aged 111).

How does Greenwood, who trained on the viola at school, see
these two methods complementing each other? 'There have
always been bits of orchestration in Radiohead,' he acknowledges.

'It's always been good to have the knowledge of music theory and I've used it all the time. A big part of what we've always done is slightly scientifically tried to copy something which we can't. It's always been like that, whether it was bits of *OK Computer* that in our heads we wanted to be like *Bitches Brew* – and the fact that none of us could play the trumpet, or jazz, didn't bother us. Which sounds like arrogance, but it's more that you aim and miss and don't let it bother you. And a lot of this film stuff is trying to do something I don't really know how to do, so I'm scrabbling around and getting a little lost and unsure, but it's been a nice way of working.'

In person, Greenwood is reserved and modest. But all the same, he becomes enthusiastic when discussing the more exciting aspects of his job. Here is a man, it seems, who even uses his down-time constructively in the pursuit of making music.

'Touring's been good for working on classical stuff,' he explains. 'I've had hours and hours in hotel rooms. The silence . . . '

So is there such a thing as a typical day for him at present, and what does he do when he's not working?

'I play the piano a lot at the moment,' he says after a pause. 'I don't know, I'm a bit low on hobbies. I used to do lots of photography . . . I don't know. What do I do? What do you do? I just generally worry about things, I think? And daydream ideas for programming.' That puts him back in his stride. 'The programming is really fun at the moment, very satisfying. I spend half my time writing music software, computer-based sound generators for Radiohead. Trying to bypass other people's ideas of what music software should do and how it should sound, going back a step. It's like building wonky drum machines, not using pre-sets, basically. It's like Mouse Trap, you construct things.'

Has he got a mathematical mind, then?

'I like a lot of popular science writing – John Gribbin and stuff. Lots of nerdy science and linguistics books. Yeah, I'm a bit trainspottery, let's not deny it.'

'As a guitar player he's extraordinary: a virtuoso, frenetic and full of personality,' testifies Bernard Butler, who views Greenwood as one of a quartet of players with distinctive styles who emerged at roughly the same moment, including himself, John Squire and Graham Coxon. 'We're all very emotional and slightly deranged guitar players and have an overwrought and melodic sensibility. I can't think of any guitar players with those qualities at the moment. It's a most un-Radiohead thing to do, but he probably did meet a devil at a crossroads somewhere, along the A1 probably.'

How, I ask Greenwood, would he like to be remembered, as a composer or as a respected guitarist?

'God, not as a "guitar stylist"!' he bursts out. 'Helping to write some very good songs, playing on them and recording them with this amazing band is like nothing else. As to what people think years from now . . . You see our record winning top album of the last whatever years, but then you see shocking albums winning the same thing twenty, thirty years ago and you think, it's nice but . . . all that really matters is what we do next, really.'

Such a comment naturally leads to more gentle probing about forthcoming plans for the Radiohead crew.

'We've been recording and working,' he allows. 'We're in the frame of mind of wanting to finish things and then decide what to do next. The old-fashioned way of thinking, when we had a record label, was: "You need to book the tour today, even though you're only halfway through the record." And we can't do that anymore. We just want to finish something and be satisfied.'

Leaving EMI to go it alone has meant, not surprisingly, 'you lose the structure, but then you are a bit freer. None of us are very nostalgic for those days of waiting for somebody's approval of your recording. But I've always said [that] at EMI we had a good relationship compared with some people.'

But in the age of digital distribution and the increasingly invisible presence of music on the high street, and given that *In Rainbows* was launched with its radical pay-what-you-like policy – plus an extraordinary, free, televised late-night gig at east London's Rough Trade store – chances are, however the next record ends up, there'll be something of a fanfare.

'I don't like how music dribbles out,' he announces as we wrap things up. 'I like events. That's the only thing, really.'

6

Review of
Atoms For Peace's *Amok*

Wyndham Wallace, bbc.co.uk,
February 2013

A supergroup they may ostensibly be, but it's hard to shake the impression that – despite the presence of Radiohead producer Nigel Godrich, Red Hot Chilli Peppers bassist Flea, regular Beck drummer Joey Waronker and Brazilian percussionist Mauro Refosco – in reality *Amok* is the second chapter in Thom Yorke's solo career.

It's hard, too, to avoid comparing *Amok* with Radiohead, given Yorke's distinctive voice and talent for an unusual tune, both of which remain central to his new project. Here, however, he immerses himself fully in the glitchy electronica that's inspired him since working on *Kid A*. Though there are traits familiar from recent 'head albums – *The King of Limbs*' 'Feral', for instance – *Amok* has its own restless, simultaneously sophisticated and gauche personality.

In fact, it displays the same twitchy rhythms and occasionally genial sincerity that Yorke displays with his onstage dancing. Built from three days of studio jamming around existing laptop sketches, its intent is to lend electronica a sense of songcraft, to create a world where digital and analogue blur, and frequently it succeeds. Yorke's ghostly falsetto traces an easily followed line through the agitated percussion and nebulous textures of 'Before Your Very Eyes . . . ' and 'Unless', while 'Stuck Together Pieces''s defining features are a rolling bassline and rippling guitar that drift amidst the muted clatter of programmed beats.

'Judge, Jury and Executioner', meanwhile, buries acoustic guitars in a cloudy chorus of incorporeal vocals, its slightness deceptive thanks to a weirdly infectious melody, and there's a sense of claustrophobia inherent in 'Ingenue''s befuddled atmosphere and oddly tropical backdrop. But the more one delves into *Amok*'s spasmodic content, the more one perceives the characteristics that make Radiohead so special: the unexpected breakdown, the unforeseen musical diversion. Here, though, divorced from his band's familiar expressive delivery, their genesis as abstract ideas generated in solitude is occasionally too conspicuous.

Nonetheless, while *Amok* – like *The Eraser* – is unlikely to arouse the same passions as, for instance, *In Rainbows*, it's an often fulfilling and fascinating indulgence. Yorke remains consistently inventive, whatever company he keeps.

7

In a Room with Radiohead

Adam Thorpe, *Times Literary Supplement,*
18 May 2016

___

Colin has contacted me to say he'll be recording with his band 'nearish you', outside Saint-Rémy-de-Provence. We would have most of the morning to chat, as recording is usually between midday and the early hours. I have never before seen a band at work in the studio, and the band in question – Radiohead – is notoriously secretive about its methods. Would I get a glimpse?

The route keeps to the ancient Via Domitia between olive groves and ripe vineyards: joining the road just metres away from our flat in central Nîmes, I leave it an hour later for a country lane, down which the studios are reached between two stone pillars. La Fabrique was once a nineteenth-century mill where madder root was crushed into red dye and artist's pigment. In 1889, Van Gogh voluntarily entered the asylum in Saint-Rémy, producing dozens of paintings; perhaps he paid the mill a visit.

At any rate, his spirit would be a suitable presiding genius for the band's sojourn here: what I have understood through Colin is that Radiohead achieve their music through a kind of obsessional persistence, much of it by trial and error. Years ago, Colin played me the taped result of a week or so's exploration in their Oxford studios; it was a mere sketch and I wondered how on earth those basic rhythms and chords could become one of the intricate, haunting and eccentrically original numbers, streaked by Thom Yorke's bright voice (frequently ranging into a crystalline falsetto), that have turned Radiohead from a sixth-form band into the world's most inventive.

I park in the front courtyard and Colin appears in a dark blue jersey, jeans and white trainers, greeting me warmly. The plan is to start with breakfast as the rest of the band trickle in. I haven't seen them since they played the huge Roman arena in Nîmes three years before. Colin was nervous at the time: over supper in our flat, he reminded us that this gig was their first since the tragic accident in Toronto, when the lighting rig collapsed onto the stage and the tour's drum technician, Scott Johnson, was killed. The Nîmes concert was remarkable, ending with multiple images of Scott. Backstage afterwards there was a palpable sense of relief.

The old mill, a three-storey edifice of vast length and many glassed-in arches, sits in two hectares of parkland and is famous for its varied acoustics: the likes of Morrissey and Nick Cave have recorded here. After coffee and croissants in the cosy dining room, Colin takes me on a tour, from the music library holding the biggest vinyl collection in the world to a gargantuan grain storehouse now full of dusty film canisters and boxes containing unplayable digital tapes (an early misstep in the march of progress).

The studio itself is strange: a sunlit suite of rooms with antique rugs, ornate fireplaces and elegant period furniture, lined with books in wooden cabinets and invaded by recording equipment, as if the teenage scion of a stately home has taken advantage of his parents' absence. A whiteboard shows only a list of tracks in black marker pen, starting with 'Daydreaming' and ending with 'Burn the Witch'. The rejected James Bond film tune, 'Spectre', floats in the middle, slightly separate. Colin points to the main console, a vast sweep of knobs, buttons and faders. 'This is a Neve 88 R, seventy-two channels, made in Burnley. Worth about a hundred thousand. It's analogue, like this reel-to-reel Studer, but we also use digital. It's all about looping and layering.' In the older, vaulted section, part of the floor is stone, with a giant hieroglyph chiselled out. 'Probably Roman,' he explains, 'where the millstone went.'

This is all layers as well, a *mille feuille* of epochs and moments and seems perfectly attuned to Radiohead's methods. We wander out into the grounds: tree-surrounded lawns, large swimming pool, further courtyards and barns, decayed cottages and a softly roaring mill-race. In one of the larger *granges*, numerous canvases display abstract explosions of colour. The barn's speakers are wired up to the recording studios: the band's resident artist Stanley Donwood reacts in acrylic to what he hears, the results to be modified and manipulated on computer for the LP's cover.

Colin is discreet about his role, playing the straight man to his charismatic younger brother Jonny, whose gaunt good looks seem forever obscured behind loops of lamp-black hair. Colin once told me, half-jokingly, that he reckoned he was 'rubbish' at playing, that he really had to concentrate on the complex rhythms, the bass line often holding everything together: in concert he keeps his back to the audience, bowed over the guitar, with a little rhythm-marking jump now and again, as if over an invisible rope. It's at moments like these that I sense the band dissolving back into its sixth-form origins: as if my own distant memories of tootling on a sax in a cellar to my school friends' blasts of guitar and drums might just have ended up in a similar place, being roared at by hundreds of thousands of fans. I once asked Colin what that was like. 'You focus down on the stage, which becomes your own intimate space. You're just playing in your room with friends.'

Phil the drummer greets us in one of the courtyards. I tell him that my grown-up children watched him perform solo recently in Victoria Park in London and they thought he was the best. 'Oh, blimey,' he says, touchingly pleased. 'I looked around and realised I was the oldest participant, apart from Patti Smith.' The five members of Radiohead have been worrying about their age for some time: dining with the band one evening in an Arles square thirteen years ago, I heard Thom Yorke announce that he would quit rock music when he was forty. He didn't want to be a Mick Jagger, still prancing about in his withered old age. Fifty now looms, but when he appears crossing a lawn in a kind of Flaubertian dressing gown and towel turban, cool behind reflective shades, he could be twenty, aside from his salt-and-pepper stubble. He agrees that the last Nîmes concert was 'pretty emotional'. Knowing he has another long day of intense creating in front of him, we leave him be.

Colin and I catch up on personal things at the table on the gravel sweep between mill and garden, with a view of clipped box shrubs in ornamental vases, and brawny Ed, the genial six-foot-three guitarist, basking shirtless a few yards along. I ask Colin if he's pleased with the recording so far: expectations are high after five years. 'I can't talk about it much, as Nigel [the producer] is really secretive about our ways. But I like a lot of it. It's beautifully lyrical in places. There's one with a straight chord sequence, so that can go next to the cold spy one. The fluffy puppy next to the warthog!' I ask if the band are perfectionists. 'Oh, I don't know. I suppose we can't be or we'd never release anything. And we all have different likes.'

Back in the studio, the youthful technicians are checking things over. Jonny, ever restless, is in a brass-studded leather chair crouched over his home-made sound machine (little hammers hitting various objects) and its accompanying laptop, and Ed is listening to him in front of his long row of guitars. Jonny establishes a rhythm, part-calypso, part-reggae, with his yoghurt cartons, tubs, bells and mini-tambourine. 'Sounds a bit like Marvin Gaye,' Ed comments.

For all the priceless equipment, we have indeed come back to lads tinkering in their rooms: perhaps this is the heart of all this fertile imagining, its idiosyncrasies not so far from a poet's manner. Colin ushers me gently out, the secret ceremony about to begin. I mention Freelance [a regular column in the *Times Literary Supplement*]; he's a *TLS* fan (he read English at Cambridge). 'That'd be cool. It might be the only one, we're not commissioning anything. A literary piece, written by a poet! Just make sure you call me the more handsome of the Greenwood brothers,' he adds, grinning, and I drive out of the gates into the ordinary world.

Contributors

Pat Blashill wrote about rock and pop for *Rolling Stone, SPIN* and *Details* from 1987 to 2003. He grew up in Texas, consuming a steady diet of Butthole Surfers records and Ed Wood movies. He now lives in Vienna, Austria, and still writes about stuff for the Munich newspaper *Sueddeutsche Zeitung.*

Stephen Dalton began his career on the *NME* at the dawn of the 1990s, surviving acid house, Madchester, grunge, Britpop, electroclash, New Grave, New Rave, and at least four 1980s synth-pop revivals. Over the last 20 years he has also been a regular contributor to *The Times, Uncut, Electronic Sound, Classic Rock, Hollywood Reporter* and various other publications.

Tom Doyle is an acclaimed music journalist, author, and long-standing contributor to *MOJO* and *Q.* His work has also appeared in *Billboard,* the *Guardian, The Times,* and *Sound on Sound.* He is the author of *The Glamour Chase: The Maverick Life of Billy MacKenzie,* which has attained the status of a classic rock biography since its original publication, and biographies of Paul McCartney and Elton John. He lives in London, England.

Ted Drozdowski is a freelance journalist and musician living in Boston, Massachusetts. His work has appeared internationally in a wide variety of publications including *Tracks*, *Rolling Stone* and *Musician*. Before freelancing, he was associate arts editor at the *Boston Phoenix* and an editor at *Musician*.

Andy Gill has written for *NME*, *Q*, *MOJO*, the *Independent* and numerous other publications. He is the author of, among other books, *Don't Think Twice, It's Alright: Bob Dylan, the Early Years* (Carlton).

Ian Gittins is a music writer for the *Guardian*, formerly of *Melody Maker* and *Q*. He was co-author with Nikki Sixx of Mötley Crüe of the *New York Times* bestseller *The Heroin Diaries*, and with David Essex of his *Sunday Times* No. 1 bestselling autobiography *Over the Moon*. He is the also the author of *A Perfect Dream*, a 2018 biography of the Cure, and is currently writing a book with Billy Connolly.

Mark Greif is an author, educator and cultural critic. His most recent book is *Against Everything*. One of the co-founders of *n+1*, he is a frequent contributor to the magazine and writes for numerous other publications. Greif teaches literature at Stanford University.

John Harris is the author of *The Last Party: Britpop, Blair and the Demise of English Rock* (2003), *So Now Who Do We Vote For?* which examined the 2005 UK general election, a 2006 behind-the-scenes look at the production of Pink Floyd's *The Dark Side of the Moon*, and *Hail! Hail! Rock'n'Roll* (2009). He now writes about music for *MOJO* and *Q*, while devoting most of his working time to reporting, commentary and video journalism at the *Guardian*. He was named Political Commentator of the Year at the UK Press Awards for 2017.

Will Hermes is the author of *Love Goes To Buildings On Fire: Five Years in New York That Changed Music Forever* (Farrar, Straus & Giroux, 2011), an acclaimed history of the New York City music scene in the 1970s. A contributing editor for *Rolling Stone* and a long-time contributor to NPR's *All Things Considered*, his work appears periodically in *The New York Times*; he has also written for the *Village Voice, Spin, Slate, Salon, The Believer, GQ* and other publications. He co-edited *SPIN: 20 Years of Alternative Music* (Crown/Three Rivers, 2006), and his writing has been included in the *Da Capo Best Music Writing* series.

Barney Hoskyns began writing for *NME* in the early '80s and is a former contributing editor at British *Vogue* and US correspondent for *MOJO*. He is the author of the bestselling *Hotel California* (2006), the Tom Waits biography *Lowside of the Road* (2009), and *Trampled Under Foot* (2012), an oral history of Led Zeppelin. He has written for the *Guardian, Uncut, Spin, Rolling Stone* and *GQ*. *Small Town Talk*, his history of the music scene in and around Woodstock, New York, was published in 2016.

Nick Kent was one of the most important and influential music journalists of the 1970s and remains a hugely respected commentator to this day. He wrote for *New Musical Express* and *The Face* and is the author of *The Dark Stuff*, a collection of his journalism.

Nick has written for numerous publications and lives in Paris with his partner, Laurence Romance, and their son. His memoir *Apathy for the Devil* was published by Faber in 2010.

Clare Kleinedler began her career at groundbreaking online zine *Addicted to Noise* in the mid-'90s. She went on to serve as the music editor for *WIRED* magazine in early 2000. Her work has been published in numerous publications including the *Los Angeles Times*, the *San Francisco Chronicle*, *BAM*, *Paper* and *XLR8R* among others.

Paul Lester was Features Editor of *Melody Maker* and Deputy Editor of *Uncut*. Since then he has written books on Gang Of Four and Wire, and interviewed over a thousand musicians for the *Guardian*, the *Sunday Times* Culture section, *Telegraph* Arts & Books, *MOJO*, *Classic Rock*, *Classic Pop* and *Prog*. He is currently the editor of *Record Collector* magazine.

Paul Moody is a writer and musician. His first band, The Studio 68!, recorded an album called *Portobellohello* in 1992. He later joined the *NME* and then toured the world in psychedelic renegades Regular Fries. More recently he co-wrote a book called *Looking For The Moon Under Water*, based on George Orwell's description's of his perfect pub (published by Orion). He now lives in Hastings, England, and dreams of the perfect wave.

Ronan Munro is the editor of Oxford music monthly *Nightshift*, originally *Curfew*, and was the first journalist to write about and interview On A Friday, the five-piece band that became Radiohead.

CONTRIBUTORS

Peter Murphy is a writer, spoken-word performer, journalist, musician and actor. He has published two novels, *John the Revelator* and *Shall We Gather at the River* (Faber), while his non-fiction work has appeared in *Rolling Stone*, the *Guardian* and *Hot Press*, and he has released two albums with the Revelator Orchestra. He is a regular contributor to the *Irish Times* and RTE's arts show *Arena*, and currently performs and records under the name Cursed Murphy.

Ann Powers is a critic for NPR and a contributor at the *Los Angeles Times*, where she was previously chief pop critic. She has also served as pop critic on *The New York Times* and an editor at the *Village Voice*. Powers is the author of *Weird Like Us: My Bohemian America*, a memoir; *Good Booty: Love and Sex, Black & White, Body and Soul in American Music*, on eroticism in American pop music; and *Piece by Piece*, co-authored with Tori Amos.

Simon Price is an award-winning British music critic. His three-decades-plus career includes nine years at *Melody Maker* magazine and twelve at the *Independent on Sunday* newspaper, during which time he was voted Live Reviews Writer of the Year on three consecutive occasions at the Record of the Day Awards. He currently contributes to publications including *Q* magazine, the *Guardian*, *Metro* and *The Quietus*. Price currently lectures in Music Journalism at the BIMM Institute in Brighton.

Simon Reynolds is the author of eight books about pop culture, including *Shock and Awe: Glam Rock and its Legacy* (2016), *Retromania: Pop Culture's Addiction to Its Own Past* (2011), *Rip It Up and Start Again: Postpunk 1978–84* (2005), and *Energy Flash:*

A Journey Through Rave Music and Dance Culture (1998). He started his career as a music critic at *Melody Maker*, where he was a staff writer from 1986 to 1990. Since then he has freelanced for magazines including *The New York Times*, the *Village Voice*, the *Guardian*, *Pitchfork*, and *The Wire*. Reynolds operates a number of blogs centred around the hub Blissblog http://blissout.blogspot. com/. Born in London, a resident of New York during much of the 1990s and 2000s, he currently lives in Los Angeles.

Robert Sandall wrote for *Q*, *Rolling Stone*, *The Word* and *GQ* magazines. He was the chief rock critic for the *Sunday Times* from 1988 and later wrote regularly for the *Daily Telegraph*. He was best known for presenting, with Mark Russell, BBC Radio 3's *Mixing It* programme from 1990 until 2007. After ending on Radio 3 the show moved to Resonance FM in London, where it continued under the name *Where's the Skill in That?* for a further two years. Sandall also presented editions of the BBC's *Late Junction* and contributed to BBC Radio 4's *Front Row*. He died in July 2010.

Will Self is the author of ten novels, five collections of shorter fiction, three novellas, and five collections of non-fiction writing. His work has been translated into 22 languages; his 2002 novel *Dorian, an Imitation* was longlisted for the Booker Prize, and his novel *Umbrella* was shortlisted for the Man Booker Prize. His fiction is known for being satirical, grotesque, and fantastical, and is predominantly set within his home city of London. His subject matter often includes mental illness, illegal drugs and psychiatry. He is a regular contributor to publications including the *Guardian*, the *New Statesman*, *The New York Times* and the *London Review of Books*.

CONTRIBUTORS

R.J. Smith has been a senior editor at *Los Angeles* magazine, a contributor to *Blender*, a columnist for the *Village Voice*, a staff writer for *Spin*, and has written for *GQ*, the *New York Times Magazine*, and *Men's Vogue*. He is the author of *The Great Black Way*, the James Brown biography *The One*, and *American Witness: the Art and Life of Robert Frank*. He lives in Cincinnati.

Jim Sullivan began writing freelance music reviews and features for the *Boston Globe* in 1979. He also wrote for such national music publications as *The Record*, *Creem* and *Music-Sound Output*. He joined the staff of the *Boston Globe* in 1988, specialising in pop music and culture until 2005. He also freelanced for the *Boston Phoenix* and the *Christian Science Monitor* and currently does the same for Boston public radio station WBUR's arts website, the ARTery, the *Cape Cod Times* and Best Classic Bands. He also hosts a podcast/video show called Boston Rock/Talk.

Adam Sweeting was the features editor of *Melody Maker* and was rock critic for the *Guardian* as well as contributing to *Q*, *Uncut*, *GQ* and *Esquire*. He has written regularly for the *Daily Telegraph* and *The Times Saturday Magazine* and is a prolific obituarist for the *Guardian*. He is a co-founder of, and regular contributor to, the arts website theartsdesk.com.

Adam Thorpe is a Franco-British poet and novelist whose works also include short stories, translations, radio dramas and documentaries. He is a frequent contributor of reviews and articles to various newspapers, journals and magazines, including the *Guardian*, the *Poetry Review* and the *Times Literary Supplement*. His most recent book is *Notes from the Cévennes: Half a Lifetime in Provincial France*.

Wyndham Wallace's first book *Lee, Myself & I* (about his friendship with Lee Hazlewood) was published in 2015 by Jawbone Press. He writes regularly for *Uncut* and *Classic Pop*, as well as contributing to other publications including the *Guardian* and *The Quietus*. He's also the co-editor of Norwegian guide-book series *The Poor Man's Connoisseur*, translates German films for English speakers, and can be seen in *Almost Fashionable: A Film About Travis*.

Rob Young is a Contributing Editor of *The Wire* and also writes for *Uncut*, *Sight & Sound*, the *Guardian*, *Frieze* and *Artforum*. His books include *All Gates Open: The Story of Can* (Faber and Faber, 2018), *Electric Eden: Unearthing Britain's Visionary Music* (2010), *Rough Trade* (2006) and *Warp* (2005). He lives in Oslo.

Index